Nantucket and Other Native Places

I0878382

Betty Little at Miacomet

Nantucket and Other Native Places

The Legacy of Elizabeth Alden Little

Edited by

Elizabeth S. Chilton

and

Mary Lynne Rainey

SUNY PRESS

Cover image of "The Shack" courtesy of Mary Lynne Rainey

This publication was partially funded by the Massachusetts Archaeological Society which received the Louis Brennan Award for the book project from the Eastern States Archaeological Federation.

Published by State University of New York Press, Albany

Printed in the United States of America

For information, contact State University of New York Press, Albany, NY
www.sunypress.edu

Production by Diane Ganeles
Marketing by Michael Campochiaro

Library of Congress Cataloging-in-Publication Data

Nantucket and other native places : the legacy of Elizabeth Alden Little / edited by Elizabeth S. Chilton and Mary Lynne Rainey.
p. cm.
Includes bibliographical references and index.
ISBN 978-1-4384-3253-3 (hardcover : alk. paper)
ISBN 978-1-4384-3254-0 (pbk. : alk. paper)
1. Indians of North America—Massachusetts—Nantucket Island—Antiquities. 2. Indians of North America—New England—Antiquities. 3. Nantucket Island (Mass.)—Antiquities. 4. New England—Antiquities. 5. Little, Elizabeth A. I. Chilton, Elizabeth S. II. Rainey, Mary Lynne.

E78.M4N36 2010
974.4'97—dc22 2009045179

10 9 8 7 6 5 4 3 2 1

Contents

Illustrations

Tables

Preface

Dr. Elizabeth Alden Little (1926–2003) was an accomplished physicist, archaeologist, and anthropologist who devoted over thirty years of her life to the advancement and dissemination of scholarly research on Nantucket's Native American and Colonial population. She received her PhD in physics from MIT in 1954 and her MA in anthropology from the University of Massachusetts Amherst, in 1985. From 1971 to 1999, she collected and analyzed Nantucket Island data and self-published over thirty manuscripts on behalf of the Nantucket Historical Association (NHA). These manuscripts divulged complex details about Native American life and Colonial interactions from the Precontact period through the Indian sickness period of 1763–1764. Little's research canvassed topics such as Native American diet, settlement patterns, community centers, architecture, Indian whalers, and sachems of note. In addition to her NHA manuscripts, Little maintained a steady and prolific academic publishing career that elevated her status in the professional archaeological community throughout the Northeast and elsewhere. She is widely recognized today for her extensive primary manuscript research on Nantucket and for enlightening the academic community on many topics, including radio carbon dating analyses and stable isotope analyses of human bone, a technique that can reveal the primary components of the human diet. In honor of Little's accomplishments and influence, this book is a Festschrift of chapters written by archaeologists and scholars who were influenced by her work. The thematic contributions capture many of her areas of expertise, including Nantucket Island archaeology, and reflect the widespread influence she maintains.

Chapters in this volume were written by archaeologists who knew Little well. The chapters are thematic and linked to many of Little's research interests. Topics include the Jethro Coffin House, Native American architecture on Nantucket Island, coastal settlement patterns, maize, Indian sachems, wampum, and Contact period archaeology on Nantucket Island and the mainland. Little's final manuscript, as edited by

Elizabeth Chilton, in draft at the time of her death, is also included here. A biography of Little's life has been written by Dr. Dena Dincauze, and a comprehensive bibliography of Little's publications has been compiled by Dr. Dena Dincauze and Mary Lynne Rainey.

This work is a joint venture between the Massachusetts Archaeological Society (MAS), which received the Louis Brennan Award for this book project from the Eastern States Archaeological Federation, and State University of New York (SUNY) Press.

The editors would like to thank the other members of the MAS Publications Committee, Tonya Largy and Dr. James Bradley. They also wish to thank Gary Dunham of SUNY Press for his support throughout this project and for supporting Northeast archaeology in general. Most importantly they wish to thank the Little family for helping them find a way to honor Betty's memory, her life, and her work.

The cover image of "The Shack" was taken by Mary Lynne Rainey, and the following excerpt is a quote written by Betty Little about The Shack at Miacomet (Little 1989): " 'The Blue Heron,' an old gunning shack moved to the west side of Miacomet Pond near the ocean by ~1900, stood there until 1944, when it was burned down, probably by vandals. The present shack was once part of the old White Elephant hotel on Easton Street and was moved here when the hotel was rebuilt about 1965. 'The Shack,' a name which was applied to the site even during the 20 years when there was no shack on the property, has been used every summer by my family all of my life, and, according to my mother's photograph album, at least once a summer since about 1924. My earliest recollections are of shack picnics, all day expeditions involving large numbers of family, through 5th cousins three times removed. [ ] The ocean swimming there can't be beat!"

1

The "Ancient Dwelling" on Sunset Hill

Preliminary Archaeological Investigations at the Jethro Coffin House

Duncan Ritchie

The Jethro Coffin House is one of Nantucket's (Massachusetts) important historical landmarks, representing the dwelling of a prominent early settler on the island. This historic structure, constructed in about 1686, is owned and maintained by the Nantucket Historical Association (NHA). An element of the Nantucket Historical District since 1955, the Jethro Coffin House was designated as a National Historic Landmark in 1968. In observance of the 1986 tercentennial year for the Jethro Coffin House, the NHA initiated a comprehensive study of this historic site. Located on the crest of Sunset Hill, the house is a highly visible symbol of Nantucket's past that has been visited by tourists and photographed since the Victorian era. With its enigmatic wishbone/horseshoe design in raised brick on the chimney and association with the Coffin and Gardner families, it is an icon of early European-American settlement on Nantucket.

Initial consideration of an archaeological investigation began in 1984 when plans to construct a Colonial-period garden at the Jethro Coffin House raised the possibility of conducting an excavation in the proposed location of the garden bed. Elizabeth Little, as vice chairman of the NHA Archaeology Committee, proposed that the archaeological survey be expanded to include the entire Jethro Coffin House property. In January 1985, she prepared a draft proposal for a project with the primary goal of locating the archeological remains of outbuildings, fence lines, garden plots, or other features within the Jethro Coffin House lot to reconstruct land-use patterns and the lifeways of past occupants of this property. The proposal reflected her interest in a multidisciplinary approach to the study of archaeological sites. A grant proposal prepared by Victoria Hawkins (NHA curator of Collections) was submitted to the Massachusetts Council on Arts and Humanities as a source of funding for the proposed archaeological study.

Innovative in its use of interdisciplinary approaches to collecting information about this historic property, the Jethro Coffin House project employed architectural history, documentary research, folklore, remote sensing, archaeological survey, and paleobotany. Research utilizing various primary and secondary sources such as deeds, probates, maps, and historic photographs was conducted by knowledgeable NHA staff. The Public Archaeology Laboratory (PAL) was among the organizations and individuals that participated in the study. It became involved in the Jethro Coffin House project through the invitation of Little, who was the head of the NHA's Archaeology Committee.

The following section of this chapter presents the general objectives and a research framework for the archaeological survey conducted by PAL. This is followed by a summary of the construction, occupation, and abandonment of the Jethro Coffin House based on architectural study and documentary research. The results of the remote sensing study, subsequent archaeological survey of the property, and paleobotanical analysis are then discussed.

Project Background

The primary goals of the archaeological survey conducted by PAL were: (1) a review of the documentary materials assembled by the NHA; (2) an intensive (locational) archaeological survey of the house lot to identify potentially important subsurface features and deposits; and (3) the analysis and synthesis of the archaeological information, incorporating what had been learned from documentary research. Recommendations for managing and protecting the archaeological component of the property were also developed. The award of a technical assistance grant to the NHA from the Massachusetts Council on Arts and Humanities in February 1986 provided funding for the archaeological survey. Fieldwork for the survey was conducted in April 1986, and a report was submitted to the NHA later that summer.

Primary components of the research design for the project were a review of documentary sources, remote sensing, and archaeological surveys of the Jethro Coffin House lot and paleobotanical analysis of soil samples collected from suspected garden plots. Completion of these tasks was a group effort, reflecting the multidisciplinary nature of the project. The documentary information related to the Jethro Coffin House included deeds, probates, tax lists, federal census data, and other vital records. Other sources were photographs taken over the last 130 years, several architectural studies, and research on the Coffin family done by NHA members Helen Winslow Chase (1986) and Elizabeth Little (Little 1986; Little and Morrison 1986).

The remote sensing survey of the house lot was organized and conducted by members of the NHA Archaeology Committee and John Pretola from the Springfield Science Museum under the guidance of Richard Gumaer from the University of Massachusetts Amherst. The archaeological survey, artifact analysis, and flotation processing of soil samples were conducted by PAL staff. Steven Mrozowski, then archaeologist for the city of Boston, conducted the analysis and interpretation of paleobotanical material recovered from soil samples.

Research Framework

Three historic contexts provided a basic interpretive framework for the archaeological survey. They were: (1) the core-periphery relationship of Nantucket to the mainland; (2) eighteenth- and nineteenth-century land use patterns; and (3) economic decline on Nantucket circa 1840 to 1880. The contexts were based on themes recognized in the results of documentary research on both the Coffin family and the Coffin House, done as part of the tercentennial year project by the NHA (Chase 1986; Little 1986; Little and Morrison 1986).

These contexts were made more meaningful by the way Coffin family history and the Jethro Coffin House reflected larger processes on Nantucket from the late seventeenth to the late nineteenth centuries. The house was built in the period of initial European settlement and was continuously occupied through the expansion of maritime activities, including whaling, and an economic crash in the mid-nineteenth century that was followed by the decline of whaling. During the last quarter of the nineteenth century, when there was substantial population loss on Nantucket due to the general decline of maritime commerce on the island, the Jethro Coffin House was abandoned. Its final restoration by the Society for the Preservation of New England Antiquities (SPNEA) was funded by Coffin family descendants and linked to a renewal of interest in island history between 1880 and 1928.

Documentary evidence suggested that the patterning of activities within the Jethro Coffin House lot may not have changed much through the eighteenth and nineteenth centuries, reflecting a pattern of conservatism and tradition in land use on Nantucket. After construction of the Paddack House (ca. 1726–1740) on a section of the original Coffin lot, certain features such as the driveway/cart path and the well remained mostly unchanged and were shared by occupants of both houses. They may have also shared some outbuildings such as sheds or barns.

With the demise of the whaling industry on Nantucket in the mid-nineteenth century, economic conditions on the island suffered a steady decline. Nantucket was unable to compete with mainland ports and had been devastated by a major disaster with the Great Fire of 1846. The subsequent movement of island residents to the mainland caused a significant reduction in the population of Nantucket and the relative value of property. This process was reflected in the eventual abandonment of the Jethro Coffin House as a dwelling in the late 1860s.

Summary of Construction, Occupation, and Abandonment, 1686–1867

The Jethro Coffin House and the lot on which it was built went through four stages, from construction through occupation by members of Coffin and other families from about 1686 to1867 and from abandonment and finally reconstruction/restoration in the late nineteenth and early twentieth centuries. The year 1686 has generally been accepted as the likely construction date for the Jethro Coffin House, based on Coffin family tradition. However, the circumstances surrounding this event are not clear, since no deed or other document describing the initial granting of ownership to Jethro Coffin is known to exist. Physical evidence of this construction date allegedly appeared during the first phase of renovation in 1881, when the date 1686 was found inscribed into mortar on the west face of the chimney in the attic. Tradition also relates that the house was built as a wedding present for Jethro and Mary (Gardner) Coffin, whose marriage represented a significant reunion between two of Nantucket's most prominent early European families. In a dispute over the division of common lands known as the Half-Share Insurrection, the Gardner and Coffin families had been members of opposing factions. The property on which the house stands was given to Jethro Coffin by John Gardner, while timber used in its construction was provided by Peter Coffin from his landholdings in Exeter, New Hampshire.

In its original form, the Jethro Coffin House was a hall- and parlor-type structure of one and three quarter story height. On the front of the house, two gables projected from the roof, and there was a small porch over the front door (see Figure 1.1). Another distinctive feature was the use of a horseshoe-shaped motif in raised brick on the face of the chimney. This motif has been interpreted as a symbol of the joining of the Coffin and Gardner families, or, as Lancaster (1972, 20) has suggested, it may only be a decorative Jacobean-style chimney arch used in modified form. Phillips's (1984) architectural study and measured drawings from the 1927 restoration indicate that the original house was 30.5 by 39 feet in dimension, with its sills resting on a shallow stone foundation about 4 feet deep. This foundation extended across the entire front and about 16 feet toward the rear of the house, forming a small, shallow cellar. At the rear of the house the sills probably rested on a few large stones. Included under a 10½-foot deep lean-to at the rear of the structure was a kitchen flanked on the east by a milk room and to the west by a chamber. In this configuration, as a center chimney, lean-to structure, the Jethro Coffin House survived relatively unchanged into the late nineteenth century. Fire allegedly destroyed a portion of the rear lean-to prior to the 1860s. However, architectural studies found no convincing evidence of fire damage to the structure (Phillips 1984; Lancaster 1972, 20–22, Forman 1966). A late-nineteenth-century photograph shows the configuration of the lean-to at the rear or northwest corner of the house.

Figure 1.1. Jethro Coffin House, Built 1686

In relation to the general pattern of seventeenth-century settlement on the north shore of Nantucket, the Jethro Coffin House was located near the eastern end of the English town of Sherburne. Initial settlement in the 1660s was concentrated in an area north of Hummock Pond and west of Reed Pond, with a small harbor at Capaum (Capaum Pond) as the focal point. English settlement gradually spread to the southeast in the direction of Nantucket harbor in the 1670s. Other early developments were mills at Wesco Pond and a tidal mill, shoemaking and weaving shops, and warehouses in the harbor area. Further intensive settlement in Sherburne was initiated by the laying out of the Wesco Acre Lots in 1678 (Forman 1966, 22–25; Starbuck 1924, 23, 24).

Compared to other seventeenth-century house sites on Nantucket, the location of the Jethro Coffin House lot is somewhat anomalous. Little noted the unusual choice of location for this house in a 1985 proposal for a comprehensive archaeological survey of NHA properties. The Jethro Coffin House occupies the crest of an elevated knoll with a northerly aspect, while other contemporary homes were placed in more sheltered settings. Use of this exposed location may reflect other non-functional, possibly symbolic, considerations involved in the construction of the Jethro Coffin House.

Historical Background

Documentary research conducted for the 1986 tercentennial study yielded a wealth of information on the families that occupied the Jethro Coffin House from the late seventeenth to mid-nineteenth centuries (Chase 1986). From about 1686 to 1708, Jethro and Mary Coffin occupied the house, and six of their eight children were born in this period, between 1689 and 1704. The earliest possible reference to gardens or cultivated land owned by Coffin dates to before 1701, when blacksmith Nathaniel Starbuck charged him a fee for plowing an acre of ground. The small size of this plow land suggests that it could have been within the 1½-acre lot containing the Jethro Coffin House.

Jethro Coffin sold the house in 1708 to Nathaniel Paddack for the sum of 95 pounds. This transaction included the entire 1½-acre lot, a barn, other outhouses and shops, a well, easements, and garden fences. The Coffin family moved in 1708 to Mendon, Massachusetts, where Jethro became involved in cutting timber and iron making, possibly to support boat building for the early offshore whaling industry on Nantucket. Some other former Nantucket residents joined the Coffin family in Mendon, forming a small colony there. After Jethro's death in 1726,

Mary Coffin returned with the rest of the family to Nantucket (Little and Morrison 1986, 7–9). The lengthy occupation of the Coffin house by the Paddack family began in 1708, when Nathaniel Paddack bought it and moved there with his wife Ann and their first child Daniel (born 1707). Nine other children were born between 1709 and 1724, probably in the Jethro Coffin House. Paddack listed his occupation as weaver, but other documentary evidence indicates he was involved in offshore whaling. In 1714, six years after buying the property, Paddack had paid to Jethro Coffin the sum of 117 pounds, 5 shillings, and sixpence. It is unclear if this amount included the 95 pounds paid to Coffin at the original purchase in 1708. By 1726, Nathaniel and his sons Daniel and Paul were active in shore whaling. Between 1726 and 1740, Nathaniel Paddack built a house (Paddack House) a short distance southeast of the Jethro Coffin House. This new house was probably occupied by Daniel and Paul Paddack and their families. From about 1726 to 1752, various members of the Paddack family occupied both the Paddack and Jethro Coffin houses (Chase 1986).

After Captain Daniel Paddack's early death while on a whaling expedition in 1743, his father Nathaniel mortgaged the Coffin House and all of his other property to three persons—Paul Paddack and two sons-in-law, Jethro Coleman and George Swain, each held mortgages for 100 pounds. This mortgage was likely arranged to provide for Daniel Paddack's widow Susanna and her children. In 1747, Nathaniel Paddack was able to pay the 300 pounds needed to release his property, and he probably owned both the houses (Paddack, Coffin) on Sunset Hill. A few months later, Nathaniel sold to his son Paul "one half of my lands and other real estate," excluding the Coffin House, for 150 pounds. This transaction gave Paul half of the Paddack House, and a few years later, in 1752, he acquired full ownership of it from his father. In 1754, Paul Paddack sold a half interest in the house to mariner Henry Smith, which included the west end of this structure, one rod of land to the north, the use of a cartway or path to the house, and rights to the well and pump. This pattern of shared use of the cart path and the well by occupants of the Coffin and Paddack houses was established by this time and continued into the nineteenth century.

In the early 1760s, Paul Paddack mortgaged his half of the Paddack House to Joseph Swain, a boatwright. At that time, the house was rented to tenant Joseph Dawes, a tailor. Paul and his family could have been sharing the Coffin House with his widowed mother during this period (Chase 1986, 15–17). Other occupants of the Paddack House in the last half of the eighteenth century were the Smith and Fosdick families. In 1763, Henry Smith acquired the entire house for his family, along with rights of access to the cartpath and the well or pump near the Jethro Coffin House. John and Elizabeth Fosdick purchased the Paddack House from Smith in 1776. Fosdick was a joiner and cabinet-maker with a large family of ten children and occupied the house until he and his wife died in 1809.

Paul Paddack apparently continued to live in the Coffin House through the latter part of the eighteenth century, and in 1786 he sold half of it and surrounding lands to his son Nathaniel II. A provision of this sale was that Nathaniel would receive the remaining half of the house upon the death of his parents. In 1801, two years after his father's death, Nathaniel mortgaged the Coffin House for $250. This debt would not be paid until 1820 (Chase 1986, 18–22).

After the deaths of both John and Elizabeth Fosdick in 1809, the Paddack House passed through several short episodes of ownership. Sailmaker Edward Brown purchased the house in 1810 for the sum of $450. Two years later, in 1812, Brown sold the property to Nantucket mariner and trader Joseph Earle. In 1818, Robert Calaway (Calloway) purchased the house from Earle for the same amount Earle had paid for it six years earlier (Chase 1986, 18).

The first official land survey of the Jethro Coffin House and property took place in 1839 in connection with the sale of Nathaniel Paddack's estate to his son George. Since that time, this survey has formed the basis of all deeds describing the property. When Nathaniel Paddack died in 1840, George sold the Coffin House to George Turner, a cooper, for $300. Turner, his wife Mary, and their five children were the last residents of the house and lived there until about 1867. Tax records for that year indicate that the house, a half-acre lot and one acre "mowing lot," had a value of $225. A photograph taken circa 1863 reveals three outbuildings, possibly sheds and a privy, standing on the property along the rear (north) lot line. Although the Turners did not actually live in the Coffin House after the period 1867–1868, George Turner's widow Mary retained ownership of the property until 1881. At some point between around 1867 and 1881, the unoccupied Jethro Coffin House was used as a barn for storing hay (Chase 1986, 24–30).

Repair and Restoration, 1881–1928

The Coffin family reunion held on Nantucket in August 1881 marked the beginning of a period of repair and restoration of the Jethro Coffin House. A prominent participant in the reunion, Judge Tristram Coffin, of Poughkeepsie, New York, was made aware of the Jethro Coffin House and decided to save this ancestral homestead from further deterioration. Together with his brother O. Vincent Coffin, Tristram Coffin bought the house from the heirs of George Turner and had it repaired in 1881. The restored house became one of Nantucket's primary tourist attractions and was opened for summer visits between 1897 and 1923. In 1923, the Nantucket Historical Association acquired the Jethro Coffin House from Tristram Coffin. A few years later, another Coffin descendant, Winthrop Coffin, of Boston, offered to fund a more extensive restoration of the house. Coffin stipulated that the restoration be carried out under the direction of William Sumner Appleton, secretary of SPNEA. Winthrop Coffin also donated a parcel of land north of the Jethro Coffin House to the town of Nantucket for use as a park. A primary purpose of this gift was to preserve some of the open space around the house on the crest of Sunset Hill.

Restoration work began in June 1927 and involved raising and shoring up the chimney, replacing wood sills, and installing a new masonry foundation under the entire house. The burned lean-to structure at the rear of the house was also replaced. Timbers, lath, and other structural elements were taken from the nearby Paddack House, which was dismantled to provide authentic materials for the restoration. The Jethro Coffin House was rededicated in its restored condition in 1929. The 1927 restoration by Appleton and his project supervisor, Alfred Shurrocks, was summarized by Morgan Phillips of SPNEA as part of an initial inspection report in 1984. Documentation of the restoration work was carefully done with numerous photographs, measured drawings by Shurrocks, and other notes. Some of the important architectural information recorded by Shurrocks included evidence for the existence of two front gables and an original front entrance porch, in addition to many other details of the construction techniques used on the house (Stackpole 1969, 34–36; Phillips 1984; Chase 1986, 30–38).

Archaeological Investigations

Prior to 1986, one other archaeological investigation had been done on the Jethro Coffin House lot. Conducted in the summers of 1975 and 1976, under the direction of Dr. Selina Johnson, the excavations were limited to a single test trench near the northeast corner of the Coffin House. An inventory of the artifacts from the 1975–1976 excavations, including photographs of the fieldwork in progress, was prepared by the Archaeology Committee of the NHA (Jacobson et al. 1986). The artifact assemblage from the test trench was inspected during background research for the PAL survey. The mixture of eighteenth- and nineteenth-century ceramic types ranged from white Staffordshire stoneware and creamware to transfer-printed pearlware and hard whiteware. Together with other interesting items, such as part of an export porcelain tea caddy, a wooden button, slate pencils, and clay marbles, the ceramic assemblage clearly showed that the yard surrounding the house contained some potentially important archaeological deposits. A small-stemmed projectile point of quartz was the first evidence that the property contained a Precontact period Native American component, possibly dating to the Late or Terminal Archaic period (ca. 4,500 to 3,000 years ago).

The 1985–1986 Tercentennial Project

Remote Sensing

A remote sensing study of the rear yard of the Jethro Coffin House lot was the first actual step in fieldwork for the NHA tercentennial project. Remote sensing of the yard around the house with electrical resistivity was expected to yield information on subsurface anomalies that might mark the location of archaeological features such as former outbuildings, trash pits, and fence lines. It was an opportunity to test the effectiveness of this nonintrusive technique on a historic site where any anomalies could be examined by follow-up sampling with shovel test pits during the archaeological survey.

The electrical resistivity survey of the Coffin House lot was the first time that a remote sensing technique had been applied to an archaeological site on Nantucket. Soil resistivity had been successfully used by Rick Gumaer and other University of Massachusetts Amherst, archaeologists to examine other historic sites in New England for subsurface features (Gumaer et al. 1984). The nonintrusive nature of a soil resistivity survey was an advantage for the Coffin House lot survey because of its open lawn and frequent visits by tourists.

A soil resistivity survey of the rear yard area north of the Jethro Coffin House was done over a two-day period in the summer of 1985 under the direction of Gumaer. NHA Archaeology Committee members Elizabeth Little, Clinton Andrews, and Tim Lepore, as well as John Pretola (Springfield Science Museum), volunteered to assist in carrying out the survey. Gumaer provided the electrical resistivity equipment and technical expertise to collect and analyze the resistivity data.

The resistivity survey covered an area of about 200 m^2 extending from the rear wall of the Coffin House to a fence marking the northern boundary of the property. This area was divided into a one-meter square grid pattern with resistivity readings taken at each grid point. Identified anomalies ranged from small, localized "hot spots" to a fairly large "patch" extending in a northeasterly direction from the northwest corner of the house. Anomalies along the eastern edge of the rear yard conformed to previous archaeological excavations done in 1975 and the probable alignment of a water pipe leading to an existing outhouse. Part of the large "patch" anomaly was suspected to be the site of outbuildings (outhouse, shops) mentioned in a 1708 deed for the property (Jacobson et al. 1986; Little et al. 1987) (see Figure 1.2).

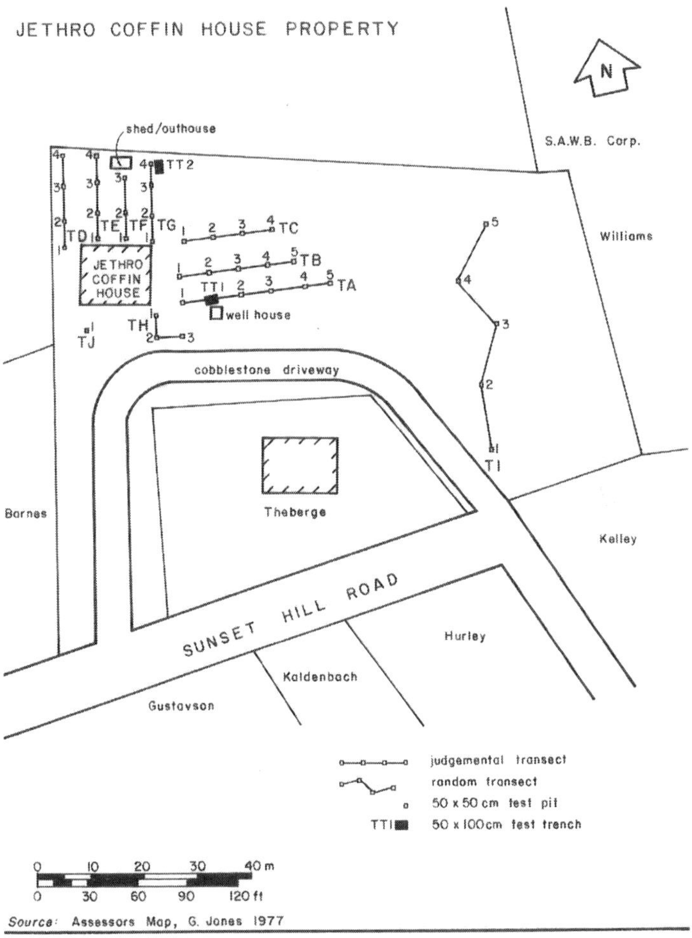

Figure 1.2. Location of Subsurface Testing on Jethro Coffin House Property

Intensive Survey

In April 1986, PAL conducted the fieldwork phase of the intensive archaeological survey. The general objective of this survey was to intensively sample the open property or lot surrounding the Jethro Coffin House. Specific goals were to assess the type, condition, and research potential of archaeological deposits and to identify locations of former outbuildings and garden plots. Condition was important, since it was expected that restoration and stabilization work done on the house in 1927 had likely disturbed older archaeological deposits around the foundation.

To organize the subsurface testing, the Jethro Coffin House lot was divided into four sections that were investigated using different sampling methods. These sections included the side yard east of the house and a low meadow swale below it, the back yard to the rear (north) of the house, and the front yard and a densely wooded area in the extreme east/southeast portion of the property.

Sets of parallel transects with 50 × 50 cm test pits placed at 5-meter intervals were used to sample the most archaeologically sensitive parts of the property. These were the back yard, side yard and swale east of the house, and the front yard. The back yard had anomalies from the soil resistivity survey and possible outbuilding sites; the side yard and swale was a likely location for former gardens and deposits of household refuse. The three parallel transects placed in the side yard and swale and four transects in the rear yard formed a 5-meter grid over these sections of the property.

The area of lowest archaeological sensitivity was the wooded southeastern part of the lot extending from the swale to Sunset Hill Road. Shovel test pits in this wooded area were placed at a 10-meter interval along a single randomly oriented transect. Two 50 × 100 cm trenches were used to investigate small features first encountered in test pits. These included a deposit of brick-and-mortar rubble along the northern property line and a brick-and-cobble paving found on the north side of the well in front of the Coffin House.

Side Yard and Swale

A few test pits in the side yard showed evidence of disturbance such as mixed loam topsoil and sandy subsoil with coal ash from either landscaping or installation of an exterior water faucet on the Jethro Coffin House. In the meadow swale east of the house test pits revealed a 30–80 cm deep accumulation of sandy loam that appeared to be a typical plow zone enhanced by erosion and slope wash. A gray sand podzol or leached zone separated the plow zone from a coarse sand subsoil horizon.

The ceramic assemblage from the deep sandy loam in the swale consisted of predominantly glazed and unglazed redware (150 sherds). Other diagnostic ceramic types had median manufacture dates ranging from 1730 to 1791. Creamware (69) was most frequent followed by decorated delft (35), smaller amounts of lead-glazed (combed and dotted) slipware (14), and fine white stoneware (15). English brown or Westerwald stoneware and Chinese export porcelain were limited to a few sherds. Late eighteenth to early nineteenth century wares—with median dates ranging from 1800 to 1830—were mostly undecorated (55) and transfer printed (15) pearlware. A small amount of whiteware was found in the disturbed fill of a trench containing a water pipe running across the side yard.

Vessel forms included a basal sherd from a small slipware cup or bowl, a white stoneware plate rim in a "barley" pattern (ca. 1740–1770), and two sherds from a stoneware bowl and cup with an overglaze hand-painted decoration in brown, blue, and green enamel. A few rim sherds were from pearlware plates with a shell- or feather-edged treatment. Among the small samples of glass artifacts from the swale were a fragment of a large, hand-blown bottle with a deep basal indentation and a fragment of a wineglass with an engraved decoration. The thirty-one tobacco pipe stem fragments had bore diameters ranging from 4/64" to 7/64", producing a mean date of 1735. This is close to the median dates for some of the eighteenth-century ceramic types found in the meadow swale area.

Structural materials (brick, window glass, nails) and faunal remains such as pieces of shell, mammal, and fish bone were widely dispersed across this part of the site. A distinct concentration of bone fragments in two test pits on Transect B may have marked the location of a trash pit disturbed by plowing. A few fragments of brown-yellow European flint and a piece of coral may have been brought to Nantucket as ship's ballast. Various occupants of both the Jethro Coffin and Paddack houses were mariners and could have brought these materials to their homes.

Precontact period Native American material found in the swale included a midsection fragment from a projectile point of tan rhyolite and a large, bifacial blade of quartz. Six pieces of chipping debris were recovered and were made of argillite, quartzite, and an unidentified metamorphic rock. All of these items were in the deep sandy loam topsoil or plow zone and the upper subsoil horizon.

The only feature found in the meadow swale area east of the house was a loose paving of cobbles and brick fragments in a test pit on the northeast side of the well house. Buried under a thin loam deposit, this paving suggested that some attempt was made to prepare the ground surface around the well to facilitate rapid drainage and to prevent erosion. It also was good evidence that the present location of the well house corresponds to the well or "pump" referred to in numerous deeds for the Jethro Coffin and Paddack houses.

Back Yard Area

Four evenly spaced transects created a grid of test pits across the back yard of the Jethro Coffin House lot. Fourteen test pits were excavated at 5 m intervals along these transects, which also conformed to the north-south orientation of the 1 m-meter grid used to organize the earlier soil resistivity survey. Several test pits within the grid were on the locations of anomalies identified in the soil resistivity survey. A single 50 × 100 cm trench (Test Trench 2) was excavated on a suspected feature corresponding to the former location of an outbuilding near the rear fence line.

Soil profiles exposed in the back yard were varied and showed much more evidence of alteration from diverse activities than those in the side yard swale section of the property. Filling or landscaping, restoration of the house, and installation of utility lines were all sources of previous disturbance to this part of the yard. The least altered soil profiles were along Transect D near the western edge of the back yard and consisted mostly of two zones of dark-brown sandy loam extending to about 50 cm below the surface. Closer to the center of the back yard, test pits along Transect E were composed of an upper-loam topsoil with coal ash about 30 cm in depth overlying a grayish-brown, sandy loam A-horizon. This buried A-zone appeared to be an older yard surface and contained ceramic sherds, glass, and other eighteenth- and early-nineteenth-century artifacts. The B_1 subsoil horizon across the entire back yard was a typical dark-yellow/orange coarse sand.

Near the exterior rear wall of the Jethro Coffin House, test pits on Transects E and F exposed evidence of the 1927–1928 restoration work in the form of redeposited loam topsoil and subsoil, which extended from the surface to a depth of 30 cm. The first test pit excavated on Transect F (F1) uncovered a 15-cm layer of brick-and-mortar rubble above an undisturbed sandy loam A-horizon. This restoration-related disturbance appeared to be limited to a narrow zone next to the exterior wall of the house and may not extend more than 1 m into the back yard. Another recent disturbance from water and sewer lines installed along the eastern edge of the back yard was found in test pits on Transect

G (G2, G3). In both test pits, cast iron and ceramic water and sewer pipes leading to the existing outhouse were found under mixed-loam topsoil and sandy subsoil fill.

A trash pit feature containing a dense deposit of ceramic sherds and glassware was found in the location of a strong anomaly identified in the electrical resistivity survey. In test pit F2, a thin deposit of loam topsoil and dense coal ash about 20 cm thick covered the top of the trash deposit. This feature was a concentration of ceramic sherds, glass, and structural materials (brick, nails, window glass) that extended to about 45 cm below surface. At this depth it appeared to intrude into an older, late-eighteenth-century deposit in the upper B_1 subsoil horizon.

Ceramic sherds in the trash deposit were primarily early-nineteenth-century types such as hand-painted and transfer-printed pearlware with lesser amounts of domestic stoneware, glazed redware, and cream-colored ware. Although the sherds were highly fragmented, identifiable vessel forms in the trash pit assemblage included pearlware plates with a feather -edge and transfer-printed decoration, a small jug or pitcher with a hand-painted floral design in blue, and what could have been a child's mug or cup of red-and-green, transfer-printed whiteware. A chamber pot of glazed redware was represented by a single-rim sherd. Glass items found in the trash pit included a very small hand-blown, light-green bottle about 1½ inches in height and a molded, aqua-colored bottle base with embossed lettering that likely held patent medicine or other preparations. The basal portions of a large clear tumbler with beveled sides, a dark-green wine bottle, and an aqua- colored beverage bottle were also found. Brick and window glass in the trash deposit showed no obvious evidence of burning from the fire that allegedly damaged part of the rear lean-to on the house in the 1860s. The B_1 subsoil horizon under the trash deposit contained eighteenth-century white stoneware, redware, and creamware sherds and fragments of dark-green bottle glass.

The suspected location of another feature in the back yard was investigated with a 50 × 100 cm trench (Test Trench 1). A mid-nineteenth-century photograph of the Jethro Coffin House showed two small outbuildings, one of which appears to be a privy, in this location. A shallow depression filled with brick, mortar rubble, and a few boulders was excavated to about 50 cm below the surface, but no evidence of a filled privy or outbuilding was found at this depth. A filled privy or other feature could still be present below this rubble deposit.

Ceramic sherds from test pits in the back yard included primarily redware, creamware, and various pearlware (plain, transfer-printed, hand-painted polychrome). A group of ninety-seven sherds, with median date ranges from 1730 to 1791, consisted of mostly creamware and white Staffordshire stoneware with a few pieces of delft, lead-glazed yellow slipware, and English brown stoneware. This was a smaller, less diverse assemblage of eighteenth-century ceramics in comparison to that collected from the side yard and swale area of the property. In the back yard, these ceramic types were dispersed in a buried sandy loam (A-horizon) assumed to contain artifacts relating to late seventeenth- and eighteenth-century occupations of the Jethro Coffin House.

Nineteenth-century ceramics, with median dates ranging from 1800 to 1860, comprised the largest category of sherds. Most of the sherds (228) in this grouping were all pearlware, predominantly plain and transfer painted with smaller numbers of hand-painted polychrome and blue- or green-edged wares. Included in this total are the pearlware sherds from the trash deposit described earlier. Domestic stoneware, whiteware, and a few pieces of yellowware made up the remainder of this grouping. These mostly mid-to-late-nineteenth-century ceramic types were found as small sherds scattered throughout the loam topsoil forming the upper half of soil profiles in the back yard.

An analysis of twenty-eight white clay tobacco pipe stem fragments from the back yard using the Binford (1962) regression formula yielded a mean date of 1734. This date is very close to the one (1735) calculated for pipe stems from the side yard and swale section of the house lot. It was somewhat later than most of the median dates for ceramics found in the back yard, dominated by early-to-mid-nineteenth-century types.

In addition to the concentration of window glass and nails in the trash deposit, other interesting structural materials found in test pits were three machine-cut iron spikes about 3½" to 4" in length and four large nails of copper or bronze of the type used in shipbuilding. No concentration of brick, nails, or other structural materials was found near the northern or rear edge of the house lot where it was expected that these materials might help locate former sheds or other outbuildings.

The sample of about 200 pieces of faunal material from the back yard area consisted of mammal, bird, fish bone, and shellfish remains. Most of these faunal remains were unidentifiable, but there were ten recognizable fragments of long bone from large- or medium-size mammals, possibly from a cow, pig, and/or a sheep. Other domestic animal remains included a broken boar tusk and six other teeth from a sheep and a pig. A dense concentration of bone fragments found near the exterior rear wall and northeast corner of the Jethro Coffin House was in an area disturbed by restoration work. It was likely part of an interior, subfloor refuse deposit that was excavated and reburied during the 1928 stabilization work on the foundation. Quahog (*Mercenaria* sp.)

comprised most of the sample of eighty-eight pieces of shell found in test pits across the back yard.

Precontact period Native American cultural material from the back yard was limited to two pieces of quartz shatter and a tabular fragment of gray-green argillite chipping debris found in test pits near the rear of the house. The Native American archaeological component probably extended from the lower meadow swale area on to the slightly elevated portion of the site later selected as the location for the Jethro Coffin House.

Front Yard Area

A subsurface sampling of the front yard part of the site was conducted with four test pits placed along two short transects. Transects H and J originated on the southeast and southwest corners of the Jethro Coffin House and extended south/southeast toward the driveway. Soil profiles showed little evidence of a previous disturbance. A dark-brown sandy loam topsoil 20–35 cm thick covered a lower deposit of lighter gray-brown loam extending to about 50 cm below the surface. This lower deposit of sandy loam appeared to be an older, buried A-horizon and contained mid-to-late-eighteenth-century artifacts. The underlying B_1 subsoil horizon was a pebbly, dark-yellow sand, similar in color and texture to the subsoil observed in other parts of the house lot.

The thirty-six sherds of red earthenware from the front yard included black-glazed redware such as that found in other sections of the house lot with buried domestic refuse. Another forty sherds were eighteenth-century ceramic types such as fine white stoneware, creamware, delft, combed slipware, and Westerwald and English brown stoneware with median manufacture dates ranging from circa 1730 to 1791. These ceramics were found within a lower, gray-brown sandy loam that appeared to be a buried A-zone soil. This soil zone contained a typical sheet refuse deposit of household debris, such as ceramics, bottle glass, bone, and shell fragments associated with the late-seventeenth-to-eighteenth-century occupation of the Jethro Coffin House. The small size of the sherds and glass fragments was consistent with their being dumped on an active surface such as the front dooryard or driveway, where they would have been easily broken and trampled into the soil.

Southeast Section of the House Lot

The wooded southeast part of the Jethro Coffin House lot was investigated with a single randomly oriented test pit transect. Transect I extended from the extreme southeast corner of the property in a northwesterly direction toward the open meadow/swale below the house. The soil profiles in this densely wooded area were very uniform, consisting of a dark-grey sandy loam topsoil or plow zone about 30 cm thick over a grey quartz sand podzol or leached zone. Below, about 40 cm to 45 cm from the surface, was a strongly oxidized orange-brown B_1 subsoil horizon. Near the poorly drained eastern edge of the house lot, this oxidized subsoil was replaced by a very deep podzol and brown-to-black muck soils. The plow zone in this part of the house lot yielded a scatter of eighteenth- and nineteenth-century ceramic sherds and brick and nail fragments such as those found in greater amounts in the nearby swale. One quartz flake was the only Precontact period Native American object. The most interesting artifact was a tubular bead of dark-blue glass found in test pit I-5, closely resembling the glass trade beads found in seventeenth-century contexts on other Native American and Colonial sites in southern New England.

Paleobotanical Analysis

The use of plants by the former occupants of the Jethro Coffin House was a topic of interest from the earliest stages of this project. The design and installation of a Colonial-period garden was part of the tercentennial year plan for the property. Little's proposal for an archaeological survey first suggested that paleobotanical research should be part of the project. Like the remote sensing survey, the proposed archaeological investigation was an opportunity to apply a technique that had not yet been used on any historic period site on Nantucket. The flotation of soil samples from other sites in urban settings such as Newport, Rhode Island, had demonstrated that floral remains such as seeds could be recovered from feature fill. These floral remains (unburnt and carbonized seeds, fruit pits, plant parts) indicated the types of plant foods making up the diet of occupants of houses and small-scale changes in the landscape, such as vegetation succession in vacant lots, yards, and other open spaces (Mrozowski 1979, 1984). Soil flotation analysis was expected to indicate something about the past location of garden plots used for vegetables or herbs, as well as larger parcels of plow land used for crops (grains, flax, etc.).

A set of eleven, one-liter soil samples for paleobotanical analysis was collected from specific parts of the property during fieldwork. Nine of these samples were taken from test pits along three transects in the overgrown meadow or swale east/southeast of the house. The swale was thought to have been a garden plot and contained relatively dense deposits of household refuse in a deep loam probably representing a plow zone horizon. Two other soil samples were from test pits in the back yard. They contained a shallow deposit of eighteenth-century artifacts and a dense trash deposit or pit feature containing early-to-mid-nineteenth-century ceramic sherds and bottle glass. Both deposits appeared to be associated with distinct depositional events on the site.

The set of eleven soil samples was processed in a flotation tank at PAL, and the recovered floral remains were identified and interpreted by Steven Mrozowski. A preliminary analysis of the thousands of seeds from these samples was able to identify specimens from ten plant families or species and was considered good evidence of gardening on the property. The samples included *Chenopodiaceae* (chenopodium), *Compositae* (flowering weeds), and *Leguminoseae* (possibly bean and alfalfa). The chenopodium and flowering weed species were plants that frequently become established in areas of disturbed or open soils such as an open plowed field or garden plot.

Summary

A substantial amount of information was collected from the below-ground component of the Jethro Coffin House during the archaeological survey. A majority of the house lot was found to contain intact and potentially significant archaeological deposits related to most of the occupation span (ca. 1690 to the 1840s) of the house. Most of the previously disturbed areas were of limited size and in close proximity to the house on the north (rear) and east sides, with the exception of several modern utility lines extending across the back yard from the northeast corner of the house. The specialized studies such as remote sensing and paleobotanical analysis yielded more information than originally expected.

Subsurface testing within the back yard area of the property was planned so that soil anomalies identified during an earlier remote sensing survey using electrical resistivity could be investigated. The discovery of a dense deposit of nineteenth-century household refuse on the location of one of the strongest resistivity anomalies in the back yard was an important finding of the archaeological survey. This trash pit feature contained ceramic sherds and bottle glass that provided a majority of the information now available for activity at the Jethro Coffin House during the early nineteenth century, circa 1800 to 1830. A paleobotanical analysis also yielded a set of data that was larger and more complex than first expected. The eleven soil samples collected from selected sections of the house lot yielded seeds and plant remains that provide good evidence for the existence of open, cultivated land such as a garden plot on the Jethro Coffin House property.

Other information was relevant to the historic contexts guiding the interpretation of archaeological data from the property. While it was expected that some evidence of the arrangement of outbuildings on the house lot would be uncovered, no physical remains of this type of structure was found in the archaeological survey. Ephemeral buildings such as sheds or workshops may not have been placed on foundations of stone or brick. However, there was also a noticeable absence of other evidence, such as concentrations of nails, window glass, rotted wood, or other structural debris or items that might have been stored in these outbuildings. Photographs of the house and lot showed that by the mid-to-late nineteenth century, outbuildings were located against the rear fence line, and it is possible that they were always on that part of the property. Despite the lack of structural remains, these photographs and the continuity evident in other use of space within the house lot, such as the well, garden plot, and driveway, make it likely that outbuildings were located near the rear lot line.

Since no evidence of a barn was found, it is also possible that occupants of the Jethro Coffin House used one of the outbuildings on the adjacent Paddack House lot, an area that was not tested as part of this survey.

Depositional patterns reflected by the distribution of artifacts and features provided evidence of continuity or conservatism in the arrangement of activities on the Jethro Coffin House lot. One of the most distinct depositional patterns illustrated by the archaeological data was the presence of typical sheet refuse deposits around the house and in the lower meadow/swale area. In the front yard, a discrete layer of eighteenth-century artifacts and faunal remains was in a buried sandy loam topsoil zone. Similar deposits appeared to be present in the back yard but were altered to some extent by later, nineteenth-century events such as filling/landscaping with coal ash and the disposal of household refuse in a trash pit. In the late seventeenth to eighteenth centuries, depositional processes included the disposal of large amounts of domestic refuse such as ceramic sherds, bottle glass, animal bones, and shellfish remains in the lower meadow/swale area. There is good evidence that this part of the property was actively used as cultivated land, possibly a garden plot, and that household trash would have been dumped there to enrich the soil. An analysis of floral remains found in soil samples suggested that the meadow/swale was used for agricultural purposes. Large numbers of seeds from several species of low-lying weeds commonly found in disturbed or open ground such as gardens were identified in soil samples processed by flotation. They indicate that a garden could have been located there over a long period of time in the eighteenth to nineteenth centuries. An 1863 photograph shows a patch of open land inside a fence next to the well house that stands on the western slope of the meadow/swale area.

Other archaeological evidence in the form of a brick-and-cobble paving indicated that the well on the Jethro Coffin House lot was always in its present location. This feature was found on the north side of the existing well house and contributed to a better understanding of documentary sources that describe how the well was shared by occupants of the Jethro Coffin and Paddack houses over a span of approximately ninety years.

Some use of the space within the Jethro Coffin House lot probably changed in the early nineteenth century. In particular, the disposal of household refuse appears to have shifted from the side yard and meadow/swale to the back yard. The early-nineteenth-century trash pit feature found in the back yard may have been the result of a change in occupancy of the house, possibly from the Paddack to Turner family in 1840. The ceramic sherds, bottles, and other household refuse in this feature could have been cleaned from the house and then buried in a pit excavated in the back yard. Coal ash also appears to have been used in filling, grading, and/or landscaping the back yard and was widespread over this part of the house lot. After the first decades of the nineteenth century, there appears to have been much less disposal of household refuse in the meadow/swale part of the property.

The abandonment of the Jethro Coffin House as a dwelling in the 1860s was reflected in the archaeological assemblage as a whole. Artifacts from the mid-to-late nineteenth century, particularly ceramics, were present only in very small amounts relative to older eighteenth- and early-nineteenth-century types. The abandonment and eventual change in function from a dwelling to a storage outbuilding (hay barn) were related to a larger episode of economic decline on Nantucket. Within this larger context, the late-nineteenth-century treatment of the Jethro Coffin House before repairs in 1881 stands in sharp contrast to its relative value in the late seventeenth and early eighteenth centuries, when the house was a prominent display of the political and socioeconomic achievements of two important Nantucket families (Coffin and Gardner).

The Jethro Coffin House is now one of the most extensively studied historic properties on Nantucket. The study described here was the first systematic sampling and interpretation of the archaeological component of a historic period standing structure on Nantucket. The comprehensive documentary research done by members of the NHA was of great value for enhancing the interpretation of the archaeological assemblage. It provided insights into family and household composition, property transfers, and the occupations or trades of persons living in the Jethro Coffin House from the late seventeenth through the mid-nineteenth centuries. The findings of this multidisciplinary study should provide a useful benchmark for any future archaeological investigations of similar historic properties on the island.

Works Cited

Binford, Lewis R. 1962. A New Method of Calculating Dates from Kaolin Pipestem Fragments. *Southeastern Archaeological Conference Newsletter* 9 (1).

Chase, Helen Winslow. 1986. *Jethro Coffin House Chronology 1686–1986*. Unpublished ms. in possession of author.

Forman, Henry Chandler. 1966. *Early Nantucket and Its Whale Houses*. New York: Hastings House.

Gumaer, D. R., R. Paynter, D. Weston, and R. Del Gizzi. 1984. Geophysical Applications and Horizontal Site Structure in New England Historical Sites. Paper presented at the 34th Annual Meeting of the Northeastern Anthropological Association.

Jacobson, Marlo, J. C. Andrews, Louise Hussey, and Elizabeth Little. 1986. Inventory of Artifact Finds from the 1975–1976 Archaeological Excavations at the Jethro Coffin House. In *Background Essays for an Archaeological Study of the Jethro Coffin House Lot*, ed. Elizabeth A. Little, 1–14. *Nantucket Archaeological Studies* 7. Nantucket, MA: Nantucket Historical Association.

Lancaster, Clay. 1972. *The Architecture of Historic Nantucket*. New York: McGraw-Hill.

Little, Elizabeth A. 1986. Title Search for Jethro Coffin House in Mendon, Massachusetts. In *Background Essays for an Archaeological Study of the Jethro Coffin House Lot*, ed. Elizabeth A. Little, 1–40. *Nantucket Archaeological Studies* 7. Nantucket, MA: Nantucket Historical Association.

Little, Elizabeth A., T. Lepore, R. Gumaer, J. C. Andrews, J. Pretola, and J. N. Little. 1987. *Resistivity Study at the Jethro Coffin Houselot*. Archaeology Committee. Nantucket, MA: Nantucket Historical Association.

Little, Elizabeth A., and Margaret Morrison. 1986. The Mendon-Nantucket Connection, 1708–1737. In *Background Studies for an Archaeological Study of the Jethro Coffin House Lot*, ed. Elizabeth A. Little, 1–32. *Nantucket Archaeological Studies* 7. Nantucket, MA: Nantucket Historical Association.

Macy, William F. 1929. *Nantucket's Oldest House*. Written and compiled for the Nantucket Historical Association. Nantucket, MA: The Inquirer and Mirror Press.

Mrozowski, Stephen A. 1979. *Archaeological Investigations in Queen Anne Square, Newport, Rhode Island.* Manuscript on file at the Department of Anthropology, Brown University, Providence, Rhode Island.

Mrozowski, Stephen A. 1984. Middle Range Theory, Households, and Floral Analysis in Historical Archaeology. Paper presented at the Annual Meeting of the Society for Historical Archaeology, Williamsburg, Virginia.

Noel Hume, Ivor. 1985. *A Guide to the Artifacts of Colonial America.* Reprinted, originally published 1969. New York: Alfred A. Knopf.

Phillips, Morgan. 1984. *Jethro Coffin House, Nantucket, Massachusetts.* Report of Initial Inspection, April 1984. Boston, MA: The Society for the Preservation of New England Antiquities.

South, Stanley. 1978. Evolution and Horizon as Revealed in Ceramic Analysis in Historical Archaeology. In *Historical Archaeology: A Guide to Substantive and Theoretical Contributions,* ed. Robert Schuyler, 68–82. Farmingdale, NY: Baywood Publishing.

Stackpole, Edouard. 1969. The "Oldest House" Becomes a National Historic Landmark. *Historic Nantucket* 17 (2). Nantucket, MA: Nantucket Historical Association.

Starbuck, Alexander. 1924. *History of Nantucket.* Boston, MA: C. E. Goodspeed.

2

Native American Architecture on Nantucket Island, Massachusetts

Mary Lynne Rainey

In southern New England, the search for archaeological remains of Native American residences, community structures, or specialized building forms has been driven by a broad set of regional ethnohistoric descriptions, archaeological site data, and nineteenth- and twentieth-century imagery believed to encompass the physical reality of Algonquian vernacular architecture. Vernacular architecture can be defined in this case as an expression of Native control of the layout and construction of residential and institutional buildings within the social, cultural, and environmental context of the people (Kapches 1993, 138). The collective emphasis among historic and contemporary writers on wigwams as a universal Native house form has greatly influenced how archaeologists working in Algonquian territory have approached the potential for their discovery. Despite the well-defined and analyzed longhouse footprints, residential complexes, fortifications, and other features of Iroquoian structures and settlement patterns, the archaeological signature of traditional Indian households or buildings in general has remained illusive throughout southern New England. In a synthesis of regional (southern New England) sites containing architectural information, Juli and Lavin (1996, 86) note, "It is clear that the archaeologically recovered structural data from the region are sparse. Several of the reported house forms are in excavation contexts that are either unclear, or poorly dated. Even the most careful excavations in this region are often hampered by poor preservation, overlapping elements from several periods and indistinct subsoil features." New discoveries in recent years are beginning to reveal the regional diversity in the styles and functions of traditional Native American structures that existed and evolved for thousands of years.

On Nantucket Island, most nineteenth- and twentieth-century historians have generalized the terms for Indian residences of the seventeenth and eighteenth centuries as either "wigwams," referring to traditional construction, or "English-style houses," referring to those constructed using boards. In both primary and secondary documentary records, Native institutional structures fall under the interchangeable words "meetinghouse," "church," and "school." Despite a substantial Indian population on Nantucket into the first half of the eighteenth century, standing wigwams in Squam in 1797, and a wood-framed Indian meetinghouse adapted as a Colonial residence until 1839, there are no known written descriptions of the appearance, construction materials, or design and engineering of residential, ceremonial, or institutional buildings built and used by the Nantucket Indians of the seventeenth and eighteenth centuries. This disregard for the details of daily Indian life can be attributed in part to the Christian Indian movement on Nantucket during the pre-Colonial and post-Colonial era, combined with widespread Colonial exploitation and the marginalization of Indians in the context of the whaling industry.

To address the topic of historic Native American architecture, Dr. Elizabeth Little scoured deeds and probate records, resulting in an inventory of sixty seventeenth-to-eighteenth-century Indian houses, which were recognized by the English as property of value, and presumably constructed using boards and hardware in the English-built style (Little 1981). It was her contention that traditional wigwams, on the other hand, had no market value for the English and, therefore, were not inventoried or referred to as houses in the records (Little 1981, 6). While drawing a strong case for Indian-built wooden houses to exist today in Siasconset Village, originally a seventeenth-century group of small fishing shelters on the eastern elbow of the island, Little's comprehensive manuscript underscores the lack of written records that describe indigenous building forms on Nantucket.

With limited documentary records containing detail on the subject, a clear understanding of traditional Precontact, Contact, and Colonial period vernacular architecture on Nantucket must draw from the archaeological record. In order to identify these sites, archaeologists working under contract to assist project proponents in meeting their regulatory requirements on Nantucket consider several different lines of evidence. These include the regional and local ethnohistoric and historic records of Indian building forms, characteristics of residential archaeological sites from elsewhere in the region, Nantucket Indian deeds and probate inventories, island merchant account books, Christian Indian material culture studies, and the Native American cultural context and landscape history of the specific area under study. Since 1997, this multidisciplinary approach to the archaeology of Nantucket has contributed to the discovery of seven systematically excavated archaeological sites containing evidence of Native American traditional domestic and institutional architecture prior to and after European settlement (see Figure 2.1). Analyses of these sites are leading to a better understanding of the diversity and antiquity of indigenous architectural traditions on Nantucket.

This chapter reviews key primary and secondary documentary sources that reference regional (New England) and local (Nantucket Island) Native American building forms and provides an abbreviated historic context within which Indian vernacular architecture adapted on Nantucket. Although Indian probate records and merchant account books inform us of material culture types (including purchased building materials) that could, if discovered in an archaeological context, support a domestic site interpretation, these records do not describe Indian homes or reveal elements of the natural environment used in traditional architecture. For this reason, material culture is not a central topic of this chapter. Rather, this chapter synthesizes the nature of archaeological work on Nantucket through the present and focuses on recent and systematic projects, driven by federal and state legislation, that have provided new information about Native American vernacular architecture.

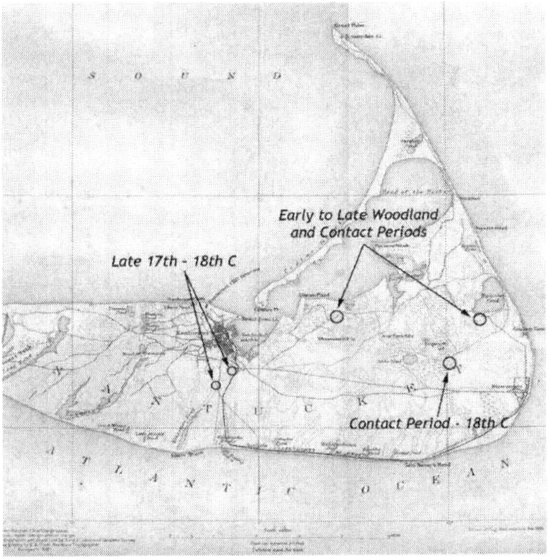

Figure 2.1. Nantucket Archaeological Sites Containing Information on Native American Vernacular Architecture Plotted on 1893 USGS Topographic Map

Ethnohistory of Algonquin Architecture: A Regional Review of Sources

Ethnohistoric accounts, historic photographs, and renderings of Algonquin structures are numerous and encompass a broad territory. From Massachusetts, Connecticut, Rhode Island, southeastern New York, and coastal regions to the north and south, Contact and Colonial period descriptions and illustrations derive from seamen and explorers, missionaries, naturalists, entrepreneurs, and adventurers. Among them, Giovanni de Verrazzano in 1524 (Wroth 1970), Samuel de Champlain from 1604 to 1618 (Champlain 1907), Henry Hudson in 1609 (Laet [1625]1841), Daniel Gookin in 1621 (Gookin 1806), John Josselyn from 1638 to 1663 (Josselyn 1865), William Wood from 1629 to 1630 (Wood 1977), and Roger Williams in 1643 (Williams 1936[1643].) all remarked to some degree on aspects of regional Native American architecture. With the exception of Roger Williams's detailed accounting of Narragansett Indian lifeways in Rhode Island, these men generally took note of two principal building forms, the wigwam and longhouse. Specifications on materials and method of construction techniques compare well, while allowing for significant variation in overall dimensions; for wigwams, round to semi-spherical, from 10 to 60 feet in diameter, constructed of bent saplings tied together at the top, covered with woven mats or skins, typically with a mat or skin-covered doorway or two, with a center hearth and smoke hole in the roof. Other commonly noted variations include the use of double mats, round and square sapling poles, bark coverings of walnut, birch, chestnut, and other hardwood trees, skins, rushes, and sedge. There is occasional mention of house framing left in place during seasonal moves, with only the mats and possessions carried off.

For archaeologists and historians, one of the challenges in addressing architectural variability such as this is due to the fact that by the 1630s, the term *wigwam* preempted more specific architectural terms on a regional basis and was assigned to any building occupied by an Indian (Nabokov and Easton 1989, 56). Still, many reported examples of vernacular residential architecture reveal more detail and demonstrate the great depth of this regional variability. For example, an illustration of an oval-shaped traditional residence from Niantic, Connecticut, derived from notes and sketches by Ezra Stiles, provides one of the most detailed architectural records for southern New England available, especially with regard to the interior use of space (Sturtevant 1975). In Pequot territory, Vincent (1638, 105–106) described houses within a Pequot fort, as "huts or little houses, framed like our garden arbors, something more round, very strong and handsome, covered with close wrought mats, and hempen threads, so defensive that neither rain, though ever so strong, can enter. The top through a square hole giveth passage to the smoke, which in rainy weather is covered with a plover." These types of references reveal elements of community-specific architecture that are uncommon and valuable to archaeologists challenged with discovering these sites.

The "longhouse" is the second most common building form described in historical records, generally characterized as a larger, more elaborate, dome-shaped building also constructed with a sapling frame but covered tightly with tree bark (Nabakov and Easton 1989, 52). Josselyn (1865, 99) observed Massachusetts longhouses from 60 feet (18.28 m) to 100 feet (30.48 m) long by 30 feet (9.14 m) wide, lined inside with painted rush mats. William Wood (1977, 8), who lived in Massachusetts from 1629 to 1633, noted the winter longhouse 50 feet (15.24 m) or more in length and housing forty or fifty men, however, it is unclear if this information was a direct observation or recorded by Wood during interviews with other settlers.

Aside from wigwams and longhouses, alternative house forms and specialized building types designed, constructed, and used by Native people have received nominal mention in secondary histories, and most have not been identified archaeologically. For example, Roger Williams's (1936[1643]) seventeenth-century interactions with the Narragansett Indians of Rhode Island resulted in the recognition of summer houses (a variant of the circular wigwam), watch houses (erected in cornfields to prevent scavenging), temporary hunting houses, menstrual houses, playhouses (in which stores of wampum were hung and games were played), distinctive ritual longhouses, and hot houses (a round, 6-to-8-foot diameter cell or cave with a door, typically built near a freshwater stream). In another case, an early-twentieth-century reference by Dr. Frank Speck (1909, 187) suggests that traditional Mohegan residences were square, partly subterranean structures with sod- and brush-covered roofs. These references add to the potential broad range of architectural site types that could be expected in the region and on Nantucket. Nonetheless, by 1919, the Smithsonian Institution, Bureau of American Ethnology (Bushnell 1919, 58), subsumed Native residences of the "eastern tribes" as belonging to two characteristic structures, the circular, dome-shaped wigwam and the more quadrangular longhouse with an arched roof—a common tidewater Virginia form documented in northeastern North Carolina by John White in the latter part of the sixteenth century. Of note, Bushnell's (1919) work also represents a thorough review of the ethnohistory of eastern Native architecture, including detailed descriptions of a wide range of residential and nonresidential building styles, construction methods, and functions, rarely consulted by popular historians of the twentieth century.

Review of Principal Ethnohistoric and Historic References to Native American Settlements, Buildings, and Praying Indians on Nantucket

On Nantucket, a small number of ethnohistoric and historic references fueled speculation about the lifeways of Indians from 1659, when the island was settled by colonists, through the first quarter of the nineteenth century. By then only a few Indians still residing on the island were integrated into a mixed ethnic community on the outskirts of town and were no longer a recognizable culture group. Little's thorough research on Nantucket Indian houses (1981, 2–3) summarized several of the key references to Native American buildings and the general distribution of settlement areas on the island. Included in her summary are cursory notations made by J. Hector St. John de Crevecoeur (1971), an eighteenth-century writer; Zacchaeus Macy (1792a, 1792b), an eighteenth-century island resident who had spent considerable time with the Indians; and Obed Macy (1972), a nineteenth-century island historian. The writings of Zachaeus Macy (1792a, 1792b) represent the principal and perhaps only firsthand account of the political and social structure of the Nantucket Indian communities, including sachem lineages, territories, anecdotes of well-known individuals, and, to a lesser degree, daily life. Although an invaluable reference for historians, details of the Indian-built homes and meetinghouses he witnessed are lacking.

De Crevecoer (1971) was a French-born American farmer who authored a series of descriptive and philosophical letters upon visiting Nantucket, Martha's Vineyard, and other parts of New England prior to the Revolutionary War. The letters were first published in England in 1782. During his time in Nantucket, the Indians were a nominal community who, in his words, "still live together in decent houses along the shores of Miacomet pond, on the south side of the island" (123). There is no descriptive detail, however, to suggest that he actually visited the Miacomet community and may have elected to favorably characterize their dwellings for his European audience.

Obed Macy (1972) published the first comprehensive history of Nantucket in 1835, just seventy-two years after an epidemic took the lives of an estimated 222 Nantucket Indians (Macy 1972, 58). Macy stated, "The Indians lived scattered over the island in such parts as best suited themselves. Although emigrants early purchased their land, they were still allowed to till and improve as much as was necessary for their subsistence" (54). He further characterized their homes as "neat framed houses patterned after the English" and their lifestyles as "comfortable" (57). He also refers to the existence, at one time, of four meetinghouses where Indian ministers held religious services, including "at Myercommet, a little south from the town" (56).

The foremost early-twentieth-century history of Nantucket by Alexander Starbuck (1924) is a comprehensive treatment of local social and political developments from the first settlement through the nineteenth century. Additional remarks on Native architecture by Obed Macy in 1842 were included as memoranda (Starbuck 1924, 611–13). In reference to one of their meetinghouses at "Ockorwaw," Macy (Starbuck 1924, 11–12) states, "This Meetinghouse was built of wood, according to the common practice of the time, but at what time it was built, or by whom, is not known. After these Indians had left that part of the Island the Meetinghouse stood many years. About in the year 1770, Peleg Swain removed it to Town and placed it toward the southern part of town and occupied it as a dwelling house, for which purpose it was used until the year 1838, when it was taken down." A second "memoranda" (Starbuck 1924, 612–13) includes a broad characterization of Indians dwellings and settlement patterns and the notation of the Miacomet meetinghouse standing "until about the year 1782." In contrast to his earlier remarks from 1835, Macy recalled (Starbuck 1924, 612–13) that Indian dwellings were "constructed of frail materials," "easily moved from one place to another," and "mostly wigwams; some few English built houses toward the latter part of their being called a people."

It is important to mention several contemporary historians who have integrated both primary and secondary sources, as well as oral traditions, in their treatment of Nantucket Native American history. Of note are the works of Edward Byers (1987), Nathanial Philbrick (1994), and Frances Karttunen (2005). Byers's (1987) extraordinary primary research on the sociopolitical developments of Nantucket from 1660 to 1820 confirms the absence of documentary records pertaining to Indian daily life. Philbrick (1994, 16) notes that for shelter, the Indians of Nantucket built wigwams constructed of bent saplings and mats that were moved on a seasonal basis. Based on a 1724 secondhand comment from an island visitor, Philbrick (16) suggests that Indians also built "sweat houses," temporary, cavelike structures dug into the Nantucket hillsides for use by men. Karttunen (2005), like Philbrick (1994), refers to Nantucket Indian residences as wigwams covered with grass mats and frequently moved about.

Records of missionaries reporting on Nantucket Indians are another source of general information about seventeenth- and eighteenth-century meetinghouses, which served to unite the various Congregational Indian communities across the island and to reinforce Native cultural identity (Philbrick 1994, 103). These reports were not intended to describe the human condition and in most cases are accounts of missionary success, such as numbers of Indian converts and numbers of meetinghouses. Congregational minister Timothy White preached to Nantucket Indians for over a decade beginning in 1728, and his notes, preserved at the NHA, are limited to names of pupils in attendance, payments received, and sermon ideas (NHA 1727–1759). The earliest published record of Christianized Indians on Nantucket is based on the personal experience of Daniel Gookin and his interactions with the Mayhews of Martha's Vineyard and other ministers (Gookin 1809, 166). In a very brief discussion he indicates that in 1674 there was one church on Nantucket at the eastern end of the island in a place called "Oggawame," where John Gibbs was the minister. According to the passage, the Nantucket Indians were at that time meeting in three places, including Oggawame, Squatesit, and Wannisquam. A postscript states that by 1694, there were approximately 500 adult Indians on Nantucket, five assemblies of praying Indians, and three churches (John Gardner's 1694 letter published in Gookin 1809). Gookin's discourse is also the first reference to the Indian Hiacoomes, a Martha's Vineyard convert under Thomas Mayhew, having been sent to Nantucket to assist with religious conversion.

In 1698, the Reverends Grindal Rawson and Samuel Danforth traveled through Massachusetts visiting several Indian communities and documenting the progress of the missionary efforts (Rawson and Danforth 1809). All of the communities mentioned were actually visited by Rawson and Danforth in May and June 1698. In a brief paragraph about Nantucket, five Indian congregations are recognized under the leadership of nine different Indian preachers. Rawson and Danforth (1809) mention two churches in existence on the island but do not say where they are located. Their estimation of a total of 500 adult Indians may have been derived secondhand through John Gardner, as he estimated the same in 1694 (Gookin 1809). They (Rawson and Danforth 1809, 132) also stated, "Three schools were upheld among them, though at present none, for want of primers. A good meeting house is building here; the frame whereof, at their desire and charge, is already procured by the worshipful captain Gardner. Here we preached to them in their own language, twice in one assembly, unto which they were generally convened on the Lord's day." This account suggests that a meetinghouse was under construction as a wood-framed structure similar to the English buildings of the period.

The Reverend Freeman of Boston was born in 1759 and was the first Unitarian minister in the United States. His notes on the natural resources, environment, and general culture of Nantucket in 1807 were clearly derived firsthand, although the information on Native Americans appears to be secondhand information from oral tradition gained in his discussions with island residents (Freeman 1807). In describing the divisions of the island, he states (Freeman 1807, 26), "South of the town is Miacomet, where another Indian village formerly stood." A section titled "The Indians" relates much of the information provided earlier by Zachaeus Macy and does not elaborate on their homes or meetinghouses.

In addition to these sources, countless nineteenth- and twentieth-century authors of popular Nantucket history have generalized Indian residences under the word "wigwam," and later, "English-style houses," and institutional structure types fall under the interchangeable words "meetinghouse," "church," and "school." Remarkably, although a few wigwams were still standing until 1796, there are no written descriptions or drawings of their appearance (Forman 1966, 10). Ceremonial or institutional buildings also existed in the second half of the eighteenth century, although it is unclear just how they were constructed or what they looked like. As noted earlier, the wood-framed Occawa Christian Indian meetinghouse, once situated in a traditional settlement area in the Plainfield region of Nantucket, was salvaged and relocated to town for use as a home by a prominent Colonial resident in the 1780s. The building was never described architecturally however. Zacchaeus Macy (1792a, 1792b), who participated in their meetings and wrote extensively about the Indians, did not discuss building details. Others who wrote in the late eighteenth through the twentieth centuries provide nominal and somewhat conflicting characterizations of Native residences, including wigwams, "hovels," decent houses, neat-framed houses, residences constructed of frail materials, or similar descriptions (Macy 1972; de Crevecoeur 1971; Douglas-Lithgow 1911; Starbuck 1924).

In two contemporary cases the topic of architecture is treated in more detail. Nantucket Native architecture is discussed by Henry Forman (1966) in *Early Nantucket and Its Whale Houses* and by the late Dr. Elizabeth Little (1981) in a manuscript entitled "Historic Indian Houses of Nantucket." Forman (1966, 9–11) suggests that three styles of wigwams existed on Nantucket: circular, beehive huts with a domed roof, arbor houses similar to the Quonset hut with vaulted roof, and a conical tepee with inside and outside supports. He claims that skins were not used by Nantucket Indians as they were not available, and that arbor houses were much like the first English dwellings, similar to those used by gypsies and called "tans." These statements and his illustrations are not supported with references, so it is unclear exactly where these ideas came from. Forman's (1966, 10) brief section on Indian architecture refers to an 1829 sketch map of Tuckernuck Island by Eliza Gardner (original in the NHA holdings), which depicts a subterranean dwelling labeled "Uncle Black's cave." He presumes Uncle Black to be a Native American imitating English work. Forman (1966) also attributes fishing stages to Native American invention—small shelters with lookout platforms along the coastline from which to spot whales. Little (1981) examined land evidence and probate records, account books, missionary records, and other primary documents with the goal of an inventory and a map of historic Native American residences, meetinghouses, and fish and whale houses. It was her contention that wigwams were not recorded in probate or land court, as they would not be recognized by the English proprietary as viable property (Little 1981, 6). The study identified the records of sixty Native wood-framed houses and forty-two fish and whale houses. In her manuscript, Indian property owners were organized by the Native territory in which they lived, and estimated house sites were plotted on a map. Little (1981, 21–22) believed that the rapid growth of the Siasconset fishing village at the eastern elbow of the island following the 1763–1764 epidemic was the result of Indian fish and whale houses relocated to the colonial village. As a result, she proposed that Native-influenced architecture could be discovered in Siasconset buildings (Little 1981, 26–27). She also found that wigwams were not probated or transferred and suggested that indentured or poor Indians were probably permitted to build wigwams on common land (Little 1981, 6; 1989).

A Historic Context for Nantucket Indigenous Architecture

In the search for archaeological remains of indigenous architecture, it is important to understand the degree to which life changed for Indians living on Nantucket during the period of Colonial settlement and the resulting social context of marginality for Nantucket's seventeenth- and eighteenth-century Indian population. In 1642, Thomas Mayhew, having secured patent rights to the islands south of Cape Cod, sent his son Thomas (age twenty-six) to Martha's Vineyard to begin a settlement (Worth 1902, 7). The young Mayhew quickly learned the Algonquian language of the Native inhabitants and began the work of converting Native Americans to Christianity. Although the Mayhew family's missionary efforts on Nantucket were well under way by the late 1640s, Native converts were soon used to facilitate the process (Byers 1987, 27). As a result, direct contact between the Mayhews and Nantucket

Native Americans was limited, and basic descriptive information about Native life was apparently never recorded. According to the extensive primary research conducted by Edward Byers (1987, 18–19), "Not even the Mayhews of Martha's Vineyard, who began missionary work on Nantucket in the late 1640s, left a record of Indian life."

Kellaway (1961, 245) stated that attempts to "civilize" the Native Americans on Nantucket were far more haphazard than on Martha's Vineyard. It seems that the process of religious conversion via Vineyard Native Americans resulted in the recognition of nearly all early-eighteenth-century sachems of authority as either ministers or teachers. Reverends Grindal Rawson and Experience Mayhew, upon visiting Nantucket in 1709, selected Samuel Wiswall of Harvard to learn the Algonquian language and catechize young Native Americans there. He refused, as did his brother Peleg, also a Harvard graduate, the following year, despite the monetary offers. According to Kellaway's research (1961, 246), by 1717 Wiswall had somewhat mastered the language and was pastor of Edgartown on Martha's Vineyard. However, when asked to preach to the Eastern Native Americans on Nantucket, he gave "a positive denial" (Kellaway 1961, 246). In 1731, Native American Minister Japhet Pannis was compensated 20 pounds by the commissioners for his efforts preaching to a small Anabaptist congregation of Nantucket Native Americans, and Timothy White was employed as a minister in residence from 1728 to 1749, preaching to Indian groups for about thirteen years (Kellaway 1961, 246). Despite the presence of the occasional appointed ministers from off-island, it is clear that most of the religious instruction on Nantucket on behalf of the Christianized Native Americans was delivered by Native Americans. As Byers (1987, 63) states, "A degree of autonomy was maintained by the Indian church as well, resulting as much from English neglect as from their acceptance of religious diversity." He claims that Peter Folger was the only English inhabitant of the island who took an interest in the religious life of the Native converts, at least until 1728, when Timothy White arrived. Prior to that time, the Christian Native Americans were left to run their own religious affairs (Byers 1987, 63).

Zacchaeus Macy (Macy 1792a) provided what may be the only detailed, firsthand account of their meetings, stating:

> They were very solid and sober at their meetings of worship, and carried on in the form of Presbyterians, but in one thing imitated the Friends or Quakers, so called: which was to held meeting on the first day of the week and on the fifth day of the week, and attended their meetings very precisely. I have

> been at their meetings many times and seen their devotion. (in Starbuck 1924, 122)

By the mid-eighteenth century, Native American complaints to the Massachusetts General Court were frequent, and they reveal the social and moral conflicts that had begun to overcome them. In 1747, for example, the eastern Native Americans complained that they were prevented from worshipping on the Sabbath day because they were forced to row after whales all day (Starbuck 1924, 155). The case goes on to relate, "and nantuckket English men say nantuckket Indions are no christions. It is true we cannot be a true Christions for we haue no Books that we may haue under standing by them but we are willing to do what we can to serve God In all times Especially on the Sabbath days" (Starbuck 1924, 122, original language). Another mid-eighteenth-century petition claimed that the English come to Indian towns on the Sabbath to look for men to cut whales, wash fish, and lay them out to dry and to skin sheep. As a result, the petition states, no more people come to the meetings on the Sabbath day (Byers 1987, 162). Court records testify to a number of social processes that effectively rendered many Native American families without property and reliant on the English by the mid-eighteenth century. During this period, it is apparent that there was a rapid transformation of the majority of Native American residents from being autonomous and self-sufficient to being indentured and relatively poor by English standards. Byers (1987, 99) concluded that about three fourths of the Native Americans hired for whaling crews between 1725 and 1733 were servants whose earnings were given to their masters upon the conclusion of a voyage.

The process of indentured servitude created a succession of Native American complaints that triggered a 1718 bill in the Massachusetts General Court designed to ensure that Native Americans only entered labor agreements by choice (Byers 1987, 97–98). A subsequent act in 1725 reinforced earlier laws and required parental consent for the "binding" of a child or spouse, while recognizing the economic benefits of whaling and fishing employment for both English and Native American communities. What is particularly intriguing about the act, as paraphrased by Byers (1987, 98), is the stipulation that the master, for a fee, was to assist in building houses on his servants' land, furnishing servants and their families with fuel and the like during the period of the indenture. If this was actually implemented on Nantucket, then it might explain why some of the Native American houses owned by Native American whalers disappear from the records after the 1763 epidemic. It also reinforces Little's suggestion that many Indians were living in traditional wigwams as squatters on common lands. Those who retained sachem status or direct sachem lineage in the Indian community through this period were fortunate to also retain the power to negotiate land and shares in sheep and horse commons and, for a limited time, profit (Byers 1987; Little 1996). A small proportion became successful tradesmen and whalers who had managed to prosper despite oppressive English laws, rapidly diminishing traditional homelands, and a growing movement on the part of the English toward ethnic marginalization (Byers 1987; Little 1990, 1992, 1996).

The Archaeology of Nantucket Island: A Historic Context

Amateur archaeology on Nantucket began sometime after the near-total demise of the last cohesive entity of living Native Americans, and it has been a common island pastime since the latter half of the nineteenth century. Still, local fascination with the buried remains of this once robust population was prevalent in the early nineteenth century and documented within a few years after the publication of Obed Macy's (1972) *The History of Nantucket*. Although descendants of Indians were undoubtedly living within the mixed ethnic community of Newtown, by 1835 the notion of the Native American had become a newfound curiosity for antiquarians and self-proclaimed historians. In 1835, the subject of phrenology had become a topic of public debate on Nantucket (Karttunen 2005). Phrenology evolved in the mid-1790s from the theories of Viennese physician Franz Joseph Gall, who believed that the surface of the skull was an index of an individual's psychological aptitudes and tendencies (Van Wyhe 2004). A specialist could run her or his fingers over an individual skull and provide a character analysis, often for a fee (Van Wyhe 2004). According to Van Wyhe (2004), many phrenologists were political and social reformers, some were radicals, and others were secular.

The Nantucket Atheneum opened in 1838 and launched its public outreach with a phrenological lecture series (Karttunen 2005, 57). According to Dr. Karttunen, the Reverend Henry F. Edes delivered the inaugural address at the Atheneum in January 1838. That spring, his brother Richard's fiancée, Mary Cushman, visited the island to meet the Edes family, and in April she wrote a letter to her mother about social activities on the island. The letter was printed in the 1949 Proceedings of the Nantucket Historical Association (NHA 1949) and stated, "We were engaged to go to a Phren'l society this evening, but I was too tired and stupid, so the gentlemen went without us. R. just came in from there to get two skulls (which he found Saturday afternoon in exhuming from the Native American burying place) to carry back." Karttunen (2005) also discovered that by 1846 the burial place of the victims of the Indian sickness had been so thoroughly mined by phrenological enthusiasts that Charles Dyer wrote in his diary, "One mile from town is the old Indian burial where many graves have been dug over to get the skulls. Some of the other bones are left in the ground but too much decayed to be worth bringing away." The exact location of the cemetery was forgotten within a few decades, as evidenced by the historic Ewer (1869) map placement of the landmark. In 1980, it was accidentally discovered during construction of a housing development and confirmed by the Massachusetts Historical Commission as the Miacomet burial ground (Simon 1989).

Throughout the late nineteenth and twentieth centuries, amateur archaeology was a widespread Nantucket activity for year-round residents and seasonal visitors. It was not until the last few decades of the twentieth century that information collected from island sites began to inform the scientific community beyond the goal of classifying material culture and interpreting cultural chronologies. As a result, despite the large numbers of excavated or otherwise destroyed sites on Nantucket prior to the implementation of federal and state guidelines, only traces of details specific to an understanding of Native building traditions were collected by the 1980s. After the implementation of federal and state legislation, more formalized and analytical practices in applied archaeology were integrated into the discipline, and archaeology for the sake of public recreation was no longer promoted. Nonetheless, artifact collecting remains a modern local pastime.

The discovery of Native American archaeological sites on Nantucket can be attributed to the efforts of five principal groups, each with a different history and set of objectives. They include local or seasonal resident artifact collectors, members of the Massachusetts Archaeological Society (MAS), university-sponsored field schools (University of Massachusetts and Temple University), members of the NHA, and cultural resource management (CRM) companies. In addition, since the early 1980s, occasional salvage excavations of Native American burials have been carried out by the staff of the MHC as a result of accidental discoveries during construction projects.

Artifact collectors as a group have the longest history and are responsible for the discovery of the largest proportion of prehistoric sites on Nantucket. As a recreational pastime, artifact collecting has been popular among year-round residents and seasonal visitors from the early nineteenth century to the present. However, the availability and research value of the information held by past and present artifact collectors varies. In the 1970s, several older island residents donated their artifacts and, in rare instances, field notes or records to the NHA (Little 1980, 76). Around the same time a number of early-twentieth-century collections were donated to the Peabody Museum of Harvard University in Cambridge and the Robert S. Peabody Museum in Andover.

The MAS was active on Nantucket from 1939 through 1965. The first organized MAS excavations were directed by Ripley Bullen and Edward Brooks in 1939 (Little 1989, 54). At least three sites were targeted during the early "digs" of Bullen and Brooks, including the Squam Pond, Herrecater Swamp, and Hughes sites (Brooks 1939, 1941, 1942; Bullen and Brooks 1947, 1949). The Herrecater Swamp site contained eighteenth-century artifacts indicative of a residence (Bullen and Brooks 1949) and interpreted by Little (1981, 5) as Native American, however, no information on architecture was collected. Apparently there was no MAS activity on Nantucket during the World War II years, circa 1941 to 1945. Controlled excavations resumed after the war, when the Shawkemo chapter of the MAS was formed in 1957 (Little 1989, 54). Efforts were focused on several larger sites during the course of about eight years, beginning with the Top Gale, Ram Pasture I, and Pocomo sites. Aspects of the excavation results were published by Stanley Roy (1958), Joseph Waters (1965), and Bernard Stockley (1964a, 1964b, 1968). For the Top Gale and Ram Pasture I sites, assemblage analyses and excavation details were never disclosed, however, Stockley's efforts at Ram Pasture I and Pocomo were undertaken in a more scientific manner, including some post-fieldwork analysis.

In the mid-1960s, MAS activity on Nantucket declined radically with the dissolution of the Shawkemo chapter and the introduction of a new academic focus to Nantucket archaeology. This trend was inspired by the development and implementation of federal cultural resource management legislation regarding the identification and preservation of significant archaeological properties. Within the next decade, advances in the field of archaeological method and theory, combined with an increasing awareness of Nantucket's diminishing cultural resources by the newly formed NHA Archaeological Committee, also influenced the overall decline in amateur excavations on the island.

University-affiliated field schools were held at a number of archaeological sites on Nantucket during the period 1965–1978 concurrent with the decline of MAS-sponsored work and the formation of the Massachusetts Historic Preservation Office and the NHA Archaeology Committee. In 1965, the University of Massachusetts (UMass) Amherst, initiated an archaeological studies program that included an on-island field school under the direction of Dr. Ronald Spores (Little 1980, 76). The first field school excavations were conducted at the Norcross site, an extensive oyster shell midden on the margins of Sesachacha Pond. The Norcross site had already been identified by local collectors, and MAS excavations had also taken place there in 1964. In 1966, Dr William Harrison directed a second UMass Amherst field school at the Marshall site, another shell midden located in Shimmo near the central interior part of the island. The Marshall site was the subject of a 1973 master's thesis and was later summarized in a journal article (Pretola 1973; Pretola and Little 1988, 47–68). In 1978, Dr. Barbara Luedtke of the University of Massachusetts, Boston, organized and directed a field school on the 115-acre University of Massachusetts Nantucket Field Station in Quaise (Luedtke 1980, 95–122). Unlike the earlier, site-specific field schools, Luedtke undertook a survey to determine the patterning of prehistoric activities within the field station property. The field station survey resulted in the first comprehensive treatment of archaeological site patterning within a definable study area on Nantucket. Concerned about the rapid depletion of archaeological sites, in 1972 the NHA formally assumed leadership and responsibility for any ongoing archaeological program under administrator LeRoy H. True (Little 1980, 76). In 1974, the NHA archaeological division began several years of excavations at the Quidnet site (Locus Q-6), just northwest of Sesachacha Pond (Morris 1976). Paul C. Morris, chairman of the archaeology division, reported that (Morris 1976, 61) "more than 85 enthusiastic diggers" worked at the site through the entire second field season in 1975.

It was in 1973 that Little, then an archaeology student at the University of Massachusetts Amherst, and summer resident of Nantucket, became involved with the NHA's efforts. Initially a volunteer and later a field director at the Quidnet site, she began to influence the quality of excavation and the direction of subsequent analysis and publication of results. The Quidnet site is one of the few published efforts by the NHA that revealed aspects of Native American architecture. In a 1984 summary of the excavations (Little 1984, 13), a site map depicted the relationship of sixty-six 7–10 cm diameter post molds, twenty-two of which formed a 4.75-meter arc; this was interpreted as the partial outline of a structure or structures. Many of the post molds appeared to be in pairs, suggesting that a specific support system was designed to consider improved structural stability that would not be achieved with a single-pole arrangement. The study was largely focused on assemblage and landscape analyses, and detailed aspects of the architectural style were not identified in the field or speculated on in the analyses.

In 1978, the NHA obtained a matching grant-in-aid from the Department of the Interior, Heritage Conservation and Recreation Service, through the MHC, to inventory Nantucket's prehistoric archaeological sites (Little 1980, 77). This work was coordinated by Little and Cynthia Young, chairperson of the archaeology division at the time, with Dr. Dena Dincauze, professor at the University of Massachusetts Amherst, serving as consultant. The concurrent survey of the field station by Dr. Luedtke was designed to consider the comparative results between the two different types of investigations. Objectives of the NHA project were considerable, given the history of artifact collecting and completed excavations prior to the inventory. The research team attempted to develop a comprehensive list of prehistoric cultural resources on the island by obtaining records and reports of excavated sites, interviewing collectors and property owners, identifying, cataloging, and photographing artifact collections, visiting and photographing the sites, and describing and mapping confirmed site locations. The project ultimately resulted in a report of all known Native American sites on Nantucket, which was provided to the NHA and MHC (Little 1979). In addition, MHC state site forms were prepared for inclusion in the state's cultural resource inventory.

Data gathered through the NHA project were used to develop a predictive model for prehistoric site distribution within broad environmental zones across the island (Little 1983). From 1979 through 2003, Little researched, composed, and published dozens of manuscripts addressing the history and prehistory of Nantucket Island as a director of archaeology and prolific research associate affiliated with the NHA. Consideration of her work proved essential to the success of CRM projects beginning in the late 1970s, not only for the development of valid predictive statements and research designs for archaeological surveys but also in the formulation of interpretive contexts for sites and assemblages discovered through these projects. The first multidisciplinary archaeological research project carried out on Nantucket Island was completed in 1986 on the property surrounding the NHA-owned Jethro Coffin House. Spearheaded by Little and supported by the firm PAL (see Duncan Ritchie, chapter 1 of this volume), the study exemplified the foundation of scholarly standards that Little initiated and upheld on Nantucket for decades.

The catalyst for the development of CRM standards in the United States is the National Historic Preservation Act of 1966, which recognized the importance and finite nature of archaeological resources and provided a mechanism to ensure that federal undertakings would consider their effects on significant historic and archaeological properties. Subsequent federal and state legislation augmented the same principles and formalized the objectives of three stages of archaeological investigation: identification, evaluation, and mitigation. Since the early 1980s, approximately sixty CRM surveys have been undertaken on Nantucket so that projects requiring federal or state approval would be in compliance with the law. The archaeological sites discovered through these surveys have added new and significant information about Nantucket prehistory and history. Detailed technical reports and curated collections required under these federal and state guidelines serve as permanent records for future research.

The Archaeology of Vernacular Architecture on Nantucket

Due to their relative scarcity in the regional archaeological database, the process of identifying archaeological sites that represent the Precontact through Contact periods as well as seventeenth-to-eighteenth-century buildings built and used by Indians must take into account a range of potential feature types and artifact assemblages. It is a potentially complex site type whose principal elements can be expected to vary widely (Chilton 2002, 295), although, to date, regional discoveries are extremely rare relative to the documented archaeological site database. Without an actual structure, archaeologists must interpret specific data sets in the archaeological record in order to make inferences about the design and construction methods and materials of what once stood on a site. Those data sets can include features preserved in the soil, such as organized post mold arrangements, builder's trenches, excavations into the natural topography, berms created for structural support, and artificial substrate created to improve drainage under a living area. Unfortunately, on multicomponent sites or sites that were plowed after residential occupation, post molds are often not patterned to the degree necessary to estimate the physical placement of a former structure or overall dimension and shape. In addition, the introduction of nineteenth- and twentieth-century or modern cultural materials and activities can result in the amalgamation of older features and activity areas, making it difficult to isolate the components of the original site.

The interior features of a former structure can also contribute to the interpretation of architectural elements, including hearth placement, post mold arrangements, or other features representing household furniture, soil compaction reflecting high-traffic areas, and activity areas marked by artifact accumulations that reflect the interior use of space influenced by the structural components of the building. Artifact types can also reveal the primary building materials used, including the obvious items such as wood and bark fragments, nails, window glass, and clumps of daub, and less obvious items such as grass or sedge seeds that may have accumulated as a result of the preparation of exterior wall coverings. Species identification of charred wood samples can lead to a better understanding of the forest composition at the time of occupation and, in turn, construction materials available to the community.

On Nantucket, residential Native American sites that were established before European occupation of the island would have been situated in traditional settlement areas that were familiar and within proximity to reliable resource procurement areas. These sites could have been occupied on a seasonal basis over the course of several seasons, or annually, depending on the overall environmental and social conditions of the setting through time. It is important to understand that the settlement pattern was not static, and that community decisions about relocation could vary from one year to the next. The archaeological manifestation of long-term, repeated use of a locale can include dense artifact accumulations and distinct strata saturated with the chemical constituents of deteriorated organic household refuse. In contrast, based on the post-Colonial documentary record of imposed natural resource restrictions, Native American servitude in occupations away from the home, and depletion of traditional homelands, archaeological evidence of Native traditional dwellings dating to the post-settlement era on Nantucket would be expected to include low-density distributions of food remains (calcined and unburned bone, shell fragments, charred maize and beans, and charred seeds) and specific cultural material types of both Native and European manufacture, coinciding with traces of ground-disturbing human activity that might reflect architectural elements of a wigwam or house, interior use of an enclosed space, subsistence gardening, food processing, and refuse disposal.

During the late seventeenth and eighteenth centuries, most Indian families living on Nantucket were displaced from their traditional homelands as the Colonial population surpassed the Native population. Moreover, the Miacomet community is believed to have formed after English settlement as a process largely influenced by the development and growth of the whaling industry. Due to land restrictions imposed upon the Indians and forced relocations from many of the traditional settlement areas elsewhere on the island, residential site types associated with this community would have been year-round and in existence for no longer than approximately fifty to seventy-five years. The Native American population on Nantucket was integrated into the whaling economy during the seventeenth and early eighteenth centuries, with men employed as whaleboat crews and women as on-island domestic servants often in bound positions of servitude. While there is documentary evidence that some Indians held property for a time and were financially successful during the eighteenth century, it is unclear who, if anyone, actually owned the land on which they were living. There was no designated Indian reservation, and those who held indentures for Indians in their employ may have provided their residency, as explained previously.

Beginning in 1994 I was fortunate to have had the opportunity to lead archaeological studies on Nantucket for the CRM firm, PAL, under the direction of Duncan Ritchie and eventually in my role as principal investigator. It was in this capacity that I engaged with Little over, approximately, a ten-year period, incorporating her research results into each of the projects to which I was assigned. Her comprehensive knowledge of the prehistory and history of the island and her expertise in so many areas of the discipline influenced each and every research design put forth. Through her guidance, we began to apply regionally significant radiocarbon-dating corrections to all of our Nantucket samples, and we analyzed dated shell samples for carbon replacement processes to improve the validity of our interpretations. Considering her ideas and research pertaining to settlement pattern models, Indian residences and their likely placement across the island, site aspect, Indian deeds and probate inventories, and local resource availability, among many other topics, the work carried out by PAL benefited immensely and, in turn, contributed new data. In the area of Native American vernacular architecture, four separate projects completed by PAL between 1994 and 2004 successfully identified seven former Native American structure locations that reveal diversity in building size, shape, configuration, and construction fabric (see Figure 2.1). The sites are described next.

The Coffin Farm Complex 1 Site (1994–1995)

In 1994, a Phase I (locational, or identification, phase) archaeological survey was completed on a 250-acre tract of land in the eastern portion of Nantucket in an area known historically as the Native American community of Occawa. Based on documentary records, Occawa included land around Gibbs Pond and eastward through common land referred to as Plainfield, and it was known as a large Indian settlement area within the territory of the lead sachem Wannachmamach during the mid-to-late seventeenth century (Little 1996, 194–96). The 250-acre tract under study was east of Gibbs Pond, in an area where the wood-framed Occawa meetinghouse and church were suspected to have once stood.

Other than a general location of the meetinghouse on the historic Reverend Ewer map of Nantucket (1869) and notation on the map of a community garden in Occawa, there were no clear leads to guide the survey team closer to the former meetinghouse location or associated residences. It was suspected that the main concentration of the settlement was situated on the margins of Gibbs Pond further to the west, where collectors had spent decades gathering up artifacts. The initial survey resulted in the discovery of four prehistoric and four historic sites across the 250 acres. Of these, the Coffin Farm Complex 1 Site was identified near the extant Coffin Farm outbuildings and on the perimeter of a former pasture adjacent to a wetland. Several test pits contained concentrations of brick fragments, nails, and window glass, along with bone and shell. Additional testing placed around a test pit containing a felsite flake revealed a distinct artifact-free mottled soil layer below the plow zone. This unusual buried strata and the discovery of several early-eighteenth-century artifacts in the assemblage led to the conclusion that the site may include a historic Native American component dating to the late-seventeenth or early-eighteenth centuries.

To evaluate the site for National Register eligibility, a Phase II site examination was carried out by establishing a 5 m grid across the former pasture and testing on grid points across the field (Rainey and Ritchie 1996). The highest density of early artifacts, including fragments of diagnostic seventeenth-century earthenware and stoneware, dark-green wine bottle glass, white clay pipe fragments, and architectural remains, fell within a topographic contour line at 48.3 feet, just 6/10 of a foot above the surrounding field, and spanning a 15 × 20 m section of the grid (see Figure 2.2).

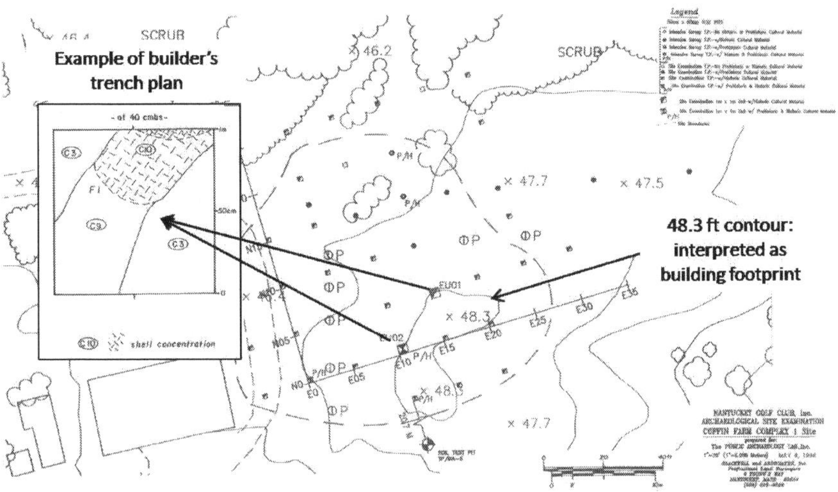

Figure 2.2. Map of the Coffin Farm Complex 1 Site with Builder's Trench Inset

In addition to increased quantities of brick, heavily patinated window glass, and nails, testing in this area recovered a fragment of a lead window muntin and a small accumulation of red daub fragments, a locally produced mixture of clay and other ingredients used as building material. Two 1 × 1 m excavation units were positioned on grid points to intersect the contour line. Both units exposed distinct linear features that corresponded to the topographic contour line, ranging from 30 to 50 cm in width and about 30 cm in depth. In both units, the linear features were packed with organic, domestic, and architectural debris, including relatively large quantities of fish and other mammal bone (both calcined and unburned), small quantities of charred maize and nut fragments, shell, pipe fragments, and bits of ceramic and glass. Remnants of what appeared to be unpatterned stake molds adjacent to the linear features were also recorded. The features in these two units were interpreted as elements of one continuous hand-dug builder's trench for an early-to-mid-seventeenth-to-eighteenth century Indian-built structure, possibly measuring as much as 10 m (30 feet) by 15 m (45 feet). The estimated building size was based on the dimensions of the irregular contour line and spatial patterning of early artifacts. Some of the test pit data beyond the limits of the linear feature documented an area with a deep, buried plow zone interpreted as a possible family garden plot or perhaps the Occawa gardens referenced by Ewer (1869).

Despite the limited archaeological sample, several artifact types suggest that the initial period of Native American residency could have coincided with the 1659 English settlement on the west end of the island. In addition to several early ceramic and stoneware types (buff-bodied, coarse earthenware, combed and dotted slipware, and German gray stoneware, for example), the collection included a mouth harp nearly identical to those found at a seventeenth-century Wampanoag burial in Warren, Rhode Island (Gibson 1980), and a red clay pipe stem dating to the early-to-mid-seventeenth century (Mrosowski 1994, personal communication).

The Coffin Farm Complex 1 Site provided evidence of a Native construction technique in which the framing of a former building was anchored in a shallow trench. The composition of the framing may have included poles as well as boards, although it is impossible to speculate on the exact structural configuration with the limited archaeological sample. If the building footprint matched the topographic contour line, as I suspect, then it is doubtful that the building was constructed in the English style. Although only eight hand-wrought nails were recovered, if the structure was predominantly made from boards, then the entire structure, or the dismantled materials, would have been recycled and reused when the site was abandoned. Still, the archaeological sample was too small to make confident statements about the composite building fabric. Based on the concentration of aged window glass, brick fragments, and one lead muntin, the structure most likely included one or more windows and a brick hearth. The discovery of the red daub is unique on Nantucket and suggests that the building fabric was reinforced and insulated for long-term and perhaps annual occupation. The exact nature of that building fabric remains a mystery, although a wide range of natural materials could have been integrated with the framing and daub. This particular region of Nantucket is characterized by clay deposits, and the original Coffin farmhouse was built upon a circular foundation of cobbles lining a cellar dug into clay not far from the archaeological site. As an anomalous architectural feature on Nantucket, the origins of the Coffin farmhouse stone cellar could lie in the Occawa settlement as a community food storage feature associated with the occupants of the Coffin Farm Complex 1 Site. The site was considered National Register eligible by the MHC, and the proponents of the golf course elected to avoid it.

Sites 19-NT-50 and 19-NT-68 (1995–1996)

In 1988, the Nantucket Planning and Economic Development Commission began the process of designing an 8.1-mile bike path from Milestone Road to Anne's Lane in Siasconset village. PAL completed the Phase I survey in 1989, reporting on many previously documented sites as well as many new ones. Phase II work to determine National Register eligibility was completed in 1991, and four Native American sites were evaluated as being significant at the national and state levels (Rainey and Ritchie 1994). Archaeological data recoveries were carried out and completed at each of the four sites in 1995, and multidisciplinary analyses of the more than 70,000 artifacts collected spanned the next few years (Rainey 2004b). Post-fieldwork analyses included radiocarbon dating, wood-species identification, faunal identifications, soil flotation and macro-botanical identifications, and phytolith analyses. Two of the four Native American sites contained domestic house floor deposits representing, in each case, the interiors of former Native American traditional residences. One site was located on an interior, slightly elevated terrace overlooking Folger's Marsh near the Quaise section of the island and the other on an interior terrace adjacent to Sesachacha Pond. Although the sites were in different environmental settings several miles apart, each of the living floors was remarkably similar, consisting of blackened, greasy soil deposits imbedded with chipped stone tools, thousands of stone flakes (the debris from tool production activity), food remains (shell and bone), and ceramics. Hundreds of interior post molds were documented, as well as several food refuse pits, center hearths, larger post molds, and, at one of the sites, plow scars from a small garden.

In the study of Native American architecture, the Polpis Road investigations provided evidence that traditional house sites were established on Nantucket during the Late Archaic to Early Woodland period, about 3,000 to 3,500 years ago. Radiocarbon-dated charcoal, shell, and maize samples provided specific time frames for site use through the Contact period (ca. 450 B.P.), while small collections of seventeenth-century ceramic and pipe fragments indicated occupation during the Contact and Early Colonial periods. These homes were articulated with the natural landscape, making use of protective slopes, slightly elevated terraces, and efficient access to critical resources. The architectural patterns observed at the two sites containing house floors were nearly identical. Based on exposure of a complete cross section of each floor, the study concluded that oval or elongated structures measuring about 8 m (27 feet) in length were constructed using small poles (averaging 5–7 cm diameter), in addition to two to three larger, interior posts (30 to 40 cm diameter) that likely supported a ridge pole (see Figure 2.3).

These deep supports were set about 1 m inside the building perimeter and spanned about 6.5 m (21 feet). The interior spatial patterning of artifacts suggested that these larger supports were also utilized as elements of interior household furniture. Because the footprints of the two structures did not change over several thousand years, I suggested that the ridge pole supports were probably left in place during periodic, and possibly seasonal, movements to other parts of the island, or to the New England mainland (Rainey 2004a, 2004b). Charred wood analyses by Dr. Lucinda McWeeney concluded that white oak and hickory were part of the local hardwood canopy when these sites were established and available resources for building materials. Phytolith analyses by Dr. Irwin Rovner and macrobotanical analyses by PAL staff shed light on local conditions at each site through time and offered insight into the potential diversity of plants available to and used by the site occupants. The wide range of faunal remains present on both sites led to the conclusion that animal skins certainly could have been used as exterior building coverings and interior bedding, however, the use of bark or reed matting may have been a more practical, efficient choice, perhaps depending on the season of the year (Rainey 2004b).

The extensive investigations and analyses concluded that domestic dwellings had been established at Sites 19-NT-50 and 19-NT-68 by the Transitional Archaic to the Early Woodland periods. Consistency in landscape positioning, architectural style, and interior use of space through multiple Early, Middle, and Late Woodland period settlements resulted in the aggregation and amalgamation of domestic refuse within the well-

BISECTION PROFILE - FEATURE 5, CONTEXT 22 - JEU 11 - FACING NORTH

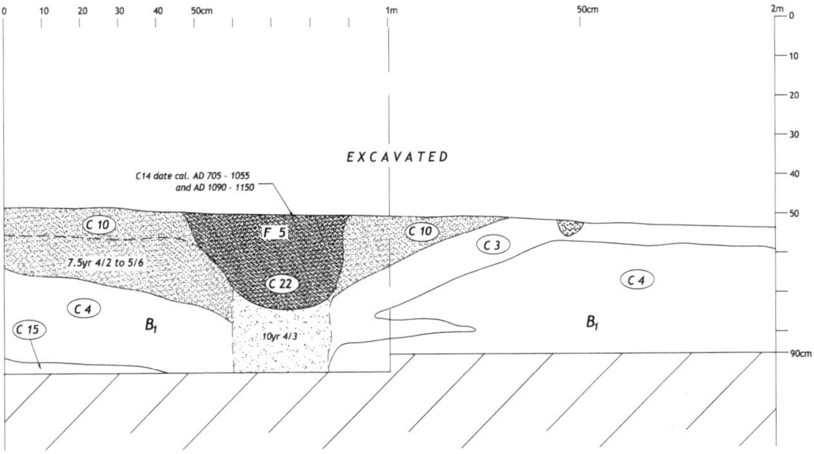

CONTEXT KEY:

C 10 10yr 3/2 very dark grayish brown with 7.5yr 4/2 dark brown - brown and 7.5yr 5/6 strong brown silty sand - Living Floor

C 3 Mottled: 10yr 4/6 dark yellowish brown, 10yr 4/3 dark brown - brown silty sand - A 1/B1

C 4 7.5yr 4/6 strong brown silty sand - B 1

C 15 10yr 5/8 yellowish brown silty sand - B 1/B2

F 5:

C 22 10yr 2/1 black silty sand with organic material and 10yr 4/3 dark brown - brown silty sand (C14 date cal. AD 705 - 1055 and 1098 - 1150)

Figure 2.3. Profile of Interior Ridge Pole Support Feature: 19-NT-50

defined limits of each house site. In each case, the sites represent the domestic domains of family groups whose principal activities were carried out inside of their homes or at the source of critical resources within the larger settlement territory. Despite some variations in the composition of artifact assemblages and radiocarbon data, the information suggests that the environmental differences between the two locations had little effect on the overall size, shape, and configuration of each building through time. The use of the ridge pole design would be a logical necessity on Nantucket due to the windy conditions much of the year.

For many generations, these sites served as familiar landscapes within which homes were constructed and families carried out their daily routines. Both sites contained very small assemblages of seventeenth-century cultural material, including ballast flint, diagnostic kaolin pipes, and earthenware, and no evidence of subsequent activity through the historic and modern periods. It was concluded that the sites were abandoned during the seventeenth century, when Indians across the island were being integrated into the whaling industry and were faced with severe natural resource restrictions and a drastically changing lifestyle.

The Dwelling Site (2004)

In 2003, PAL, to support the approval of a residential housing project, undertook an archaeological survey for Nantucket Education Trust (Rainey and Ingham 2006). The small, 1.2-acre property was set in a shallow depression behind the school and at the end of a dead-end gravel road near the upper reaches of Miacomet Pond. In terms of the cultural context, the property was within an area designated by Little in the 1970s as a Late Archaic period cremation burial district (Little 1988) and also within the boundaries of Little's reconstruction of the Miacomet Praying Indian community (Little 1981, 1988). This land was under the control of the lead sachem Attapeat during the late seventeenth century (Little 1996, 194–95).

Although no features were discovered during the initial testing program, the topsoil was subsequently machine stripped to ensure there were no human burials. This process resulted in the exposure of the footprint of a small, round structure with an entryway, a center hearth and a small bedstead outline, numerous post molds and other types of features outside of the enclosure, and an extensive linear feature composed of homogenous and compacted floor deposits running beside the gravel road and continuing underneath it (see Figure 2.4).

The smaller round structure measured 5 to 5.5 m in diameter and was marked by a linear feature of compacted soil where organic debris accumulated. The feature characteristics were reminiscent of the linear "builder's trench" documented years earlier in Occawa. Few post molds were identified on the perimeter or the interior of this continuous band of organic soil and artifacts. The material culture recovered from clearing the site and completing minor sampling was consistent with a domestic Native American residence dating to the period in which Miacomet was known as a community. White clay pipes, redware, green wine bottle glass, a variety of stone tools, domestic and wild animal and fish remains, and a small sample of calcined bone and charred maize were among the materials collected.

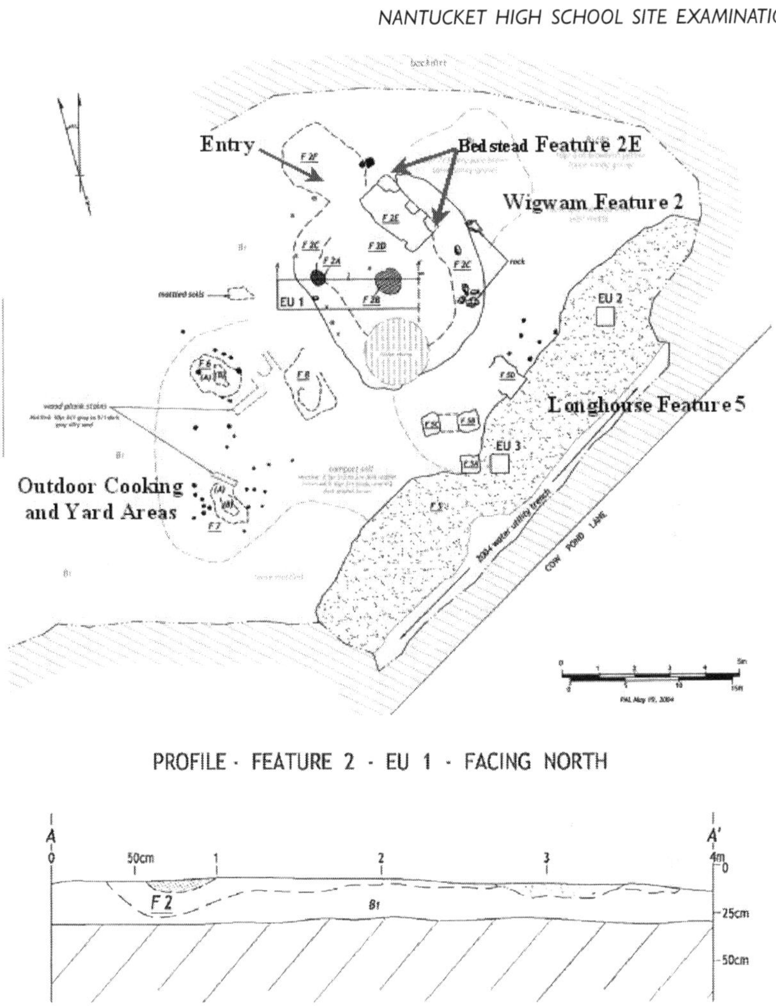

Figure 2.4. Map of the Dwelling Site, with Builder's Trench Inset

The structure was built into a slight embankment, and interior components included a center hearth and an outline of a single bedstead. An entryway was also identified on the northeast side of the house, marked by a square post and a gap in the organic berm. Analyses of bedding material by Tonya Largy (Largy and Rainey 2006) concluded that the local Pennsylvania sedge had been used as insulation, packed into the ground beneath a bed frame. Another nearby feature was interpreted as a section of a longhouse floor running at least 15 m (50 feet) in length along the narrow gravel road and continuing beneath the road. It consisted of a homogenous and distinct dark-grey brown soil, covered with small bits of bone, white clay pipe fragments, ceramics, shell, and green bottle glass. Small post molds were visible but unpatterned adjacent to the feature, and four large, square features were considered possible main supports for timber framing, or a ridge pole (Rainey and Ingham 2006). Because the entire footprint of the feature extended beneath the gravel road, it could not be fully investigated. The road, called Cow Pond Lane, ended just beyond the feature and is believed to have originated as a path leading to this Native complex.

The partial longhouse feature was interpreted as the site of the Miacomet Christian Indian meetinghouse, thought by most historians to have been constructed of wood and used as a school, church, and meeting place (Rainey and Ingham 2006). A fragment of a slate writing tablet found near the features hinted at a time when this location could have served as an Indian school, with the small wigwam sheltering an Indian teacher. The discovery of the site provided evidence to support Little's supposition (1981) that some of the Miacomet residents were living in traditional wigwams well into the eighteenth century, squatting on proprietors' common lands long after they were relinquished by leading sachems. Because these types of residences were not recorded, the search for archival records of the individual or family who lived there ends in 1797, when a member of the Starbuck family cashed in some shares in common land. The archaeological evidence of the use of sedge may also contribute to further studies of the architecture of indigenous building forms on Nantucket, as this same plant was thriving on land where the last sites discussed herein were identified.

The Poison Meadow, Valley View, and Wild Rose Pasture (2004–2005)

Soon after the discovery of the Dwelling site in Miacomet territory, PAL undertook another survey nearby of a 5-acre tract of land, adjacent to Miacomet Valley and directly across the road from the Miacomet Indian burial ground. Accidentally discovered in 1980 during the construction of a housing project, the burial ground was confirmed as the resting place of many Indians who died during the epidemic that swept through the community in the period 1763–1764 (Simon 1988). This too was the site reportedly mined for Indian skulls in the 1830s by local phrenologists (Karttunen 2005). Given the proximity to the burial ground and Miacomet Valley, the entire property was considered likely to contain historic Indian residences. With a Phase I survey sample of forty-five test pits, the PAL team identified four archaeological sites, three of which were interpreted as former dwelling areas of Miacomet Indians. The Poison Meadow and Valley View sites were characterized on the surface by thick patches of Pennsylvania sedge amidst other invasive species, such as poison ivy. These two sites contained low-density scatterings of white clay pipe fragments, calcined and unburned bone, green bottle glass, redware and other types of earthenware, and small bits of metal and hardware, suggesting Native American domestic use. The Wild Rose Pasture site was marked by patches of wild roses and concentrated eighteenth-century artifacts and other domestic debris. All three were subsequently subject to Phase II site evaluations to determine National and State Register eligibility status (Rainey and Ingham 2006).

At the Poison Meadow Site, the site examination grid testing resulted in the discovery of two nearly identical features interpreted as large post molds (see Figure 2.5). These features marked the limits of the distribution of cultural material across the site, spanning about 14 m (46 feet). Between these features, many of the test pits contained unusual mottled soils, soils with faint post molds, or compacted soils, in addition to low frequencies of domestic artifacts. In a technical report it

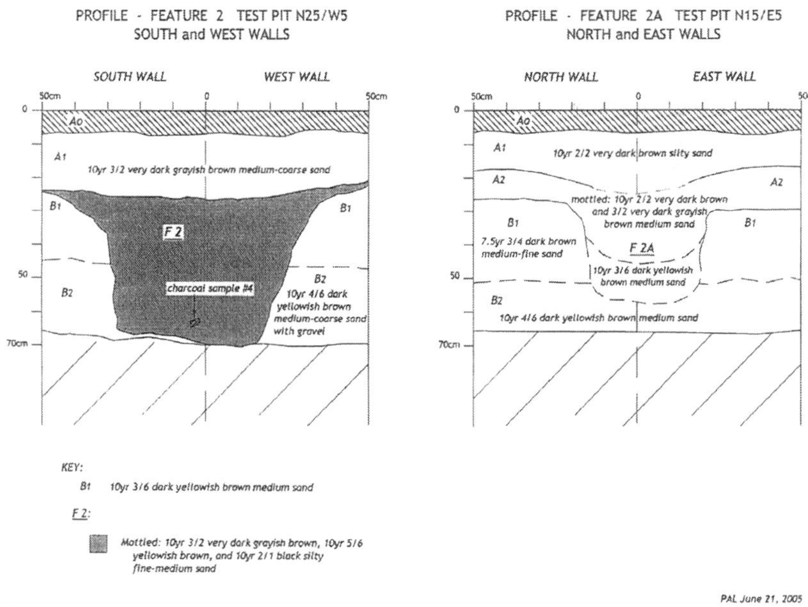

Figure 2.5. Possible Structural Support Features at the Poison Meadow Site

was suggested that a residence or large shelter constructed using a ridge pole design is a likely explanation for the archaeological evidence.

The nearby Valley View Site was located with one test pit placed within a patch of sedge overlooking Miacomet Valley. The pit revealed a mottled soil zone, just 10 cm in thickness just below the A-horizon. Three slip-decorated redware fragments were found in the mottled soils. The Phase II work extended the site from the valley rim to Miacomet Road due to the light but continuous distribution of cultural materials. Calcined bone, shell, redware, metal, wine bottle glass, and kaolin pipe fragments marked the assemblage. Like Poison Meadow, domestic refuse from occupation was thinly scattered across the area. A 1 × 1 m excavation unit placed next to the original test pit revealed a layer of mottle soils about 10–15 cm thick, with a contrasting linear band of dominant subsoil running through the center of the unit. The feature was comparable with linear features marking shallow builders' trenches for traditional residential structures at the Coffin Farm Complex 1 and Dwelling sites. Another 1 × 1 m unit revealed a complex feature marked by a blackened soil horizon overlying a mottled layer. Due to the limited sample, additional architectural information was not obtained. The feature soils contained a variety of period artifacts, including a 1723 halfpenny and a highly polished Orient fishtail projectile point, interpreted as part of the historic assemblage (Rainey and Ingham 2006). Danforth (2001) suggests that the halfpenny arrived in the American colonies sometime after 1737, when their value had diminished greatly in Ireland. Charcoal collected from the feature was radiocarbon dated and returned a conventional age of 250+/− 40 B.P. The calibrated results at 95.4 percent probability suggest the feature most likely formed from 1610 to 1690 and 1730 to 1810.

The Wild Rose Pasture site is believed to have marked the location of a sachem descendant or an individual otherwise successful in the whaling industry. Excavations identified the base of a brick and fieldstone hearth and mottled soil layers marking a former structure location (see Figure 2.6). Concentrations of window glass and nails support the conclusions that a wood frame building once stood on the site, however, the sampling was insufficient to make any conclusions about the building dimensions or actual framing. Charcoal collected from the feature was radiocarbon dated, with the calibrated results spanning the period 1650–1890, and adds little new interpretive information. The artifact assemblage included 1,118 artifacts such as tools and implements, architectural and domestic debris, and food remains, attributed to a successful and flourishing household (Rainey and Ingham 2006).

In the area of Native American architecture, these three sites provided additional evidence that ridge poles may have been a traditional element incorporated into Nantucket vernacular structures, that eighteenth-century

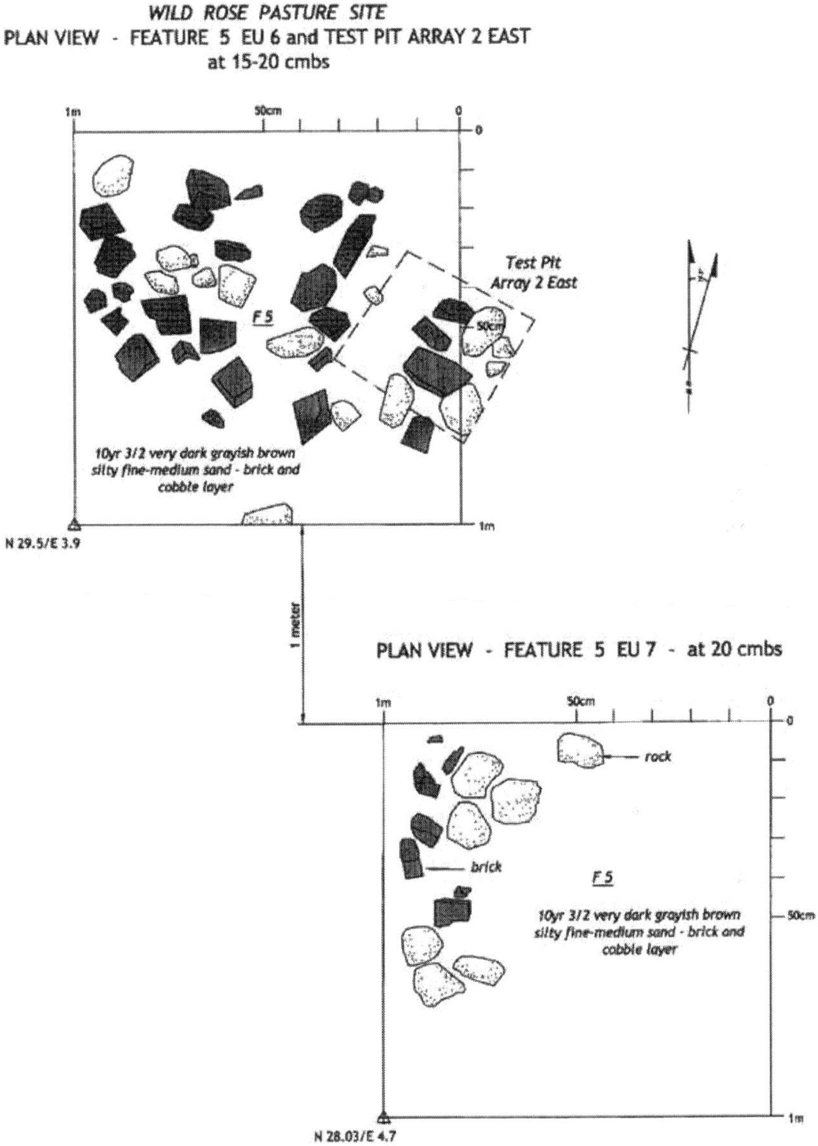

Figure 2.6. Plan View of Brick Hearth Remains at the Wild Rose Pasture Site

traditional residential sites may be marked by linear features rather than organized post mold arrangements, and that hearths constructed of brick and fieldstone can be expected as architectural elements of former Native American residences of wood-frame construction.

Conclusion

Archaeology on Nantucket has contributed a wealth of new information in the recent past that illuminates the diversity of indigenous vernacular architecture on a local level and highlights the ingenuity of a people to adapt to natural resource availability through time. The lack of detail on Indian building forms in the ethnohistoric and historic records of Nantucket, as described in this chapter, provides a great challenge to those conducting field surveys where domestic, institutional, or other types of architectural sites might be expected. While these records, by necessity, continue to present analogies to guide field discoveries and justification for interpretations, an increasing number of archaeological sites documenting former structure types serve to expand our expectations and consider a wider array of environmental and geographic variables in predictive modeling.

In the area of residential architecture, the Polpis Road investigations documented moderate-size family dwellings, oval in shape and 8 m (27 feet) long, situated in traditional settlement areas initially established several thousand years ago. Architectural data included evidence that the exterior façades of these homes, constructed with poles, were supported with an interior ridge-pole framework of substantial size and durability. This would be a logical adaptation to local conditions and was likely practiced across the island throughout the Woodland period. Reestablishing traditional home sites upon return from travel or seasonal relocations would have been facilitated by the stability of the large supports, believed to have been left in place for extended periods of time. These well-fitted homes contained ample evidence of a diverse resource base with which to produce matting, leather, fur-bearing skins, or other forms of building fabric. As these sites were not reused during the Colonial period, the final years of use during the seventeenth century likely corresponded to the elimination of hardwood resources critical to the maintenance of this architectural tradition. Other architectural attributes evident at these sites included the utilization of protective slopes and an east-west orientation to the ridge poles to maximize stability against prevailing winds.

In the traditional settlement area of Occawa, the Coffin Farm Complex 1 Site provided evidence of a considerably larger, irregular-shaped building estimated to have measured about 15 m (45 feet) by 10 m (30 feet). This site contained the first evidence of an adaptation to construction utilizing a shallow builder's trench to set framing and to add structural support. While documentation of post molds adjacent to the linear feature suggests a building constructed primarily of poles, there was sufficient architectural debris to suggest that the structure was enhanced with boards and possibly one or more windows and reinforced with clay daub. As clay is available in specific locations on the island, the use of daub in vernacular architecture of the early historic period could be expected in this particular locale. If, as I suspect, the unusual circular, stone-lined cellar of the original Coffin farmhouse was built by Indians originally as a food storage facility dug into solid clay, then it adds another intriguing aspect to the area of vernacular architecture on Nantucket.

In Miacomet territory, the full exposure of one of two Dwelling-site building features offered exceptional detail of a small, 5–5.5 m diameter, nearly round, traditional dwelling likely constructed for use by an individual or a very small family. The structure outline was identified by a continuous linear builder's trench cut into a slight embankment, and the structure entry was reinforced with framing, as evidenced by square posts. A bedstead feature, also marked by small square post molds along one wall, and a centrally placed hearth feature were the only interior elements, suggesting specialized use associated with the adjacent longhouse. While only a portion of the approximate 15-m (50-foot) longhouse interior floor was exposed, cumulative historic data point to the site as the likely location of the Miacomet meetinghouse. Several larger square post molds on the exterior of this feature were interpreted as possible structural reinforcements utilizing purchased lumber. The archaeological sample, however, was too limited to make any comments on structural enhancements such as windows, doors, and wood framing that might have been added during the eighteenth-century period of use.

The Poison Meadow, Valley View, and Wild Rose Pasture sites, also identified in Miacomet territory, all represent Native American residential sites of the seventeenth to eighteenth centuries. Because the archaeological samples were small and only portions of the residential features were exposed, the architectural information obtained was limited. Nonetheless, these sites provided evidence of vernacular architectural practices, including the use of a builder's trench at the Valley View site, a possible ridge pole at the Poison Meadow Site, and a brick-and-cobble hearth at the Wild Rose Pasture site. Taken together, however, the site data stand as direct evidence of the lifeways and possessions of a cross section of the Miacomet community.

The work discussed in this chapter offers specific detail on structural diversity, design, and building fabric while revealing the archaeological manifestations of these Native American practices that can lead future archaeologists to new discoveries on Nantucket and elsewhere in the southern New England region. The success of the archaeological investigations can be attributed, in part, to the extensive details drawn from records about Nantucket Indians scrutinized, compiled, and published by Little. The site data inform many of her research goals with supportive facts that enhance and balance Nantucket's documentary record, which will lead to a more realistic understanding of the once-robust Native American culture on Nantucket.

Acknowledgments

I express my gratitude here to Deborah Cox, president of the Public Archaeology Laboratory (PAL), and Duncan Ritchie, PAL senior archaeologist, for the many opportunities I was given to direct Nantucket investigations and work within such a beautiful, challenging, and unique Massachusetts historic context. Over the years these projects were supported by many highly skilled archaeologists and support staff at PAL, all of whom deserve recognition. Permission to use material from PAL technical reports was provided by Ms. Cox and is greatly appreciated. My introduction to the island as an employee of PAL in 1994 led me to meet Betty Little, and from that point forward, she became a steadfast advisor and supporter. I am indebted to her for the wisdom, technical guidance, and friendship she offered through many, many island projects. I also thank John D. C. Little and Betty and John's children for maintaining positive enthusiasm and personal support for this project. Special thanks to the staff of the Nantucket Historical Association Research Library and the Nantucket Registry of Deeds, who assisted me during many visits to these repositories; their expertise and knowledge of the resources are exceptional. Last, I graciously thank the volume editorial committee, including Dr. Elizabeth Chilton, Dr. James Bradley, and Tonya Largy, for their patience, guidance, and experience, and especially to Dr. Chilton for her editorial expertise and for carrying this project to publication.

Works Cited

Brooks, Edward. 1939. Our Nantucket Project. *Bulletin of the Massachusetts Archaeological Society* 1(1): 12.

Brooks, Edward. 1941. A Preliminary Report on the Second Season's Work at Site M-52/3. *Bulletin of the Massachusetts Archaeological Society* 2(2): 15–16.

Brooks, Edward. 1942. Progress Report on Site M-52/3, Nantucket, Massachusetts. *Bulletin of the Massachusetts Archaeological Society* 3(3): 34–35.

Bullen, Ripley, and Edward Brooks. 1947. The Squam Pond Indian Site, Nantucket, Massachusetts. *Bulletin of the Massachusetts Archaeological Society* 8(4): 56–59.

Bullen, Ripley, and Edward Brooks. 1949. The Herracater Swamp Site, Nantucket Island, Massachusetts. *Bulletin of the Massachusetts Archaeological Society* 10(4): 81–89.

Bushnell, David I., Jr. 1919. Native Villages and Village Sites East of the Mississippi. *Smithsonian Institution Bureau of American Ethnology* 69.

Byers, Edward. 1987. *The Nation of Nantucket: Society and Politics in an Early American Commercial Center, 1660–1820.* Boston, MA: Northeastern University Press.

Champlain, Samuel de. 1907[1619]. *The Voyages of Samuel de Champlain, 1604–1618.* New York: C. Scribner's Sons.

Chilton, Elizabeth S. 2002. "Towns they have none": Diverse Subsistence and Settlement Strategies in Native New England. In *Northeast Subsistence-Settlement Change A.D. 700–1300*, ed. John Hart and Christina B. Rieth, 289–300. Albany: New York State Museum, Bulletin 496.

Danforth, Brian J. 2001. Wood's Hibernia Coins Come to America. *The Colonial Newsletter* (August): 2213–2230.

de Crevecoeur, J. Hector St. Jean. 1971. *Letters from an American Farmer.* Reprint. Originally published 1782. New York: Everyman's Library.

Douglas-Lithgow, R. A. 1911. *The Nantucket Indians.* Nantucket, MA: The Inquirer and Mirror Press.

Ewer, Rev. F. C. 1869. *Historical Map of Nantucket Surveyed and Drawn by Rev. F. C. Ewer.* Nantucket, MA: Nantucket Historical Association Map Collection, Image Number MS2.

Forman, Henry Chandler. 1966. *Early Nantucket and Its Whale Houses.* New York: Hastings House.

Freeman, Reverend James C. 1807. Notes on Nantucket. *Massachusetts Historical Society Collections*, Series 2, 3: 19–38.

Gibson, Susan G., ed. 1980. *Burr's Hill, A 17th Century Wampanoag Burial in Warren, Rhode Island.* Providence, RI: The Haffenreffer Museum of Anthropology, Brown University.

Gookin, Daniel. 1809. Historical Collections of the Indians in New England (1674). *Massachusetts Historical Society Collections* V.1: 141–225. Boston, MA: Monroe and Francis.

Josselyn, John. 1865. *An Account of Two Voyages to New England, 1638–1663.* Boston, MA: William Veazie, reprint.

Juli, Harold D., and Lucianne Lavin. 1996. Aboriginal Architecture in Southern New England: Data from the Griswold Point Site. *Northeast Anthropology* (51): 83–99.

Kapches, Mima. 1993. The Identification of an Iroquoian Unit of Measurement: Architectural and Social/Cultural Implications for the Longhouse. *Archaeology of Eastern North America* (21): 137–62.

Karttunen, Frances Ruley. 2005. *The Other Islanders: People Who Pulled Nantucket's Oars.* New Bedford, MA: Spinner Publications.

Kellaway, William. 1961. *The New England Company 1649–1776: Missionary Society to the American Indians.* New York: Barnes and Noble.

Laet, Joannes de. [1625]1841. *Extracts from the New World or a Description of the West Indies, 1625.* New York: New York Historical Society.

Largy, Tonya, and Mary Lynne Rainey. 2006. Poverty or Natural Wisdom: Native Home Solutions in Eighteenth-Century Nantucket. *Archaeology of Eastern North America* 34: 61–70.

Little, Elizabeth A. 1979. *An Inventory of Indian Sites on Nantucket.* Report submitted to the Massachusetts Historical Commission and the Nantucket Historical Association.

Little, Elizabeth. 1980. A Brief Historical Sketch of Archaeology on Nantucket. In *Widening Horizons: Studies Presented to Dr. Maurice Robbins*, ed. Curtiss Hoffman, 75–79. Attleboro: Massachusetts Archaeological Society.

Little, Elizabeth. 1981. Historic Indian Houses of Nantucket. *Nantucket Algonquian Studies* 4. Nantucket, MA: Nantucket Historical Association.

Little, Elizabeth. 1983. *Initial Predictive Map for Prehistoric Sites on Nantucket.* Nantucket Archaeology Studies No. 1. Nantucket, MA: Nantucket Historical Association.

Little, Elizabeth. 1984. Locus Q-6, Site M52/65, Quidnet, Nantucket, Massachusetts. *Bulletin of the Massachusetts Archaeological Society* 45(1).

Little, Elizabeth. 1988. *History of the Town of Miacomet.* Nantucket Algonquin Studies No. 12. Nantucket, MA: Nantucket Historical Association.

Little, Elizabeth. 1989. Shawkemo Chapter of the Massachusetts Archaeology Society. *Bulletin of the Massachusetts Archaeological Society, 50th Anniversary Issue* 50(2): 54–55.

Little, Elizabeth. 1990. Indian Horse Commons at Nantucket Island, 1660–1760. *Nantucket Algonquian Studies* 9. Nantucket, MA: Nantucket Historical Association.

Little, Elizabeth. 1992. Indian Whalemen of Nantucket: The Documentary Evidence. *Nantucket Algonquian Studies* 13. Nantucket, MA: Nantucket Historical Association.

Little, Elizabeth. 1996. Daniel Spotso: A Sachem at Nantucket Island, Massachusetts, circa 1691–1741. In *Northeastern Indian Lives, 1632–1816*, ed. Robert S. Grumet, 193–207. Amherst: University of Massachusetts Press.

Luedtke, Barbara E. 1980. Survey of the University of Massachusetts, Nantucket Field Station. In *Widening Horizons: Studies Presented to Dr. Maurice Robbins*, ed. Curtiss Hoffman, 95–129. Attleboro: Massachusetts Archaeological Society.

Macy, Obed. 1972. *The History of Nantucket.* Reprint of 2d ed. 1880, originally published in 1835. Clifton, NJ: Augustus M. Kelley.

Macy, Zacchaeus. 1792a. Letter to Peleg Coffin: Account of the Names of the Old Sachems and Some of the Most Respectable Indians, and Their Habitations, Taken from the Best Authors That Could Be Had. 1763. Reprinted by Obed Macy, *The History of Nantucket*, 1972, 254–59.

Macy, Zacchaeus. 1792b. A Short Journal of the First Settling of the Island of Nantucket. *Massachusetts Historical Society Collections* 1:3: 155–60.

Morris, Paul C. 1976. Report of the Archaeology Committee. *Historic Nantucket* 23(3): 26–27.

Mrosowski, S. 1994. Personal communication.

Nabakov, Peter, and Robert Easton. 1989. *Native American Architecture.* New York: Oxford University Press.

Nantucket Historical Association (NHA). 1727–1759. Manuscript Collection 8: Timothy White Papers, 1727–1759. Nantucket, MA: Nantucket Historical Association Research Library.

Nantucket Historical Association (NHA). 1949. *Proceedings of the Nantucket Historical Association*. Nantucket, MA: Nantucket Historical Association.

Philbrick, Nathanial. 1994. *Away Offshore: Nantucket Island and Its People, 1602–1890*. Nantucket, MA: Mill Hill Press.

Pretola, John. 1973. *The Marshall Site: An Early Contact Shell Midden from Nantucket Island*. Master's thesis, Department of Anthropology, University of Massachusetts Amherst, MA.

Pretola, John, and Elizabeth A. Little. 1988. Nantucket: An Archaeological Record from the Far Island. *Bulletin of the Archaeological Society of Connecticut* 51: 47–68.

Rainey, Mary Lynne. 2004a. The Archaeology of the Polpis Road Bicycle Path: A Landmark in the Study of Native American Lifeways on Nantucket. *Historic Nantucket* 53(3): 8–13.

Rainey, Mary Lynne. 2004b. Polpis Road Bicycle Path Archaeological Data Recovery Program: Site19-NT-50, the Roadkill Site (19-NT-166), Site 19-NT-68, and the Folger's Marsh Site (19-NT-180), and Supplemental Site Examination of the Folger's Marsh Site, Nantucket, Massachusetts. Volumes I and II. PAL Report No. 621. Submitted to Nantucket County Planning and Economic Development Commission, Nantucket, MA.

Rainey, Mary Lynne, and Donna Ingham. 2006. Intensive (Locational) Archaeological Survey of the Nantucket High School Staff Housing Project Area, and Site Examination of the Dwelling Site, Nantucket, MA. PAL Report No. 1576.01, submitted to the Nantucket Education Trust, Nantucket, MA.

Rainey, Mary Lynne, and Duncan Ritchie. 1994. Archaeological Site Examinations, Polpis Road Bicycle Path: Including Site 19-NT-68, the Folger's Marsh Site (19-NT-180), the Norwood Farm Trust Site (19-NT-174), the Martin Site (NAN-HA-14), the Roadkill Site (19-NT-166), and Site 19-NT-50, Nantucket, Massachusetts. The Public Archaeology Laboratory, Report No. 521. Submitted to Vanasse Hangen Brustlin, Watertown, MA.

Rainey, Mary Lynne, and Duncan Ritchie. 1996. Site Examination on Fenceline, Interval, Vista, and Shadow Prehistoric Sites; and Coffin Farm Complex 1 and 2, Coffin Farmhouse 1, and Milestone Road Historic Sites, Nantucket Golf Club Project Area, Nantucket, Massachusetts. The Public Archaeology Laboratory, Report No. 718. Submitted to The Nantucket Golf Club, Edwards, CO.

Rawson, Reverend Grindel, and Reverend Samuel Danforth. 1809. Account of an Indian Visitation, A.D. 1698. Copied for Dr. Stiles, by Rev. Mr. Hawley, Missionary at Marshpee, from the Printed Account Published in 1698. *Massachusetts Historical Society Collections* 1:V.10: 129–35.

Roy, Edward Stanley. 1958. Shawkemo Chapter of the Massachusetts Archaeological Society. *Historic Nantucket* 6(1): 28–30.

Simon, Bronna G. 1988. Preliminary Field Report: Miacomet Village Elderly and Family Housing/Miacomet Praying Indian Burial Ground, Nantucket. Report on file at the Massachusetts Historical Commission, Boston, MA.

Speck, Frank G. 1909. *Notes on the Mohegan and Niantic Indians.* Anthropological Papers of the American Museum of Natural History, vol. 3. New York: American Museum of Natural History.

Starbuck, Alexander. 1924. *The History of Nantucket County, Island and Town.* Boston, MA: C. E. Goodspeed and Co.

Stockley, Bernard H. 1964a. Archaeology and History. *Historic Nantucket* 12(2): 13–19.

Stockley, Bernard H. 1964b. Some Unusual Artifacts from Ram Pasture I, Nantucket, Massachusetts. *Bulletin of the Massachusetts Archaeological Society* 25(3–4): 70–72.

Stockley, Bernard H. 1965. Preliminary Report, Ram Pasture I, A Stratified Site on Nantucket Island, Massachusetts. *Eastern States Archaeological Federation Bulletin* 24:11.

Stockley, Bernard H. 1968. An Introduction to the Prehistory of Nantucket. *Historic Nantucket* 15(3): 5–16.

Sturtevant, William C. 1975. Two 1761 Wigwams at Niantic, Connecticut. *American Antiquity* 40(4): 437–44.

Van Wyhe, John. 2004. *Phrenology and the Origins of Victorian Scientific Naturalism.* Aldershot, Hants, England: Ashgate Publishing.

Vincent, Philip. 1638. *A True Revelation of the Late Battle Fought in New England between the English and the Peqout Savages.* London: Harper & Butter.

Waters, Joseph H. 1965. Animal Remains from Some New England Sites. *Archaeological Society of Connecticut Bulletin* 33: 5–11.

Williams, Roger. 1936[1643]. *A Key into the Language of America.* Reprinted. Originally published 1643 by Gregory Dexter, London. Providence: The Rhode Island and Providence Plantations Tercentenary Committee.

Wood, William. 1977. *New England's Prospect.* Edited by Alden T. Vaughn. Originally published 1634, London. Amherst: University of Massachusetts Press.

Worth, Henry Barnard. 1902. Nantucket Lands and Land Owners. *Nantucket Historical Association Bulletin* 2(3). Nantucket, MA: Nantucket Historical Association.

Wroth, Lawrence. 1970. *The Voyages of Giovanni de Verrazanno, 1524–1528.* New Haven, CT, and London: Yale University Press.

3

Drift Whales at Nantucket

The Kindness of Moshup

Elizabeth Alden Little and J. Clinton Andrews

From before 1668 until at least 1728, Nantucket Indians engaged in a structured whaling industry, centered about drift or stranded whales. Deeds and regulations governing the ownership of drift whales show that the Indians owned rights to all the drift whales at Nantucket and retained these rights as they sold land to the English. The records of stranded whales at Nantucket today suggest the importance of drift whales as a prehistoric resource. Indian drift whaling customs, deeds, or regulations also existed at eastern Long Island, Rhode Island, Martha's Vineyard, and Cape Cod Bay. Described by Crèvecoeur (1971, 107) as "fond of the sea and expert mariners," Indians of Nantucket and these nearby shores contributed to the growth of the along-shore and pelagic whaling industry of the United States. These ethnohistoric records support the hypothesis that right whales, both along-shore and stranded, in the winter and spring, were particularly abundant along the shores of southeastern New England and eastern Long Island during the Colonial period.

Histories of the whale fishery usually start with a brief and inconclusive paragraph about whether or not Indians contributed to the beginnings of American whaling (Spence 1980, 35; Stackpole 1953, 16; Scammon 1968, 204; Browne 1968, 522). County records and historical reports of Nantucket and nearby shores provide details of the whaling activities of historic Indians. Supported by data on modern whale strandings at Nantucket, we find in the seventeenth century not just Indian use of an occasional stranded whale on an undefined coast but specific shores of the East Coast where the Indians owned rights to what were called drift whales and enthusiastically took part in the subsequent Colonial along-shore and pelagic whaling.

Historical Background

The settlement of New England coincided with the rise of the Dutch and English whale fishery in the North Atlantic, a fishery that had been dominated since the thirteenth century by the Biscayans or Basaues (Browne 1968; Spence 1980). In 1609, Lescarbot reported along-shore whaling by Biscayans in the Gulf of St. Lawrence (True 1904, 17), and in 1610 Champlain described Biscayans catching whales off the coast of New France by harpooning and lancing them from small boats (True 1904, 17, 18).

John Smith in 1614 tried whaling near Monhegan Island but found only the noncommercial finback (True 1904, 21). However, the Pilgrims in 1620 off Provincetown saw what were probably right whales. "Great whales of the best kind for oil and bone came close aboard our ship, and in fair weather swim and play about us" (Mourt's Relation [1622]1802, 204; 1832, 36). The Dutch made several attempts to whale off New York and Delaware (True 1904, 24–26). According to an English report of 1667, "The sea was rich in whales near Delaware Bay, but they were to be found in greater numbers about the end of Long Island" (Dow 1925, 12). Whaling histories do not report whales before 1750 south of Delaware (True 1904; Starbuck 1964; Dow 1925).

Even with this abundance of whales close to shore, when the English colonists finally attempted to go whaling, no one was available who knew how to kill whales at sea efficiently. For example, Macy (1835, 28) reported the tradition that a whale stayed in Nantucket harbor for three days, while the islanders "invented" and manufactured a harpoon with which to kill it. In spite of many sporadic beginnings, the whaling industry of the East Coast did not successfully get under way until after 1667 off eastern Long Island (Edwards and Rattray 1932, 197).

Although Rosier in 1605 reported that some New England Indians hunted whales from canoes with harpoons and arrows (Rosier 1843, 156), and a report of 1590 exists describing Florida Indians killing whales at sea (True 1904, 27) any such Indian along-shore whaling appears to have ceased after 1605.

The propensity of whales to strand themselves (Leatherwood et al. 1976) was reinforced by Indians in canoes, especially in shallow embayments, which provide natural traps. There are reports of trapping small whales by driving them ashore at Long Island (Ann Hartung, personal communication), at Great Point and the north shore of Nantucket, and in Cape Cod Bay (Crêvecoeur 1971, 100; Drake 1876, 343–45; Kittredge 1968). However, to summarize the historical records, although Indians made use of whales, we have no evidence that Indians harpooned whales at sea off the East Coast of Colonial America after 1605, until they became involved with English along-shore whaling.

Drift Whales, the Gift of Moshup

Rather than harpooning whales at sea, historic Indians of the East Coast were making use of the blubber, meat, and baleen of drift whales. By drift whales we mean dead whales that have stranded, drifted ashore, or washed up on shore, as well as live whales that have stranded themselves. As the Indians of Martha's Vineyard put it, "Moshup, their legendary whaleman, was kind to them, by sending whales &c. ashore to them to eat" (Basset 1792, 140). We propose that at certain coasts, drift whales were so numerous that no need had arisen to go to sea to kill them. Dead or dying whales come ashore today on the beaches of Nantucket. Andrews has recorded stranded cetaceans on Nantucket for

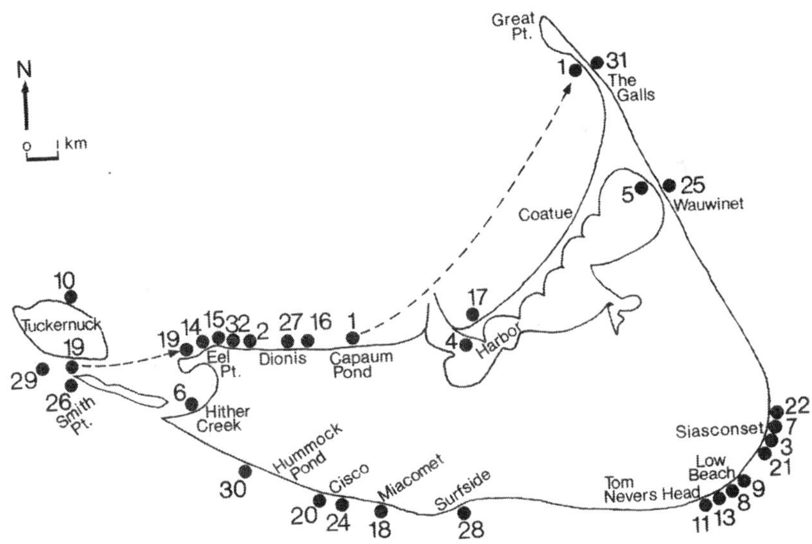

Figure 3.1. Locations of Whale Strandings at Nantucket, 1947–1980. Each numbered dot identifies a stranded whale of Appendix 1, which gives the species, date, and location. Base map after Chisholm et al. (1974).

the past thirty-three years, and from his records we have constructed the table of Appendix 1 (at the end of this chapter) and Figure 3.1. In some cases, because of decomposition, the exact identification may be equivocal. However, the data show a substantial rate of cetacean stranding, about one whale a year.

Some whales, needless to say, are large, and their weight is difficult to obtain experimentally. However, given that a 30-meter whale may weigh 90 metric tons (Leatherwood et al. [1976] state that 136 metric tons have been reported), and that a 6-meter whale may weigh 2.6 metric tons (Katona et al. 1975), we can construct a rough curve for the relation between length and weight. We assume that the weight varies with the cube of the length below about 11 meters, and linearly with length above 18 meters at a slope of 3 metric tons per meter (one ton per foot). If we now assign lengths to the unmeasured cetaceans of Appendix 1 from average species lengths given by Katona et al. (1975), then we find that a conservative estimate of the amount of blubber, bone, and meat coming ashore at Nantucket each year is about 13 metric tons. That 13 metric tons of whale annually come ashore today, when many species of whales are less abundant than formerly, suggests that before the Nantucketers began to hunt whales at sea, stranded whales could have been a significant resource for the Indians. We are, however, unwilling to extrapolate modern data on species and dates of strandings to 300 years ago, without an understanding of whale strandings on a species-by-species basis.

Drift Whaling Recorded in Nantucket County Documents

Certain details of Nantucket Indian whaling can be obtained from the county records of the island between 1668 and 1728 (see Appendix 2 at the end of this chapter; see also Figure 3.2). Although Worth (1902) reported many of these excerpts, Little has confirmed, corrected, and made additions to his transcriptions, from the original documents, where possible.

Nantucket's acknowledgment in 1673 that "all the whal [*sic*] fish or other drift fish belong to the Indian Sachims" (see Appendix 2 at the end of this chapter) was not unique to Nantucket. Indian ownership of drift whales at Martha's Vineyard and Long Island was also recognized, since the deeds for English purchase of land from the Indians at those islands often specifically included drift whale rights (see text that follows).

However, there were no sales of drift whale rights to the English on Nantucket. The Indian deed of 1684 summarizing the lands sold to

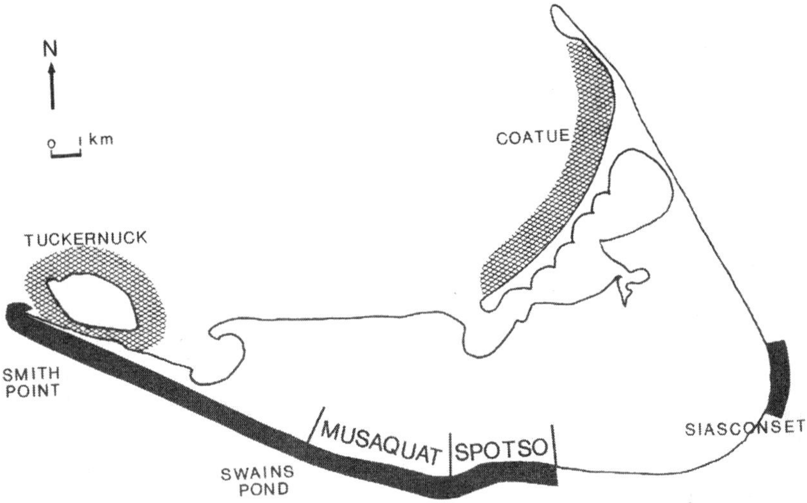

Figure 3.2. Location of Drift Whale Rights at Nantucket, 1668–1728, from Nantucket County Records (Appendix 2). Drift whale right locations known precisely are shown by solid shading, and those not known precisely are shown by hatching. Base map, after Chisholm et al. (1974) and Holland (1794), shows seventeenth- and eighteenth-century extension of the southwest shore of Nantucket to the west of Tuckernuck.

the English since their arrival in 1659 reserved the right to "what dead whales shall be cast on a shore that belong to the Indians according to former custom" (see Appendix 2 at the end of this chapter). Two other Indian-to-English land deeds reserved drift whales to the Indians. Indian retention of all drift whale rights was unique to Nantucket.

Now this is all quite interesting because, for the English, whales are royal fish and belong to the king of England, or his grantee (Edwards and Rattray 1932; Spence 1980). Indeed, between 1684 and 1687, the governor of New York tried to claim Nantucket's whales for the king (Starbuck 1924, 74). Since nothing came of this claim, we doubt that the Nantucket Indians were ever made aware of it. Quietly, as far as the records show, but firmly, the Nantucket sachems retained sovereignty over drift whales, with a possessiveness that was in marked contrast to their lack of possessiveness of land.

Although the Nantucket English were involved at the time as owners of part of the land, as arbitrators of disputes, and possibly as purchasers of oil and baleen, they not only disclaimed rights in drift whales but even awarded an Indian a judgment against an Englishman in a dispute over a whale. A spertnaceti whale, according to tradition (Macy 1835, 32), was once found dead on the southwest shore of the island and caused considerable excitement. Since ownership was disputed between the Indians, the proprietors, and the Crown, possibly the event took place in 1668 or earlier and may have occasioned the 1668 agreement with the Indians about whales (see Appendix 2 at the end of this chapter).

Indian ownership of drift whales preempted the Crown's rights (i.e., royal taxes) on drift whales at eastern Long Island (Edwards and Rattray 1932). Thus whale oil from Indian drift whales may have been exported tax-free from eastern Long Island, as well as Nantucket, which belonged to New York until 1692. This consideration may have played a role in the agreement with the Indians about whales on Nantucket, and, if drift whales were adequate to sustain an industry, it could account for the relatively late beginning of English along-shore whaling on Nantucket.

The importance of drift whales in the Nantucket economy resulted in documents that record the Indian political structure governing ownership of drift whale rights. Each of the four major sachems chose ten men for a committee to assign drift whale rights on Indian lands. In addition, whale rights on land sold to the English were assigned to sachems and other important Indians from all over the island. These rights were later inherited or transferred to appropriate successors by gift. In a rare measure of the reach of the sovereignty of Ussamequin (Massasoit), we find that the sachem at Mount Hope had once had some control over whale assignments on Nantucket (see Appendix 2 at the end of this chapter).

Geography of Drift Whaling

Several mechanisms seem to bring whales ashore. Right and sperm whales usually float when dead, whereas others, such as finbacks, will sink first and then refloat only if the water is sufficiently warm and shallow (W. E. Schevill, personal communication). Dead whales are carried ashore by currents. A shallow and sandy character of the coast appears related to live strandings. Whales come so close to shore in some places that both of the above, as well as trapping, can occur. None of these mechanisms are well understood.

Nantucket beaches with documented whale rights 300 years ago are shown in Figure 3.2. The geographic emphasis of drift whaling was on the southwest shore, with a small focus at Siasconset. Some Coatue whales may have been trapped blackfish. The differences between Figures 3.1 and 3.2, 300 years apart, are remarkably minor and reflect changes in shorelines and currents, especially the erosional changes at the west end of the island.

Both Figures 3.1 and 3.2 suggest that drift whales are more likely to come ashore at certain beaches than at others. Although occasional drift whales come ashore all along the East Coast (National Marine Fisheries Service, Gloucester), we would expect to find drift whaling customs, deeds, and regulations only where whales stranded frequently. Where do we find such records?

In 1620, the Pilgrims saw Indians near Billingsgate cutting up a beached grampus five or six paces long. "They cut it into long rands or pieces, about an eli long and two handfull broad" (Mourt's Relation 1832, 38). According to Bradford, small whales were commonly washed ashore in Cape Cod Bay after storms, a phenomenon that he attributed to the great flats of sand found there (Bradford 1898, 102). In Rhode Island, Roger Williams saw whales "which in some places are often cast up; I have seene some of them, but not above sixtie feet long: the Natives cut them out in severall parcells, and give and send farre and neere for an acceptable present, or dish" (Williams 1973, 181, original spelling). In Delaware, Indians used "whale fins" and "whale bone" for decorations (Goddard 1978, 217) (both phrases meant baleen [Starbuck 1964, 18, 40]).

Indians often deeded drift whale rights to the English along with land at Martha's Vineyard (Banks 1911, 432) and at Long Island (Schmitt 1972). More significant than deeded rights, however, are the whale rights reserved by Indians for their own use. Nantucket Indians reserved all their drift whale rights, and Martha's Vineyard Indians reserved a few (Banks 1911, 432). Nauset Indians reserved "a part of the blubber of whales that should be driven ashore" (Pratt 1844, 11), and Easthampton Indians reserved "the fynnes and tayles of all whales as shall be cast upp, and desire that they may be friendly dealt with in the other parte" (Edwards and Rattray 1932, 195, original spelling). Whale fins and tails were also reserved by an Indian at Woods Hole (Freeman 1869, vol. 2, 427).

Drift whaling regulations, including deeded ownership, first appear in town records in 1644 at eastern Long Island (Edwards and Rattray 1932, 204) and at Nauset (Pratt 1844, 11), after 1653 at West Tisbury, Chilmark, and Edgartown (Banks 1911, 1925), in 1654 at Plymouth (Starbuck 1924, 350), in 1652 and 1661 at Sandwich, Barnstable, Yarmouth, and Eastham on Cape Cod Bay (Freeman 1869, vol. 1, 243;

Allen 1916, 148), and in 1668 at Nantucket (Nantucket County Deeds [NCD] 1668, 1, 8).

Certainly drift whaling regulations may still be buried in county courthouses. A search of county records along Delaware Bay or in Rhode Island might bear fruit. However, Indian drift whaling records have not been reported in the histories of whaling at Salem (Robotti 1950) or at Maine (Martin 1975), nor have any yet been found for eastern New Jersey or the coast south of Delaware (True 1904).

We show the geographical distribution of our documented ethnohistoric drift whaling sites in Figures 3.3 and 3.4 and observe that these sites must have represented both unusually rich and reliable sources of stranded whales and Indians who were unusually interested in whales.

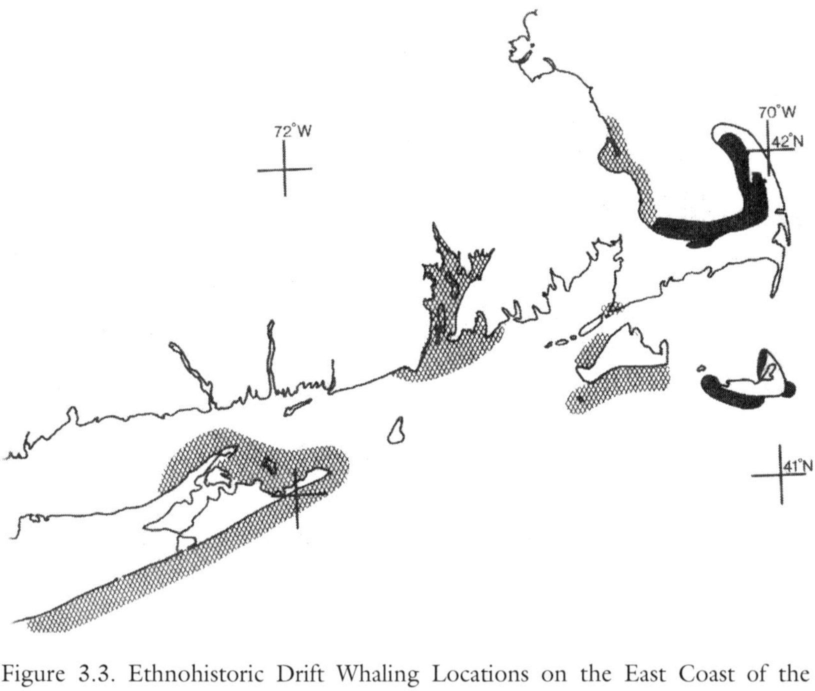

Figure 3.3. Ethnohistoric Drift Whaling Locations on the East Coast of the United States, North of New York in the Seventeenth Century, from Recorded Deeds, Customs, and Regulations. Locations known precisely are shown by solid shading, and those not known precisely are shown by hatching. Base map after National Ocean Survey (1977).

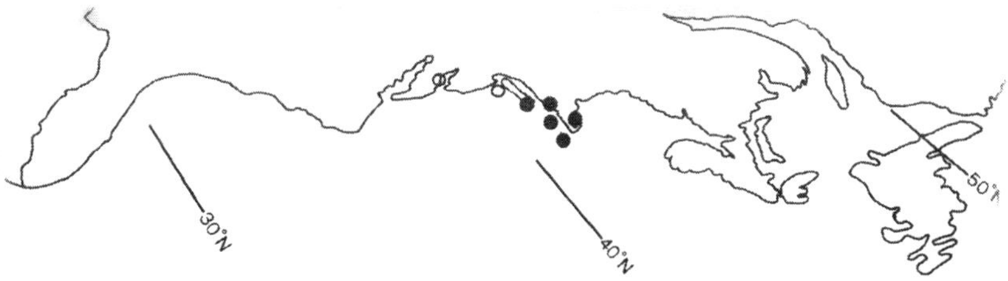

Figure 3.4. Ethnohistoric Drift Whaling Locations on the East Coast of the United States, North of New York in the Seventeenth Century, from Recorded Deeds, Customs, and Regulations. Solid circles indicate locations that are well documented, and open circles indicate locations that are poorly documented. Base map after National Geographic Society (1960).

Prehistory of Whales at Nantucket

Near the drift whaling beaches of Figure 3.3, we could expect to find evidence of the interaction of men and whales for quite some time in the past. Brereton reported in 1602 the north side of an island, somewhere south of Cape Cod, with "many huge bones and ribbes of Whales" (Brereton 1602, 6), and Shaler noted bones on Stone Horse Shoal (Shaler 1897). Although we may not subscribe to the mechanisms by which Indians explained their environment, they were good observers. Therefore, the bones of prehistoric (or possibly fossil [see Alden 1916; Macy 1792a]) drift whales may have inspired the origin myth in which Moshup waded across Nantucket Sound and discovered Nantucket with a pile of bones on it (Alden 1798, 57). For that matter, place names that refer to bones or whale bones, such as Siasconset ("great bones place") and Wasque ("whalebone') (Huden 1962, 232, 272), may, if

Figure 3.5. Along-shore and Pelagic Whaling Ports of the United States, 1715–1839 (Starbuck 1964). The major ports, Nantucket and New Bedford, are shown by stars, and minor ports are shown by solid dots. Hudson River ports were established by pelagic whalers of Nantucket.

we can trust the translations, also contribute to our knowledge of the stranding pattern of whales.

The archaeological record on Nantucket shows remains of blackfish at the Squam Pond site, and the humpback whale, identified by Glover N. Allen, at the Herrecator Swamp site (Bullen and Brooks 1947, 1949). The Ram Pasture I site, with a carbon-14 date on a piece of charcoal of 940 A.D. (M 1502), had blackfish remains and a gorget made from the vertebra of a small whale (Waters 1965; Stockley 1964, 1965). Kenneth Coffin, while digging a trench for a new house between Hither Creek and Eel Point, discovered two whalebone spades or adzes (see Figure 3.6), lying immediately above two stone celts (see Figure 3.7) (Fowler 1973), which may have been a flensing tool kit (Clark 1974, 69, 71). Loosely associated with these finds were six triangular stone tools, a grooved hammerstone, and a copper knife, attributed to the Woodland period (Paul C. Morris, personal communication). Four additional pieces of whale bone have been found on Nantucket during excavations (Nantucket Historical Association files).

These archaeological finds show only the use of whales, not the means of hunting them. No prehistoric harpoon has been unambiguously identified on Nantucket (Little 1979). Elsewhere in New England, a small number of bone toggle harpoons have been found (Fowler 1972; Moffett 1959, 1969; Scothorne 1970). Without enough data to evaluate the meaning of these finds, we will simply note that historically in southern New England the Indians hunted sturgeon with harpoons (Williams 1973; Wood 1865), but whales were the gift of Moshup.

The Relationship of Drift Whaling to Along-shore and Pelagic Whaling

Recorded Indian drift whaling appears to have been a precursor of successful along-shore and pelagic whaling on the East Coast of the United States. We propose that the basis for the distribution of all three historic whaling activities was the distribution of right whales near the East Coast in Colonial times.

Right whales, formerly more abundant than they are today, frequent temperate shores. In addition, the right whale has a placid disposition, is slow, is rich in oil, and does not sink when killed. Because of these attributes, the right whale was the chief lure that drew whale fishermen to sea in boats. At Nantucket, “The whales hitherto caught near the shores were of the Right Species” (Macy 1835, 31).

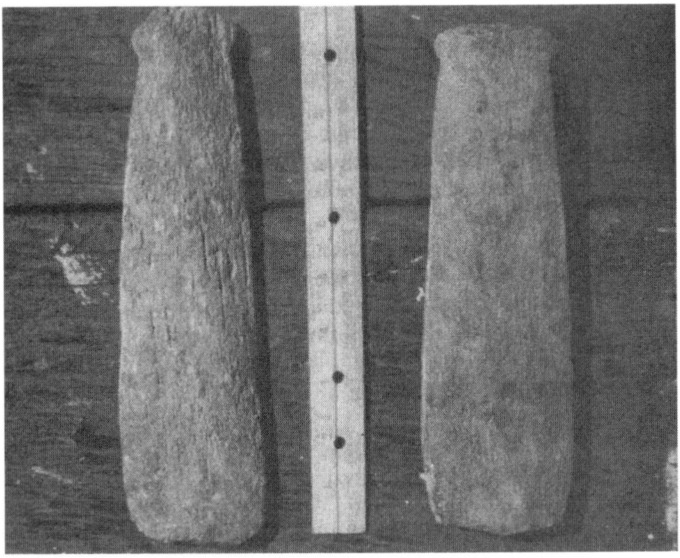

Figure 3.6. Two Whalebone Adzes, or Spades, Found at Nantucket (Fowler 1973; collection of Paul C. Morris, Nantucket)

Figure 3.7. Two Stone Celts (left: an axe; right: an adze) Found at Nantucket with Bone Adzes (Fowler 1973; collection of Paul C. Morris, Nantucket)

Along-shore whaling by the colonists began in 1667 off the south shore of eastern Long Island with James Loper, a Dutchman, as teacher (Edwards and Rattray 1932, 197), after 1688 in Cape Cod Bay (Spence 1980, 36) and after 1690 off the south shores of Nantucket and Martha's Vineyard (Macy 1792b; Banks 1911, 433; Crèvecoeur 1971; Stackpole 1953; Allen 1916, 168).

Ichabod Paddock is credited as Nantucket's teacher (Macy 1792b). Attempts at along-shore whaling also occurred before 1730 at Rhode Island (Starbuck 1964, 35), possibly at Connecticut (Alden 1916, 170), at the Isles of Shoals, New Hampshire (Josselyn 1833, 323), and at Delaware Bay (True 1904, 76; Weiss et al. 1974).

Successful American whalemen, like the Basques before them, had to go farther and farther to sea in sloops and subsequently in ships to find whales, because, by 1760, "the whales appeared generally to have deserted the coast" (Macy 1792b). By 1791 (Starbuck 1964, 90), Nantucket whale ships had reached the Pacific Ocean in pursuit of whales. In spite of their late start compared to the Dutch and English, Nantucket and New Bedford in the early nineteenth century had become the world leaders in pelagic whaling.

The geographic distribution of all U.S. ports that took part in along-shore and pelagic whaling up to 1839 (shown in Figure 3.4b) bears a remarkable similarity to the geographic distribution of recorded Indian drift whaling (shown in Figure 3.4a). Furthermore, leading whaling ports of the nineteenth century were not the chief mercantile or fishing ports of Philadelphia, New York, Boston, or Salem, but ports close to recorded Indian drift whaling, such as Nantucket, New Bedford, and Sag Harbor (Starbuck 1964).

A close relationship between Indian drift whalers and leading East Coast whaling ports is supported and clarified by historians' claims that Indians of Long Island, Martha's Vineyard, Nantucket, and Cape Cod played a key role in the growth of American whaling (Edwards and Rattray 1932; Macy 1835; Dow 1925, 23; Alden 1916, 158; Crèvecoeur 1971; see also Scammon 1968, 204). For example:

> [The Indians of Nantucket] are fond of the sea and expert mariners. They have learned from the Quakers the art of catching . . . the whale . . . and five of them always make part of the complement of men requisite to fit out a whaleboat. (Crèvecoeur 1971, 107)

> The [Nantucket] Indians, ever manifesting a disposition for fishing of every kind, readily joined with the whites in this new

> pursuit. . . . By their assistance, the whites were enabled to fit out and man a far greater number of boats than they could have done of themselves. Nearly every boat was manned in part, many almost entirely by natives; some of the most active of them were made steersmen, and some . . . head[ed] the boats; . . . they soon became experienced whalemen, and capable of conducting any part of the business. (Macy 1835, 30)

Given a supply of right whales close to shore and a labor pool of Indians with a maritime aptitude, as well as an interest in drift whales, we can readily understand the successful European introduction of along-shore whaling to southeastern New England and eastern Long Island. The success of the pelagic whale fishery, according to Crèvecoeur (1971, 116), grew out of the success of the along-shore whale fishery.

Distribution of Right Whales

Moreover, we advance the hypotheses that before 1760 the in-shore waters of southeastern New England, eastern Long Island, and possibly Delaware Bay, where along-shore and Indian drift whaling were recorded (see Figure 3.4a), experienced more right whales than any other East Coast area south of the Gulf of St. Lawrence, and that dead right whales may have contributed to the number of drift whales as well as to the Indian and English interest in drift whales on the same shores.

We support these hypotheses with the following arguments. First, right whales close to shore were fundamental to along-shore whaling, and, because of the commercial value of right whales, along-shore whaling would have been expected at any shore to which right whales resorted. Second, recorded Indian drift whaling very nearly coincided geographically with along-shore whaling. A possible explanation for this coincidence is that right whales would have tended to die and strand more often on shores that they frequented than on shores they did not. In addition, drift right whales, large and rich in oil and baleen, would have had a greater value to Indians and to the English than most other stranded whales. Therefore, the English would have been more likely to purchase Indian drift whales that included right whales than drift whales comprising chiefly, say, bottlenose dolphins or harbor porpoises. As supporting evidence for these arguments, Alden (1916, 140) reported as "curious" the fact that he found no historical records of right whales from the coast of Maine, where no Colonial along-shore whale fishery was established, in spite of attempts to do so (Martin 1975; True 1904, 21), and where no recorded Indian drift whaling has been reported.

In modern times, even with the reduced number of right whales, and the possibility that their seasonal distribution has changed over the past 300 years, one right whale has stranded at the south shore of eastern Long Island in the spring of 1979 (Richard Whitaker, National Marine Fisheries Service, personal communication), one has stranded at the southwest shore of Nantucket in the spring of 1961 (see Table 5.1), and one has stranded at Narragansett Bay (Leatherwood et al. 1976, 56).

Although we know remarkably little about the habits of right whales (Scammon 1968; W. E. Schevill, personal communication), from historical records we do know that in the seventeenth century on the East Coast of North America, along-shore whaling took place between 39° and 43° north in the winter and early spring (Alden 1916, 130–42). According to Paul Dudley (1809, 80), in 1725, right whales of New England "in the fall go westward, and in the spring eastward." Furthermore, right whale cows, calves, and yearlings were known and hunted off New England (Dudley 1809, 78) and Long Island (Ross 1902, 873). These facts are consistent with our knowledge of right whales from other parts of the world (Browne 1968, 551–72). Right whales of the southern hemisphere are known to calve in bays at 40°~45° south in the winter (Scammon 1968, 67; Payne 1974, 329; Browne 1968, 560), and right whales are known to have frequented the Bay of Biscay, at 43°~45° north, in the winter with calves (Clark 1974, 65).

In summary, we conclude from the historic and ethnohistoric evidence that there may have been a good number of live right whales and their calves, as well as drift right whales, in the winter and early spring, on the coasts of southeastern New England, eastern Long Island, and possibly off Delaware Bay in the seventeenth and early eighteenth centuries. These concentrations of right whales near specific shores would have accounted for the local Indian and English interest in drift whales, as well as for their success as along-shore whale hunters, and subsequently as pelagic whalers.

Conclusion

From the documentary records of Nantucket, as well as the histories of Long Island, Martha's Vineyard, Narragansett Bay, and Cape Cod Bay, the earliest historic Indian whaling on these shores focused on drift whales—a splendid example of people living in balance with their resources. Modern records of whale strandings at Nantucket provide evidence that drift whales could have been a more substantial resource than historians and archaeologists have heretofore considered. Based on the similar geographic patterns of ethnohistoric drift whaling, and of the along-shore and pelagic whaling ports of the eastern United States, we have identified specific shores on the East Coast along which, during the Colonial period, the Indians were whalemen, and right whales, both along-shore and stranded, must have been particularly abundant. One of the outcomes of this study has been the recognition that local ethnohistoric data may illuminate the prehistoric distribution of right whales. In turn, knowledge of the seasonal distribution of right whales would surely contribute to an understanding of coastal archaeology (Clark 1974, 62).

Acknowledgments

This chapter is reprinted with the kind permission of *Northeast Anthropology*, Sean Rafferty, editor; originally published in *Man in the Northeast* 23: 1–16 (1982).

We thank William E. Schevill for guidance to the literature of whalebone whales of New England, and Richard Whitaker, National Marine Fisheries Service, Gloucester, for access to recent records of whale strandings from Maine to North Carolina. We also thank Mrs. Louise Hussey of the Peter Foulger Museum, Nantucket, Mrs. Marcia Moss of the Concord Public Library, and the personnel of the Registry of Deeds, Nantucket, for their gracious assistance. Paul C. Morris kindly allowed photographs of the flensing took kit in his collection. We thank Dena F. Dincauze, Barbara Luedtke and William E. Schevill for comments on an early version of this study, which was presented at the San Francisco meeting of the American Society for Ethnohistory, October 24, 1980.

Appendix 1

SPECIES, DATE, AND LOCATION OF WHALES STRANDED AT NANTUCKET SINCE 1947, WITH CITATIONS TO ANDREWS' RECORDS (JCA), THE NANTUCKET INQUIRER AND MIRROR (I & M), AND LAW ENFORCEMENT BRANCH, NATIONAL MARINE FISHERIES SERVICE, GLOUCESTER (NMFS).

1. *Physetercatodon* (Sperm Whale): September 1961; drifted from Capaum Pond to strand at Galls; length: 9.1 meters (JCA; I & M, 15 September 1961)

2. *Tursiops truncatus* (Bottlenose Dolphin): 23 May 1964; North Shore near Eel Point (JCA)

3. *Tursiops truncatus*: 1 July 1968; Siasconset Beach; length: 1.7 meters (I & M, 4 July 1968)

4. *Tursiops truncatus:* 19 July 1970; west Coatue Beach (JCA; I & M, 23 July 1970)

5. *Deiphinus deiphis* (Saddleback Dolphin): 9 October 1948; Head of Harbor (JCA)

6. *Delphinus deiphis*: June 1970; Hither Creek (JCA)

7. *Deiphinus deiphis*: 12 March 1972; Siasconset Beach (JCA)

8. *Deiphinus deiphis*: February 1974; Low Beach (JCA)

9. *Deiphinus deiphis:* February 1974; Low Beach (JCA)

10. *Deiphinus deiphis:* 16 October 1974; north shore of Tuckernuck, old male (JCA)

11. *Deiphinus deiphis*: 15 February 1976; Tom Nevers Head (JCA)

12. *Deiphinus deiphis*: 22 February 1978; Coatue Beach (NNPS)

13. *Orcinus orca* (Killer Whale): 21 March 1955; Tom Nevers Head (JCA)

14. *Globicephala rnelaena* (Blackfish): 22 May 1954; Eel Point; female (JCA; Starrett and Starrett 1955)

15. *Globicephala melaena*: 22 May 1954; Eel Point; calf (JCA; Starrett and Starrett 1955)

16. *Globicephala melaena*: September 1964; North Shore near Dionis (JCA)

17. *Globicephala melaena*: 20 June 1972; Coatue Point, outside harbor (JCA)

18. *Globicephala melaena*: 10 February 1973; Miacomet Beach (JCA)

19. *Grampus griseus* (Gray Grampus): June 1975; drifted from shoal south of Tuckernuck to strand at Eel Point (JCA)

20. *Phocoena phocoena* (Atlantic Harbor Porpoise): 22 April 1967; Cisco Beach; male (JCA)

21. *Phocoena phocoena*: January 1972; Siasconset Beach (JCA)

22. *Phocoena phocoena*: 4 February 1972; Siasconset Beach (JCA)

23. *Phocoena phocoena*: 13 March 1978; Nantucket (NMFS)

24. *Balaenoptera physalus* (Finback Whale): 12 July 1948; East Cisco; length: 19.8 meters (JCA; I & M, 14 July 1948)

25. *Baleenoptera physalus:* September 1949; Wauwinet (JCA)

26. *Balaenoptera physalus*: May 1954; Smith Point (JCA)

27. *Balaenoptera physalus* [?]: 20 October 1967; Dionis Beach; length: 13.0 meters (exhibit with skeleton at Nantucket Whaling Museum), or 13.4 meters (I & M, 26 October 1967, 2 November 1967)

28. *Balaenoptera physalus:* August 1971; Surfside (JCA; I & M, 26 August 1971)

29. *Balaenoptera physalus*: June 1975; shoal south of Tuckernuck (JCA; I & M, 5 June 1975, 17 June 1975)

30. *Eubalaena giacialis* (Right Whale): June 1961; west of Hummock Pond (JCA; I & M, 9 June 1961)

31. Unknown species: 5 June 1969; the Galls; length: 18.3 meters (I & M, 5 June 1969); possibly the same whale off Tuckernuck (I & M, 22 May 1969)

32. "Dolphin": 4 September 1978; Eel Point (NMFS)

Appendix 2

July 13, 1668

"Edward Starbuck and Peter Foulger were empowered to make a bargain with the Indians concerning all whales that shall come on shore on the Island, on the Town's behalf" (NCD 1, 8).

June 20, 1672

"Ahkeiman laying claim to part of Tuckernuck his claim thereto is found no other but as he was a duke or principal man upon Nantucket; the Nantucket Sachems, together with his father, having sold Tuckernuck it is ordered that he shall have such a part or portion of land for his use at Nantucket of the present Sachems as will become one of such quality, and a portion of the whales" (Worth 1902, 137).

May 4, 1672

Grants of land and privileges to James Loper and John Savage if they will "ingage to carrey on a design of whale catching," and "follow his trade of a cooper," respectively (NCD 1, 30, original spelling). (Loper did not come to Nantucket [Edwards and Rattray 1932].)

July 19, 1673

"The Court do order that the Rack or drift whales in that bounds of the bach upon the playnes from the Pond of Richard Swayn to Smyth Poynt shal be Divided into Eight shares Washaman, Womhommin, Masaaquat, Wapskowit, Wanaquin, Kanpakanit, Wequakesoo, Obadiah" (NCD 2(b), 2, original spelling).

July 21, 1673

". . . all the whal fish or other Drift fish belong to the Indian sachims" (NCD 2(b), 4, original spelling).

March 29, 1676

"At a Court held at Sherbourn it was Concluded that Washainan is to have the head of the Drift whale for his share, and Desyer is to have halfe, along with him,—And when Washaman is hear at this Yland, then he is to go master of the share, but when he is absent then Desyer is to go master of the share" (NCD 2 (b), 2, original spelling).

June 27, 1676

"Mr Harry complayns against Spotsoo and Masaaqua for taking away or Disposing of his share of whale without his order" (NCD 2 (b), 8, original spelling).

June 27, 1676

"It is ordered that no Rack whale that com ashore in any Sachims bounds, shal be Cut up until al the Masters of the shares that belong to that whale Do Com together, upon the penalty of Twenty shillings fine, to any that shal cut up and despose of any part Contrary to the order aforesayd, and also if any master be of the Yland and leave no man to Act for him, he is to loose his share of whale for that time" (NCD 2(b), 8, original spelling).

June 5, 1677

Nickanoose gave land rights to his two brothers, "and if the whale shall happen to come shore, that whale to be theirs also . . ." (MVD 1, 38).

June 5, 1677

"Wakieaman is ordered to have such a part of whale out of Noosoquits whale as he can make appear that he used take by Ussamequi(a)s order while sd whale was in the possession of Waquakesoo. Wequash shall have such a part of whale on the Nantucket land as did belong to his ancesters in so much that it appeareth that he obtained right thereof from the Sachems. Ordered that George Nanahumoo, Mahtakegin and Obadiah with their Companies shall have the whale from Goodman Swains pond to Smiths point according to their former custom and so to be divided" (copy) (Mass. Sup. Ct. Jud. #92741, original spelling).

June 5, 1677

In a division of land between Spotso and Moosoquet, ". . . the beach and what whales come ashore shall belong to him on whose right it falleth" (Worth 1902, 138).

"24:4:1678"

"At a court of Sessions held in the Town of Sherburne the 24:4:78 it was ordered by the Court that Waquakeso, Nicanoose, Spotso, and Nusaquat shall have full power to choose each sachem ten men as a comit(ee) for the finding out the partickcular Rights in whalle of all men and having so don then this Comitty to give and accounpt to oe Court and from thence it shall transmitted to the Generall Court for Confirmation and If in cause any partickoular men should be wrounged by this Comitee the have thare liberty by petition to the General Court where the may be herd if it be done before Confirmation" (NCD 2(b), 13, original spelling).

"29th–12th 1679"

In Musaquat's complaint against Eleazer Folger for "(?) or taking away his whale," the verdict of the court was a fine for the defendant and the cost of court for the plaintiff. The plaintiff appealed to the General Court (NCD 2(b), 24).

March 6, 1681

The Coffins "desolaim any rights or interest in any whale by virtue of the land on Tuckernuck but do make over any Right that may belong unto them unto Ackeamoug and Jacob, Sons of Pattocohnet . . . including liberty of savei'ng of their whale that may come on shore on that island" (NCD 2, 38, original spelling).

August 16, 1681

"Jepta complayneth that Nickanoose and Wawinet did hinder him of his share of whale at Coatue that he formerly injoyed. The Court orders that Jepta shall have and Injoy his share thare" (NCD 2(b), 29, original spelling).

1684

Sunmary of Indian lands sold to the English, "except what dead whales shall be cast on a shore that belong to the Indians according to former custom" (NCD 3, 73).

1691

English purchase of Siasconset from sachem Jeptha, "except drift whales" (NCD 3, 51).

1701

English purchase of land previously belonging to Musaquat (see Figure 3.2) from sachem Henry Brittain; "memorandoin, the drift whale is not hearby [*sic*] sold" (NCD 3, 23).

1712

Cachahuman and Mooney to Sowacha, "all the head of Drift whales that may be stranded" or "come ashore any where nigh Tuckanucket," which Cachahuman's father, Scotsbonnet, had possessed in partnership with Pattacohonet. Upon the death of Pattacohonet, his half right had passed "successively" to "Jacob pattacohonets son," and upon his death to "Mooney now Called Pattacohonet" (NCD 3, 62, original spelling).

1712

Paunes gave half "the head of all drift whales that from time to time and at all times should come ashore or be Stranded within the Sachemship or Jurisdiction of Musacut, late Sachem" to the sons-in-law of his late partner, Johnboy (NCD 3, 68).

1728

Natakekin sold to Koskuhtukquaeinin his rights in "whale" ("pootop") (NCD 4, 62).

Works Cited

Alden, Timothy, Jr. 1798. Memorabilia of Yarmouth. *Massachusetts Historical Society Collections* l(5): 57.

Allen, Glover N. 1916. Whalebone Whales of New England. *Boston Society of Natural History Memoirs* 8(2).

Banks, Charles Edward. 1911, 1925. *The History of Martha's Vineyard.* 2 vols. Boston, MA: George H. Dean.

Basset, Dean Benjamin. 1792. Fabulous Traditions and Customs of the Indians. *Massachusetts Historical Society Collections* 1(1): 139–40.

Bradford, William. 1898. *History "Of Plimoth Plantation" [1620–1647].* Massachusetts Legislature. Boston, MA: Wright and Potter.

Brereton, John. 1602. *A Brief and True Relation* . . . London: George Bishop.

Browne, J. Ross. 1968. *Etchings of a Whaling Cruise [1846].* Edited by John Seelye. Cambridge, MA: Harvard University Press.

Bullen, Ripley P., and Edward Brooks. 1947. The Squam Pond Indian Site, Nantucket, Massachusetts. *Massachusetts Archaeological Society Bulletin* 8(4): 56–59.

Bullen, Ripley P., and Edward Brooks. 1949. The Herrecator Swamp Site, Nantucket Island, Massachusetts. *Massachusetts Archaeological Society Bulletin* 10(4): 81–89.

Chisholm, C., R. Holtzheiiner, and J. Robinson. 1974. *Nantucket Island: An Analysis of the Natural and Visual Resources.* Cambridge, MA: Harvard Graduate School of Design.

Clark, J. G. D. 1974. *Prehistoric Europe: The Economic Basis* [1952]. Stanford, CA: Stanford University Press.

Crèvecoeur, Hector St. Jean de. 1971. *Letters from an American Farmer* [1782]. New York: Everyman's Library.

Dow, George Francis. 1925. Whale Ships and Whaling, with an Account of the Whale Fishery. In *Colonial New England.* Salem, MA: Marine Research Society.

Drake, Samuel Adams. 1876. *Nooks and Corners of the New England Coast.* New York: Harper and Brothers.

Dudley, Paul. 1809. An Essay on the Natural History of Whales. [1725]. In *Philosophical Transactions of the Royal Society of London* (abridged ed.). 7: 78–84. London: C. and R. Baldwin.

Edwards, Everett J., and Jeannette Edwards Rattray. 1932. Whale Off. In *The Story of American Shore Whaling.* New York: Coward McCann.

Fowler, William S. 1972. Bone Implements: How They Were Used. *Massachusetts Archaeological Society Bulletin* 33(l, 2): 12–19.

Fowler, William S. 1973. Metal Cutouts of the Northeast. *Massachusetts Archaeological Society Bulletin* 34(3, 4): 24–30.

Freeman, Frederick. 1869. *The History of Cape Cod.* 2 vols. Boston, MA: Piper.

Goddard, Ives. 1978. Delaware. In *Handbook of North American Indians*, vol. 15, ed. Bruce G. Trigger, 213–39. Washington, DC: Smithsonian Institution.

Holland, Captain. 1794. *Chart of Nantucket Sound.* London: Laurie and Whittle.

Huden, John C. 1962. *Indian Place Names of New England.* Museum of the American Indian. New York: Heye Foundation.

I & M. *The Nantucket Inquirer and Mirror*, Nantucket, MA.

Josselyn, John. 1833. Two Voyages to New England [1675]. *Massachusetts Historical Society Collections* 33: 211–354.

Katona, Steven, David Richardson, and Robin Hazard. 1975. *A Field Guide to the Whales and Seals of the Gulf of Maine.* Bar Harbor, ME: College of the Atlantic.

Kittredge, Henry C. 1968. *Cape Cod, Its People and Their History* [1930]. 2d ed. Boston, MA: Houghton Mifflin.

Leatherwood, Stephen, David K. Caidwell, and Howard E. Winn. 1976. Whales, Dolphins, and Porpoises of the Western North Atlantic. NOAA Technical Report. *National Marine Fisheries Service Circular* 396.

Little, Elizabeth A. 1979. *An Inventory of Indian Sites on Nantucket.* Report submitted to the Massachusetts Historical Commission, Boston, MA.

Macy, Obed. 1835. *The History of Nantucket.* Boston, MA: Hilliard Ray and Company.

Macy, Zaccheus. l792a. Letter to Massachusetts Historical Society. In *The History of Nantucket*, 262–71. Boston, MA: Hilliard Ray and Company.

Macy, Zaccheus. 1792b. A Short Journal of the First Settlement of the Island of Nantucket. *Massachusetts Historical Society Collections* 1, 3: 155–60.

Martha's Vineyard Deeds (MVD). Registry of Deeds, Edgartown.

Martin, Kenneth R. 1975. *Whalemen and Whaleships of Maine.* Bath, ME: The Marine Research Society.

Mass. Sup. Ct. Jud. Massachusetts Superior Court of Judicature. Suffolk County Courthouse, Boston.

Moffett, Ross. 1959. Notes on the Small's Swamp Shell Heap, Truro, Mass. *Massachusetts Archaeological Society Bulletin* 2l(l): 1–14.

Moffett, Ross. 1969. An Unusual Indian Harpoon from Truro. *Massachusetts Archaeological Society Bulletin* 30(3, 4): 22–24.

Mourt's Relation. [1622] 1802. *Massachusetts Historical Society Collections* 1, 8: 203–39.

Mourt's Relation. 1832. *Massachusetts Historical Society Collections* 2, 9: 26–73.

Nantucket County Deeds (NCD). 1668. Registry of Deeds, Nantucket, MA.

National Geographic Society. 1960. Map of North America. In *Atlas of the United States*, 6–7. Washington, DC: National Geographic Society.

National Ocean Survey. 1977. *Cape Sable to Cape Hatteras, Chart Number 13003.* Washington, DC: NOAA, U.S. Department of Commerce.

Payne, Roger. 1974. At Home with Right Whales. *National Geographic* 149: 32239.

Pratt, Enoch. 1844. *History of Eastham, Wellfleet, and Orleans.* Yarmouth, MA: W. S. Fisher.

Robotti, Frances Diane. 1950. *Whaling and Old Salem.* Salem, MA: Newcomb and Gauss.

Rosier, James. 1843. A True Relation of the Most Prosperous Voyage by Captain George Waymouth [1605). *Massachusetts Historical Society Collections* 3, 8: 125–57.

Ross, Peter. 1902. *A History of Long Island.* New York: Lewis.

Scammon, Charles M. 1968. *The Marine Mammals of the North-Western Coast of North America [1874].* New York: Dover.

Schmitt, Frederick P. 1972. *Whale Watch: The Story of Shore Whaling in Nassau County, New York.* Cold Spring Harbor, NY: The Whaling Museum Society.

Scothorne, D. G. 1970. A Cache of Bone Implements. *Massachusetts Archaeological Society Bulletin* 31(l, 2): 28–30.

Shaler, N. S. 1897. Geology of the Cape Cod District. *U.S. Geological Survey Annual Report* 18(2): 497–593.

Spence, Bill. 1980. *Harpooned. The Story of Whaling.* New York: Crescent Books.

Stackpole, Edouard A. 1953. *The Sea Hunters.* New York: Bonanza Books.

Starbuck, Alexander. 1924. *The History of Nantucket.* Boston, MA: Goodspeed.

Starbuck, Alexander. 1964. *History of the American Whale Fishery* [1878]. Report of the U.S. Commission on Fish and Fisheries, Part IV. Washington, DC, New York: Argosy Antiquarian.

Starrett, Andrew, and Priscilla Starrett. 1955. Observations on Young Blackfish, Globicephala. *Journal of Mammalogy* 36(3): 424–29.

Stockley, Bernard H. 1964. Some Unusual Artifacts from Ram Pasture 1, Nantucket, Mass. *Massachusetts Archaeological Society Bulletin* 25(3, 4): 70–72.

Stockley, Bernard H. 1965. Preliminary Report, Ram Pasture 1, A Stratified Site on Nantucket Island, Massachusetts. *Eastern States Archaeological Federation Bulletin* 24: 11.

True, Frederick W. 1904. The Whalebone Whales of the Western North Atlantic. *Smithsonian Contributions to Knowledge* 33. Washington, DC: The Smithsonian Institute.

Waters, Joseph. 1965. Animal Remains from Some New England Woodland Sites. *Archaeological Society of Connecticut Bulletin* 33: 5–11.

Weiss, Harry B., Howard R. Kemble, and Milhicent T. Carre. 1974. *Whaling in New Jersey.* Trenton: New Jersey Agricultural Society.

Williams, Roger. 1973. *A Key into the Language of America* [1643). Edited by John J. Teunissen and Evelyn J. Minz. Detroit, MI: Wayne State University Press.

Wood, William. 1865. *New England's Prospect* [1635). Edited by Charles Deane. Boston, MA: Prince Society.

Worth, Henry Barnard. 1902. Nantucket Lands and Land Owners. *Nantucket Historical Association Bulletin* 2(3).

4

Island Queens

Women Sachems on Martha's Vineyard and Nantucket in the Colonial Period

Kathleen J. Bragdon

A salient feature of the native New England "interaction sphere" centered around the islands of Martha's Vineyard and Nantucket and the territories ringing Buzzard's Bay and Long Island Sound was the number of prominent "queen sachems," or *saunckssquûaog*, who appear to have ruled there in their own right throughout the seventeenth century. Among these were several from Martha's Vineyard and Nantucket. This chapter looks at the details of queen sachems' lives to consider women's place in these small, chiefly societies, which were themselves continuously evolving during the first century of English settlement there.

The majority of seventeenth-century English observers of Native life in southern New England implied, along with Roger Williams (1936[1643], 141), that "queen sachems" generally ruled as agents of men (see, e.g., Winslow 1910[1624], 307). Although some Native women leaders in southern New England were described as "relicts" of their sachem husbands, there are a number whose authority cannot be explained only in that way, including Askamapoo of Nantucket, Wunnatuckquanum, or "Elizabeth Queen Sachem" of Martha's Vineyard, and Hepsibah Cogenew, Queen Sachem of Chappaquiddick. These women, like others less well known, were not only powerful decision makers in their communities but also were pivotal individuals in the Native economy.

In early descriptions of southern New England Native societies written by English observers (i.e., Wood 1977[1634], Williams 1936[1643];

Winslow 1910[1624]), women's activities were rarely given the attention granted to men's, and men were understood to be the principal (hereditary) leaders and decision makers within Native society. However, the conflicts between Native polities and the English newcomers (and the documentation these generated) allow glimpses into the complexities of indigenous social organization that might otherwise have remained hidden, such as the part that women played in alliance and succession. In particular, the large number of land records that detail bequests and sales of Native lands document the principal role that the saunckсsquûaog took in the allocation of land. These cases allow us to infer a dynamic system in which high-ranking men and women's status and authority were codependent and to add further detail to what ethnohistorians can know about the historic lineage systems of Eastern North America.

Descent and Alliance in Cross-cultural Perspective

Cross-cultural studies of descent and alliance have been concerned with addressing the ways in which ideologies of descent represent "total social systems," systems that consist of "ideology and those social actions and relations which are meaningfully informed by it" (Poewe 1981, 55). For many scholars, this leads to a new appreciation for the ways in which payments at marriage and property controlled by women give clues to wider conceptual orderings within society. Marriage has dominated alliance theories of kinship largely because it highlights the role of men, and because it is only through marriage that men in many societies become total "social persons." But marriage and accompanying wealth exchange can just as easily highlight women's roles and document their centrality in social reproduction. Although women in many societies, even those for whom marriage payments have been made, often appear to lose much of their autonomy as wives, this does not appear to have been true among high-ranking women in the chiefly societies of southern New England. Lack of agreement among scholars concerning the nature of authority and descent has obscured evidence that reflects the intertwining of matrilineal and patrilineal principles, principles that are likely to have Precontact period precedents.

Marriage and Descent in Native Southern New England

Strong evidence from the indigenous languages spoken in southern New England suggests that these societies were organized into lineages, although few certainties exist about whether matrilineal or patrilineal lines were dominant (see, e.g., Simmons and Aubin 1975; Bragdon 1996). Although it is clear that male sachems typically succeeded their sachem fathers, I suggest that matrilineality was crucial in the legitimization of control over property, which in these horticultural societies was also one of the most important forms of "social capital," and the distribution of which was the principal organizer of labor. During the late seventeenth century moreover, when Native men were often incorporated into the Colonial maritime economy, women's authority helped sustain corporate landholding social groups in the face of pressures toward partibility.

In southern New England during the seventeenth century, Native women could be tied to men through various kinds of marriage arrangements, some of which were relatively impermanent (Plane 2000). In addition, high-status men were expected to be polygynous (married to more than one woman simultaneously), but only their first wives were likely to have been lifelong partners (Williams 1936[1643], 150). These variations on marriage in Native southern New England can best be understood as being largely determined by women's relative status as wives and sisters, and the economic implications of each role.

In the emergent hierarchical societies of seventeenth-century coastal southern New England, marriage, which involved bride-price payments, ensured that moveable wealth remained within a relatively small group of allied lineages who, as representatives of the communities they governed, "looked after" the property of the community. Recent scholarship also reminds us that while descent is central to social reproduction, the transactions that take place as a result of social transitions within a generation are also significant, particularly among the elite. According to Elizabeth Little (Little 1996), on Nantucket alone, hundreds of deeds involving Native people as grantors and grantees were recorded, some of which were written by Indian people themselves in the Native language, and a similar number exist on Martha's Vineyard. A smaller, but significant number also derive from the Saconnet and Nauset regions on the edges of Buzzard's Bay (see Figure 4.1, next page). I concur with Little (1996) that these deeds were representative of only the highest-ranking strata of these linked coastal societies. These documents demonstrate connections among individuals from several sachemships, hinting at marriage ties not otherwise recorded (Bragdon 2009) and reminding us that land was central to marriages as well.

Land Allotment and the Sachemship in Southern New England

The earliest descriptions of the Native societies of southern New England agree that chiefly lineages, headed by sachems, controlled use of terri-

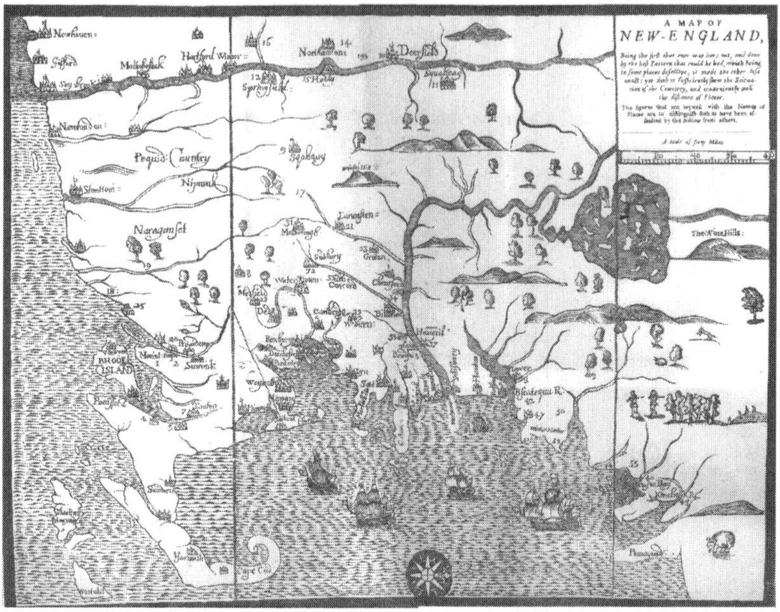

Figure 4.1. William Hubbard's "Map of New-England," 1677. It appears to have been commissioned by Hubbard for his volume *The History of the Indian Wars in New England,* published in London and Boston in 1677. It is described by Samuel G. Drake, editor of Hubbard's *Indian Wars* (1865), as "the curious Woodcut Map."

tory "in exchange" for tribute payments and loyalty. So a sachem was said to divide land for his subjects (cf. chippaht8e, or "his/her shares or divisions") (Goddard and Bragdon 1988, 613). Those for whom land had been divided owed tribute to the sachems to whom they pledged loyalty. In this way, sachems could be said to acquire "wealth in people" of a type that, according to Bledsoe (1980), "binds people to their superiors in ties of marriage, clientship, and filial obligation" (1). A sachem derived his legitimacy, hence his authority, to allot land from the alliance of his parents' families, while his children derived authority from him and his wife. This authority, as visible in recorded land transactions, was the privilege and obligation of rank, regardless of gender. And although normally female authority was "masked" by male authority, it might on occasion stand alone. It is important then to distinguish between the inheritance of property and the inheritance of authority; in Native southern New England, high-ranking men and women were not "heirs" in the English sense but "conduits" through which society continuously reproduced itself.

Rank and Bride-price in Southern New England Native Societies

That the coastal societies of southern New England were ranked societies is well known. English observers were themselves well attuned to status differences, and they rightly noted that social differences existed among the Native societies they described (Kupperman 2000, 92 ff.). Status differences were often marked in dress, deportment, the existence of a retinue of advisors and councilors, and other privileges (Bragdon 1996). Some of these differences were apparent in the behavior of high- and low-status women. Low-ranking women worked very hard, and in polygynous unions, they did the bulk of the domestic work (see, e.g., Winslow 1910[1624], 348; Wood 1977[1634], 112; Williams 1936[1643], 147).[1] High-ranking women, on the other hand, behaved very differently. Mary Rowlandson, who was captured February 10, 1675–1676, at Lancaster, Massachusetts, by allies of King Philip, described Weetamoo, Philip's sister-in-law, to whom she had been given as a servant:

> My master (Quinapin, a Narragansett sachem) had three squaws, living sometimes with one, and sometimes with another one. . . . [One] was Wattimore [Weetamoo] with whom I had lived and served all this while. A severe and proud dame she was, bestowing every day in dressing herself neat as much time as any of the gentry of the land: powdering her hair, and painting her face, going with necklaces, with jewels in her ears, and bracelets upon her hands. When she had dressed herself, her work was to make girdles of wampum and beads. (Rowlandson 1913[1682], 150)

High-ranking women had servants, and it appears that they were often entrusted with important diplomatic missions as well (Winslow 1910[1624]). Native language deeds from Martha's Vineyard written on behalf of the queen sachem Wunnatuckquanum and Askamapoo also reveal distinct discourse styles that presumably marked their high status (Goddard and Bragdon 1988, 21). These women, in short, had "charisma"—they were "charged objects" of social power (Tambiah 1984; Ferguson 1988, 507; Williamson 2003).

According to contemporary testimony, there were also status differences among a man's several wives. Some observers argued that the first wife within a polygynous marriage was of the highest rank (see, e.g., Williams 1936[1643]). On the other hand, Matthew Mayhew of Martha's Vineyard, fully familiar with Native beliefs on the island, wrote "The Blood Royal," being in such veneration that "if a prince had issue by divers wives, such succeeded as heir who was royally descended by the mother, although the youngest" (1940[1694], 7–8, emphasis added). Little suggests that on Nantucket, the sachem Nickanoose treated the children of his high-status first wife differently from those of his second, lower-ranking wife (Little 1996, 203) (see Figure 4.2).

Bride-price or bride wealth was also tied to rank in southern New England. Roger Williams suggested that a larger bride-price was paid for higher-ranking wives among the Narragansett and Niantic (1936[1643], 148), a common situation in bride-price societies with ranking systems (Collier 1987). On Martha's Vineyard and Nantucket, as elsewhere in southern New England, high-status marriages ceremonies were marked by such payments. Edward Winslow recorded this custom among the Pokanokets, and Roger Williams noted a similar practice among the Narragansett/Niantics. According to Mohegan minister Samson Occom, among the Natives of eastern Long Island, marriages were arranged

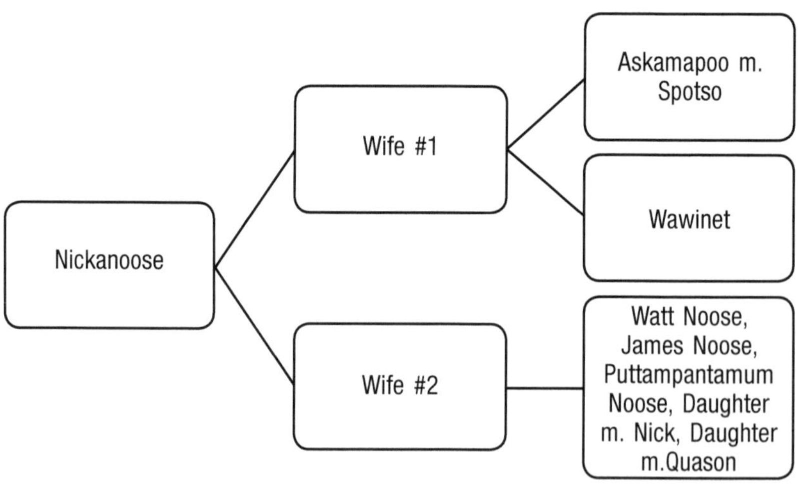

Figure 4.2. Nantucket Sachem Succession (Little 1996)

between the groom's father or mother (if the father was dead) and the bride's family, and bride wealth was paid to the woman's kin. Ann Plane (1994) notes similar payments in the Ninegret sachem family marriages until the mid-eighteenth century.

Although bride-price was paid even by less affluent men (see, e.g., Williams 1936[1643], 29, 148), other forms of marriage were not accompanied by payments and were said to be less stable (Plane 1994, 156). Bride wealth in general is found in both matrilineal and patrilineal societies but is often associated with situations in which the patrisystem requires rights to the children; it follows that in societies with a strong preference for patrilineal succession of leadership, as was the case in southern New England, the bride-price payments for high-status wives would be larger, as was also the case. On the other hand, bride-price systems can also privilege wife-giving groups, as the substantial wedding payments enrich the natal families of the brides (Leach 1971[1951], 230–31). As high-ranking Native women in southern New England were likely to remarry, often several times, significant wealth may have accrued to their families as well.

The use of wampum (beads of white and blue shell) for bride wealth exchanges in southern New England is well documented. While wampum's social and symbolic significance prior to the arrival of Europeans is poorly known (but see Becker, chapter 7, in this volume), it circulated largely among sachem families (Bragdon 1996, 97). Wampum, especially the white form made from the columella of whelk shells, had ritual significance in much of the eastern woodlands (see Becker, chapter 7, in this volume). According to Margaret Holmes Williamson (2003), white beads were "symbolically associated with power, access to the supernatural, the sky world, and to fertility" (157). If this were the case in southern New England in the first decades of the seventeenth century, then wampum would have been an appropriate "exchange" for women, as cattle were among many African matrilineal systems, because of its interconnectedness to the most central symbolic representations in those societies. Intergenerational exchanges of wampum among sachem wife-givers and wife-takers would serve to symbolically and economically bind these groups together, while at the same time consolidating their moral and economic dominance over nonparticipating family lines.

Bride wealth in southern New England not only ratified marriages but also represented the "social capital" of chiefly families. Plane (1996) notes that in the eighteenth century Narragansett/Niantic community, marriage without such payments and the feast that accompanied them failed to legitimize the succession of any children produced from it. That wampum was for a time co-opted as a medium of exchange by English traders and settlers in southern New England led some to believe that Native brides could be "bought," although this is very unlikely to have been true. In fact, in most Native language documents, wampum as payment is rarely mentioned; only English loan words such as "money" and "peny" are noted.[2]

Women's Contribution to the Consolidation of Power in Native Southern New England

The false notion that women could be bought further underscored what English observers believed: that men occupied the highest status within Native society. Certainly men wielded authority most visibly, and, to English eyes, women in general were overburdened with work (Bragdon 1996, 49–52). But high-ranking women were crucial to the process of succession, and it is in their biographies, and their disputes with the English, that we can see the workings of lineal relations, and the cooperation of matrilineal and patrilineal principles.

For example, Plane (1996, 2000) has documented two cases in which the mother's rank played an important role in the rights of their children to rule. In one, the children of the courageous Awashunks, one of the sachems of the Sakonnets and an erstwhile ally of the Plymouth colonists in the lead up to King Philip's war, were understood to have such rights (see Figure 4.3). In a letter written to her by Thomas Prince on October 20, 1671, he reminded her:

> I could have wished that [your followers] had been wiser themselves, especially your two sons, *that may probably succeed you in your government*, and your brother [a client of Philip's] also, who is so nearly tied to you by nature. (MHS 1798, 197, col. ser. 1, v. 5) (cited in Plane 1996, 173–75, emphasis added)

This document suggests that, as in many societies, the male and female children of a matriline are understood to be legitimate heirs. However, as Plane (2000) argues, the principles of matrilineal inheritance were being tested by the late seventeenth century. A separate faction of Sakonetts led by Osomehew, Posotoquo and Mamanewet decreed:

> Our Brother . . . Mamanewet should be the true proprietor and disposer of all our lands, and that our brother Mamanewet himself and his heirs shall be the chief sachem or head over

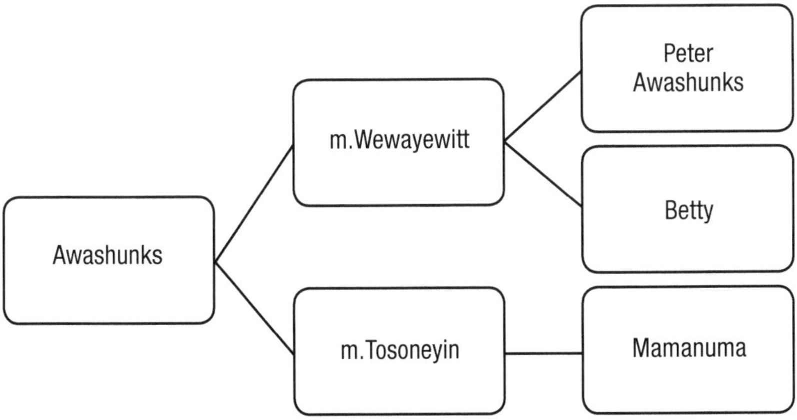

Figure 4.3. Saconnet Leadership

> us. (Town Clerk's Office, Little Compton, Rhode Island, 1672–1673, Court Records)

Mamanewet (or Mamanua) was the son of Awashonk's sachem husband Tosoneyin, and her claims to legitimacy were undermined because of her more distant blood-based relation to (her husband's?) line, according to a deed (July 4, 1673, County Clerk's Office, Plymouth, Massachusetts, Deeds [V3:286]), which stated:

> "[Awashonks] kindred . . . are of the same stock, the more remote" than Mamanua and his "bretheren the sones of Tosoneyin."

Awashunks was also the mother of Peter Awashunks, and another deed states:

> Tatuckamana, Awashunckes and those of that kindred whoe are of the same stock the more Remote may have some right to lands there as they are relations to the above said Mamaneway and have been longe inhabitants of that place. (County Clerk's Office, Plymouth, Massachusetts, Deeds [V3:286], original spelling)

Another case discussed by Plane (1994) regarding the legitimacy of children comes from a case recorded in the 1740s in southern Rhode

Island. According to contemporary testimony about Ninegret I of the Narragansett/Niantic:

> He left four children one son and three daughters which children he had by two wifes (*sic*) one daughter he had by one of his wives and one son and two daughters by the other (deposition of Sompanwat, Kouckeomotonsow and the *Old Queen, sister to Old Ninegret*). And after the death of the said sachem the tribe of Indians met together in order to choose a sachem or sachems or queen. And when the Indians got together in order to choose one of the said sachems children who was of the most royal blood and upon consulting the affair they agree that his wife by whom he had but one daughter was of the most royal blood her father being a great sachem and her mother also of the royal blood therefore thy proceeded & chose his said daughter who was of the most royal blood and made her their *sachemess or queen* and she continued to be their queen as long as she lived. (Plane 1994, 173–75, emphases added)

According to Plane (1994), Ninegret II's four wives may have been of Narragansett, Pequot, and Mohegan descent (160). Charles Ninegret, one of the disputants for leadership of the Narragansett in the 1740s, was the son of Ninegret II's fourth wife, who was from Stonington Connecticut. She recalled:

> . . . and when I was married to Ninegret the former sachem all the tribe were come together, and the elders or heads of the tribe were consulted on the matter and the whole tribe consented and contributed and the elders paid the dower and Ninegret gave the same to my mother the old Sunsk Squaw or Queen and the marriage celebrated by all according to Custom. (Records of the General Court of Rhode Island, September 3, 1746, emphasis added)

Other examples include that of Uncas of the Mohegan, who claimed descent from sachem women from both the Mohegan and the Pequot; his lineage also includes an aunt/nephew marriage as well (Burton and Lowenthal 1974). Simmons and Aubin (1975) note that the Narragansetts had a tradition that a marriage between siblings founded their sachem's line. There is also some direct evidence from eighteenth-century Narragansett marriages that a rule of matrilineal exogamy (marrying outside of the matriline) may have been in operation there.

Anthropologist Jane Collier (1987) argues that marriage is the source of and gives shape to existing social obligations. The disputes discussed earlier seem to support the notion that women who ruled as a result of their mother's status served as a "brake" against partibility, as each generation reconsolidated community property under the control of the highest-ranking persons (determined by both patrilineal and matrilineal descent). However, as Silverblatt (1987) and others have argued, as societies move toward centralization, gender hierarchies and privileges were often undermined. This seems particularly true of matrilineal societies (see, e.g., Gailey 1987; but also see Peletz 1988). These disputes, which pitted the children of different mothers or fathers against one another, revolved around the question of rank, as well as descent, and came over time, to favor male rivals. For example, Awashunks, discussed earlier, was later accused of infanticide, along with her daughter Betty, who was brought to court by another woman, perhaps representing the rival faction (Plane 1996, 150). Betty, the potential heir of Awashunk's authority, was by means of this lawsuit made ineligible to rule.

The Queen Sachems of Martha's Vineyard, Nantucket, and Chappaquiddick

Askamapoo of Nantucket, Wunnatuckquanum of Nunpaog on Martha's Vineyard, and Hepsibah Cogenew of Chappaquiddick were the daughters and the wives of sachems, and all were designated by the special English title "Queen." Askamapoo, the daughter of the sachem Nickanoose, also married the sachem Spotso, and she herself also ruled as sachem, as did her sons. Little (1990, 1996) argues that Askamapoo wielded significant authority over the allotment of land, which she inherited from her father. Askamapoo was the daughter of Nickanoose's first, and highest-status wife, and it was her son Daniel that became sachem (see Figure 4.2). Yet she clearly had status in her own right. Daniel Spotso, himself a sachem, sometimes acted according to her instructions or with her permission (Little 1996, 198–99).

Another woman ruler from the island of Martha's Vineyard was Wunnatuckquanum, "Queen Sachem of Nunpaog," also known as Priscilla, Elizabeth, or Betty Washaman. Wunnatuckquanum was the granddaughter of the sachem Towanquatuck, and the guardian, with her brother (or half-brother) Joel, to all of his lands. She was married twice, the first time to John Webscouet, the son of the sachem "Mr. Harrie" Webscoet, a high-ranking Nantucket man with close ties to the Nantucket sachem Wamechmamuck and to Wunnatuckquanum's grandfather Towanquatuck. Her second husband, Jacob Washaman, was also the son of a Nantucket sachem. In spite of these ties, Wunnatuckquanum was the principal actor in land transfers, even when her husbands were living (Goddard and Bragdon 1988, docs. 15, 16, 21, 27, 28, 31, 33, 36, 69). Washaman, in turn, was the recipient of land from the sachem Nickanoose, land in which both he and his wife had an interest (Goddard and Bragdon 1988, 253).

Hepsibah (Seiknout) Cagnehew was also known as "Queen sachem of Chapoquidick and Mosskeekett" (see Figure 4.4). Hepsibah was the wife of Samuel Cagnehew and the daughter and heir of the sachem Joshua Sieknout. Hepsibah's father and grandfather were the first-born descendants of the prolific sachem Pakeponessoo, a defiant opponent of early Christian missionaries. Hepsibah was herself the eldest of her father's children, and her son became sachem in succession.

The Chappaquiddick sachem lines demonstrate a number of aspects of a system based on descent, alliance, age, and gender and illustrate how rank interpenetrated the former categories. Queen sachem Hepsibah's grandfather Seiknout was granted land by Nickanoose and Wawinit of Nantucket, who also made alliances with the Nantucket sachem Spotso to whom he married his daughter Askamapoo. The documents show that the transfer of property between Nickanoose and Askamaboo was witnessed by two individuals: Pakeponessoo, the Chappaquiddick sachem, discussed earlier, and Papumahchohoo. Seiknout, Pakeponessoo's son, became the sachem of Chappaquiddick, as did his son and grandson.[3]

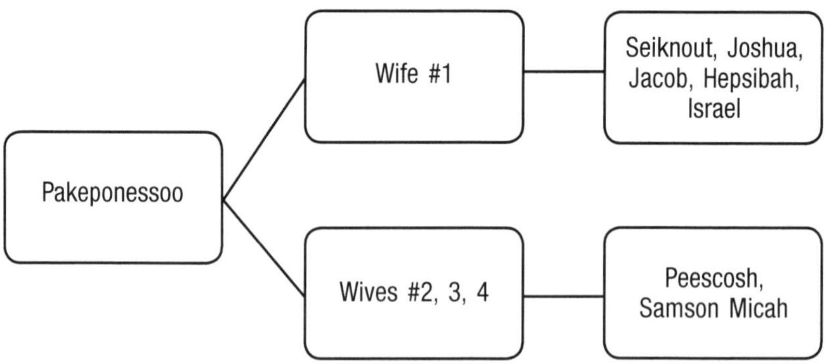

Figure 4.4. Chappaquiddick Sachem Lines

Other records demonstrate strong ties between the sachem line of Nunpaog and Chappaquiddick, as well as links among the sachem families of Nantucket. For example, Papumachohoo, noted earlier, was a frequent witness to the land transfers of Nickanoose and his son Wawinit and was also a witness to the transfer of land from the Nunpaog sachem Towanquatuck and his grandchildren Joel and Wunnatuckquanum (Goddard and Bragdon 1988, 781).

Betty Josnin, another daughter of the ruler Wampamag, left Martha's Vineyard with Joseph Josnin (variously called her cousin, or husband), in the early years of the eighteenth century and was interviewed at Bridgewater by Benjamin Smith about their "sachem rights" to another parcel at Sangekantacket in the period 1715–1716 (Goddard and Bragdon 1988, 204). That Smith felt it necessary to travel across the bay to consult with her shows that her authority as a sachem woman was significant, even in her absence.

Finally, Elizabeth Phillips of Noman's land was another who was accorded "sachem rights." She was the wife of Beniah Phillips, who may have had ties to the Phillips sachem family of Noman's land, and she was also the daughter of Ephriam Naquatim a "magistrate" on Chappaquiddick (Goddard and Bragdon 1988, 265, 459). Further research may link her family to the sachem family of Nickanoose and Spotso.

As noted previously, southern New England kinship terminology was especially rich in sibling terms and appears to have placed great emphasis on sibling ties (Bragdon 1996). The role of siblings is also central to understanding lineal organization, and many examples from southern New England suggest that leadership succession was from sibling to sibling, and then to a member of the descending generation. Little (1990, 198–99) reminds us, for example, that Askamapoo was heir to her brother Wawinet, as well as her father Nickanoose, by virtue of the high status of her mother. Wunnatuckquanum of Nunpaog was co-heir with her brother Joel as well but ruled alone after his death. Perhaps this is what Matthew Mayhew meant when he wrote that women could rule "in defect of a Male of the Blood" (1940[1694], 7–8). Hubbard recorded that leadership passed to the brother of the sachem, and then to the "sons" (Hubbard 1815[1677], 1, 84).

Conclusion

The prominence and power of women rulers on Martha's Vineyard and Nantucket were evident, despite the changes in Native societies in the seventeenth and early eighteenth centuries, which points to the continuing importance of hereditary rank in Native societies of the coastal interaction sphere, even after the land base itself was eroded. In the new Colonial context, the Native social system is more difficult to track as the land-allocation function of the sachems became curtailed, but it seems likely that traditional authority continued to be reckoned through descent from high-ranking men and women, even if these were not noticed or understood by most English observers. Even eighteenth-century documents show how the sachemship was organized and maintained through a continual series of marriage arrangements through several generations. In some parts of the islands and on the mainland, especially on Chappaquiddick and in southern Rhode Island, the system remained in operation until the nineteenth century. However, the loss of the land base elsewhere was, in a literal sense, the loss of the "social capital" upon which the sachemships were based, and rank in these situations no longer "explained" privilege or authority. In the absence of this "totalizing" ideology, queen sachems could no longer rule.

This chapter, inspired by Little's close attention to the land records and sachemships of Nantucket, has made the following arguments. First, that while (mostly male) sachems apparently inherited their leadership positions from their fathers in southern New England coastal societies, they drew their authority from their mother's line as well. In some cases, the sauncksquûaog ruled as heirs of their sachem fathers, even when there was a son to inherit. Second, the principles of matrilineal and patrilineal descent operated in tandem in establishing the right and authority to rule. Third, in some cases, a woman's rank and descent were the deciding factors in determining her authority in cases of dispute with male rivals. Thus queen sachems in southern New England were not accidental rulers but legitimate sachems in their own right.

Notes

1. For further discussion of the "squaw drudge" as an index of savagery, see Smits 1982).

2. It might be argued that the English were aware of the symbolic significance of money, as they made sure to demand it as a token of the submission of Native rulers.

3. Curiously, both Hepsibah and Wunnatuckquanum were known to the English as "Elizabeth or Betty." Two other island *saunckqsquûaog* were also given this name, including Elizabeth Josnin and Elizabeth Phillips, as were sachem women in the Ninegret and Pequot lines. Could this be a clue to their status? Is it possible that the English recognized the ruling status of these women and likened it to their former "virgin" queen, Elizabeth?

Works Cited

Bledsoe, Caroline. 1980. *Women and Marriage in Kpelle Society.* Stanford, CA: Stanford University Press.

Bragdon, Kathleen J. 1996. *Native Peoples of Southern New England: 1500–1650.* Norman: University of Oklahoma Press.

Bragdon, Kathleen J. 2009. *Indian Communities in Colonial New England: A Cultural Account.* Norman: University of Oklahoma Press.

Burton, William, and Richard Lowenthal. 1974. The First of the Mohegans. *American Ethnologist* 1(4): 589–99.

Collier, Jane F. 1987. Rank and Marriage: Or, Why High Ranking Wives Cost More. In *Gender and Kinship: Essays toward a Unified Analysis*, ed. Jane F. Collier and Sylvia J. Yanagisako, 197–200. Stanford, CA: Stanford University Press.

Collier, Jane F., and Sylvia J. Yanagisako, eds. 1987. *Gender and Kinship: Essays toward a Unified Analysis.* Stanford, CA: Stanford University Press, 1–13.

Ferguson, James. 1988. Cultural Exchange: New Developments in the Anthropology of Commodities. *Cultural Anthropology* 3:4: 488–513.

Gailey, Christine. 1987. *Kinship to Kingship: Gender Hierarchy and State Formation in the Tongan Islands.* Austin: University of Texas Press.

Goddard, Ives, and Kathleen J. Bragdon. 1988. *Native Writings in Massachusetts. Memoirs, no. 185.* Philadelphia, PA: American Philosophical Society.

Hubbard, William. 1815[1677]. *The Present State of New England. Being a Narrative of the Troubles with the Indians in New-England, from the First Planting Thereof in the Year 1607, to this Present Year 1677.* Reprint. Boston, MA: John Foster.

Kupperman, Karen. 2000. *Indians and English: Facing Off in Early America.* Ithaca, NY: Cornell University Press.

Leach, Edward. 1971[1951]. The Structural Implications of Matrilateral Cross-Cousin Marriage. *Journal of the Royal Anthropological Institute* 81: 24–29, 51–53. Reprinted in *Readings I Kinship and Social Structure,* ed. N. Belson Graburn, 223–31. New York: Harper and Row.

Little, Elizabeth. 1981. The Writings of Nantucket Indians. *Nantucket Algonquian Studies* 3. Nantucket, MA: Nantucket Historical Association.

Little, Elizabeth. 1990. *Indian Horse Commons at Nantucket Island, 1660–1760.* Nantucket, MA: Nantucket Historical Association.

Little, Elizabeth. 1996. Daniel Spotso, a Sachem at Nantucket Island, Massachusetts, circa 1691–1741. In *Northeastern Indian Lives*, ed. Robert S. Grumet, 193–207. Amherst: University of Massachusetts Press.

Mayhew, Experience. 1727. Indian Converts, or Some Account of the Lives and Dying. In *Speeches of a Considerable Number of Christianized Indians of Martha's Vineyard.* London: J. Osborn.

Mayhew, Matthew. 1940[1694]. *A Brief Narrative of the Success Which the Gospel Had among the Indians of Martha's Vineyard.* Reprint, 2nd. Ser. no. 119. Boston: The Massachusetts Historical Society.

Peletz, Michael. 1988. *A Share of the Harvest: Kinship, Property and Social History among the Malays of Renbau*. Berkeley: University of California Press.
Plane, Ann Marie. 1994. *Colonizing the Family*. PhD dissertation. Department of History, Brandeis University.
Plane, Ann Marie. 1996. Putting a Face on Colonialism: Awashunks. In *Northeastern Indian Lives*, ed. Robert S. Grumet, 140–65. Amherst: University of Massachusetts Press.
Plane, Ann Marie. 2000. *Colonial Intimacies: Indian Marriage in Early New England*. Ithaca, NY: Cornell University Press.
Poewe, Karla. 1981. *Matrilineal Ideology: Male-Female Dynamics in Luapula, Zambia*. New York: Academic Press.
Rowlandson, Mary. 1913[1682]. *Narrative of the Captivity of Mrs. Mary Rowlandson*. Reprinted in *Narratives of the Indian Wars 1675–1699*, ed. Charles H. Lincoln, 107–67. New York: Charles Scribner's Sons.
Silverblatt, Irene. 1987. *Sun, Moon, and Witches: Gender Ideologies and Class in Inca and Colonial Peru*. Princeton, NJ: Princeton University Press.
Simmons, William, and George Aubin. 1975. Narragansett Kinship. *Man in the Northeast* 9: 21–31.
Smits, David D. 1982. The "Squaw Drudge": A Prime Index of Savagism. *Ethnohistory* 29:4: 281–306.
Tambiah, S. J. 1984. *The Buddhist Saints of the Forest and the Cult of Amulets*. Cambridge: Cambridge University Press.
Williams, Roger. 1936[1643]. *A Key into the Language of America*. Reprint. Providence, RI: The Roger Williams Press.
Williamson, Margaret Holmes. 2003. *Powhatan Lords of Life and Death: Command and Consent in Seventeenth-Century Virginia*. Lincoln: University of Nebraska Press.
Winslow, Edward. 1834[1649]. *The Glorious Progress of the Gospel amongst the Indians in New England*. Preprint. Collections of the Massachusetts Historical Society, 3rd. ser., 4: 69–99.
Winslow, Edward. 1910[1624]. Relation. Reprinted in *Chronicles of the Pilgrim Fathers*, ed. Ernest Rhys, 267–356. London: J. M. Dent & Sons.
Wood, William. 1977[1634]. *New England's Prospect*. Edited by Alden Vaughan. Amherst: University of Massachusetts Press.

5

Pilgrim Subsistence

A Seventeenth-Century Profile from the John and Priscilla Alden House, Duxbury, Massachusetts

Tonya Baroody Largy and Mitchell T. Mulholland

In the late 1960s, popular archaeologist Roland Wells Robbins excavated a seventeenth-century house site in Duxbury, Massachusetts, believed to have been built and occupied by seventeenth-century settlers John Alden and Priscilla Mullins. Elizabeth Alden Little traced her ancestry to this important English family, and the results of archaeological studies conducted at the Alden House were one of her many interests. This chapter describes the archaeological faunal materials (bone and shell) recovered from the site by Robbins and what variables had to be considered to interpret their meaning. Much of the bone assemblage came from the house foundation fill in which Native American and European American artifacts were mixed, presenting a challenge for interpretation.

Background

In the late 1960s, popular archaeologist Roland Wells Robbins, with a staff of volunteers, excavated a seventeenth-century house site in Duxbury, Massachusetts. The house is believed to have been built and occupied by seventeenth-century settlers John Alden and Priscilla Mullins. The site was reported in 1969 in a notably detailed booklet (Robbins 1969), but many of the artifacts and faunal and floral samples were only summarized in tables. Robbins's notes, photographs, and other site records are curated at the Henley Library, Thoreau Institute, in Lincoln, Massachusetts. The collection of artifacts from the site was curated briefly by the town of Duxbury but later was transferred to the Alden Kindred, where it was stored in the attic of the Alden House museum. The collection remained at the Alden House for several years.

In 1996, the artifact assemblage was encountered in the attic of the Alden House by Mitchell Mulholland, in precarious curation conditions. A Public Service Endowment grant was awarded by the University of Massachusetts at Amherst to stabilize and conduct a preliminary analysis of this early collection, a partial goal of which would provide information of use in local schools. Artifacts were identified by Claire Carlson of Historic Deerfield (most of the historic period artifacts), Richard Colton of the National Park Service, Springfield Armory (metal, weapons, and military items), Eric Johnson of the Massachusetts Historical Commission (Native American lithics), and Elizabeth Chilton of the University of Massachusetts Amherst (Native American ceramics).

Largy's analysis of the faunal remains resulted in the identification of a wide range of wild and domestic mammals and birds and several varieties of shellfish remains from the collection. An analysis of the assemblage has revealed insights into potential seventeenth-century English and Native foodways, while taking into consideration the processes that led to the accumulation and preservation of the remains. The current study also has provided information about the size of early domestic species during the seventeenth century and illustrates the research value in collections from the past.

Roland Wells Robbins and the Early Alden House Site

Roland Wells Robbins was a highly popular archaeologist and lecturer in the 1950s to 1970s. His archaeological excavations were reported in popular magazines, such as *Life*. Robbins, lacking scholarly credentials, was criticized by academic archaeologists for a heavy-handed approach to archaeological excavation. Indeed, Robbins's work could be uneven. However, his work at the seventeenth-century Saugus Iron Works in the early 1950s was exemplary even by today's standards. Robbins was employed by the First Iron Works Association (a historic preservation organization that originated in Saugus in 1943) to excavate the remains of a seventeenth-century ironworks on the Saugus River and to provide archaeological information to guide the accurate reconstruction of an ironworks for a historic museum. The excavations included the accurate vertical and horizontal recordation of artifacts and features. A writer of copious field notes, Robbins also took more than 2,000 photographs of every phase of the Saugus investigation, leaving an extremely useful record of the excavation. On the other hand, some of Robbins's excavations, such as that conducted at Moore State Park in Paxton, Massachusetts, relied on destructive methods employing heavy equipment and reconstruction of historic features loosely based on archaeological findings.

Robbins has since been recognized for his contributions to archaeology. Researching his career, archaeologist Donald Linebaugh sees Robbins as a pioneer in twentieth-century historical archaeology and an early practitioner in archaeological consulting as a business (Linebaugh 1996, 2000, 2005).

Robbins's excavation at the early Alden House was sponsored by the Alden Kindred of America, a society of Alden's descendents. The association maintains a historic house museum believed to be the second Alden House built in approximately 1653. Prior to 1960, it was common local knowledge that an earlier Alden House (the first built by John and Priscilla in Duxbury) was located some 700 feet southeast of the larger house. Today this is the location of playing fields associated with Duxbury High School. A bronze and stone memorial exists at the site, erected at least as early as 1888 (Robbins 1969, 10).

In 1960, Robbins was approached by Russell Edwards of the Alden Kindred to conduct archaeological test excavations at the perceived location of the older house (Robbins 1960, 1969, 10; Linebaugh 1996, 349). Robbins excavated several preliminary test pits in the vicinity of the stone-bronze marker and found little for his efforts other than a few brick fragments (Linebaugh 1996, 351). Robbins later used a steel probe to test areas some 60 feet from the marker, and he encountered stone. Further subsurface testing revealed two buried stone foundation walls and several early artifacts that included lead cames and glass from diamond-pane windows and a silver Massachusetts Pine Tree sixpence dating to 1652 (Linebaugh 1996, 352). Robbins initially interpreted the stone walls as the part of an ell, once associated with an assumed adjoining larger structure (Linebaugh 1996, 352). Thus the suspected seventeenth-century context was supported, and Robbins was contracted to continue his investigation.

Robbins then established a master grid of 120 × 80 ft beginning in the vicinity of the stone-bronze marker (Robbins 1969, 44–45). The grid of 10-foot squares was oriented and numbered west to east and was arranged in twelve rows west to east, and nine rows north to south (see

Figure 5.1). The individual 10-foot grid squares are designated 1–96. Guided by the findings of the initial survey, three rows of six 10-foot grids then were excavated around the stone walls (see Figure 5.1). These

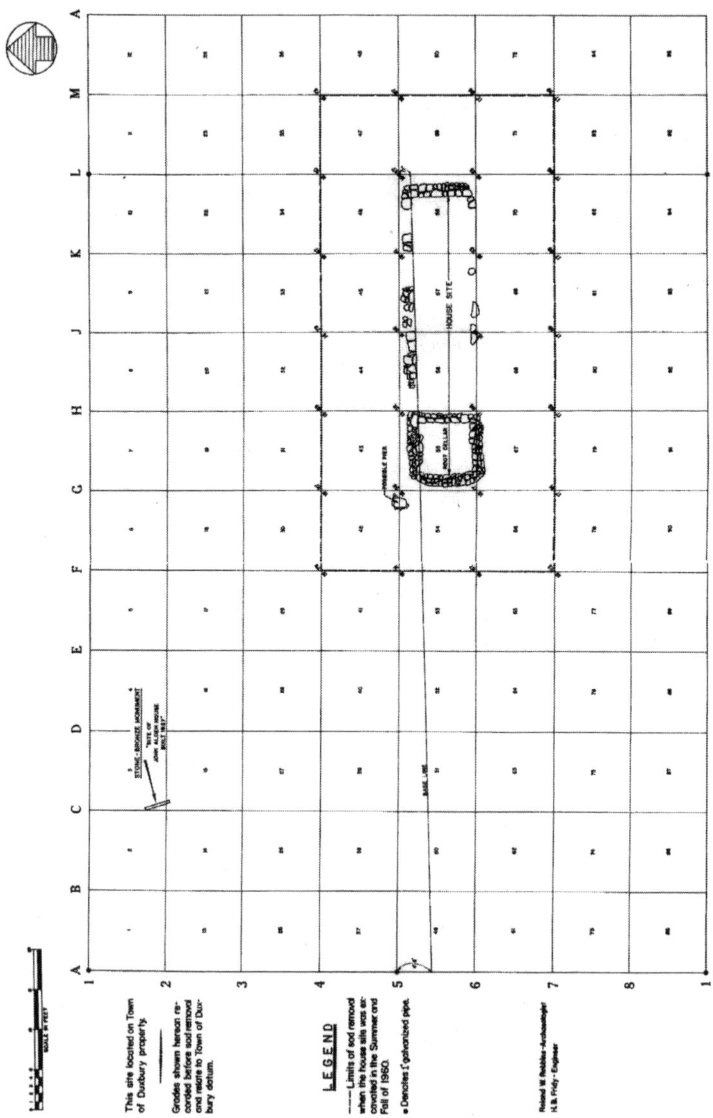

Figure 5.1. Master Plan of the Excavation Grid System Used by Robbins at the Alden House (Robbins 1969, 44–45)

eighteen grids were excavated by volunteers to a depth of 5–6 inches (Robbins 1969; Linebaugh 1996) and later were shown to include the foundations, cellar, and a 10-foot area around the small, early house site. A stone feature was encountered in this part of the excavation, located just outside of the foundation. This feature is interpreted as a stone pier, possibly associated with an as yet unidentified addition, or perhaps a support for a larger structure. A review of Robbins's site records for the 1960 survey shows no additional excavation in the units surrounding the foundation.

Subsequent excavations concentrated on the foundation, its fill, and immediate surroundings, using yet another subgrid of 2.5-foot squares (Robbins 1960) with grid designations of a number preceded by an F (e.g., F20, F21) (see Figure 5.2, next page).

Some limited excavation was conducted within 1.25 feet around the outside of the foundation. Depths of the outside units are not specified. The excavation revealed a partial stone foundation some 38 feet long and 10.5 feet wide that included a root cellar (see Figures 5.3 and 5.4), approximately 6.5 feet square and 7 feet deep in the western end. The excavation of the root cellar was broken down into three arbitrary levels (CI, CII, and CIII). All three levels were rubble foundation fill.

Faunal materials analyzed during the present study were derived from four parts of Robbins's excavation:

1. the eighteen ten-foot squares (Provenience Units 42–47, 54–59, and 66–71) surrounding and including the entire foundation, which were excavated only to a depth of approximately 6 inches (Robbins 1969, 44–45) (see Figure 5.1);

2. the interior of the foundation, divided into 2.5-foot squares (Provenience Units F1–F33 for the interior, and FA to F-H, F-J to F-Z, F-AA to F-HH, and F-JJ to F-NN for the immediate exterior), which was excavated to depths of up to 24 inches without any vertical provenience (Robbins 1969, 46–47) (see Figure 5.2); these units were excavated in the "crawl space" in the east side of the foundation;

3. the immediate exterior of the foundation, divided into 2.5-foot squares (Provenience Units FA to FZ, and FAA to FNN), which was excavated to depths of up to 24 inches without any vertical provenience (Robbins 1969, 46–47) (see Figures 5.3 and 5.4); these units were excavated around all sides of the foundation; and

4. the root cellar on the western interior of the foundation, which was excavated to approximately 7 feet. Arbitrary level CI was approximately 2.5 feet in depth; CII was approximately 4 feet in depth, and CIII, the base layer, was approximately 6 inches in depth (Robbins 1969, 46–47) (see Figure 5.2).

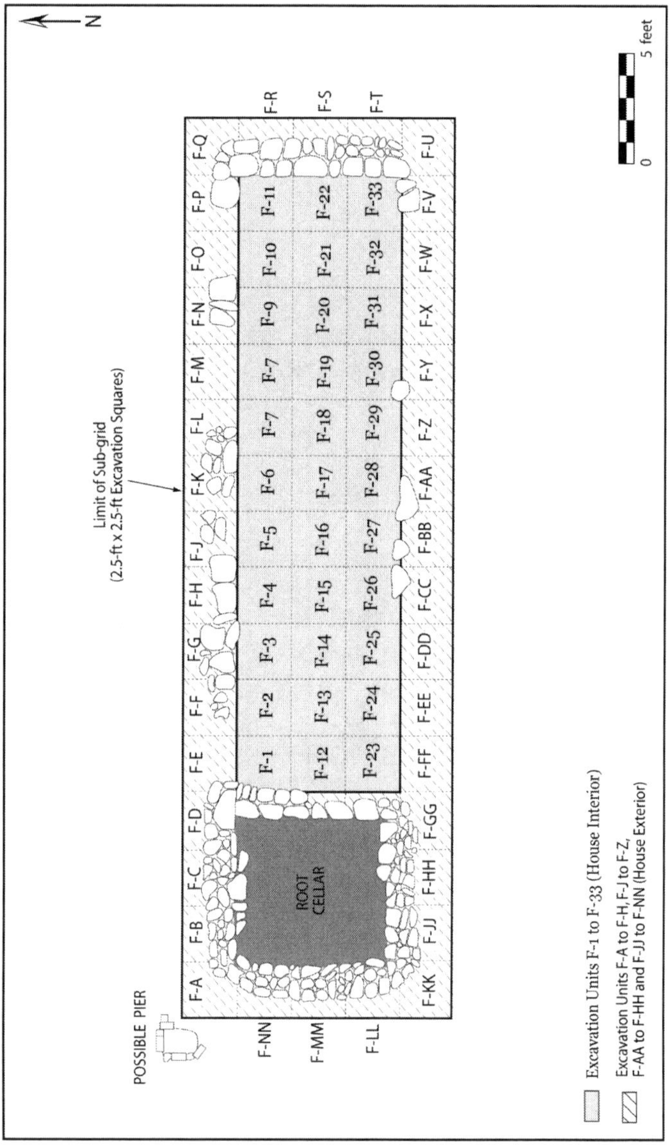

Figure 5.2. Plan of the Alden House Foundation Showing the Excavation Units (Robbins 1969, 44–45)

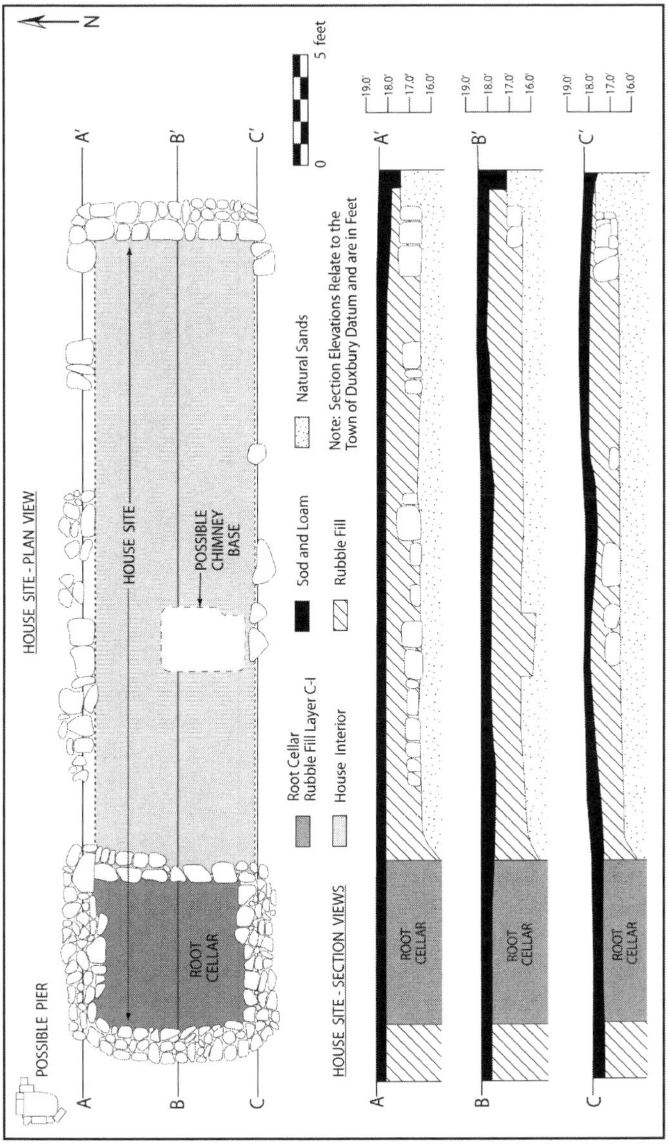

Figure 5.3. House Site Plan of the Alden House with Profiles of the Foundation (Robbins 1969, 44–45)

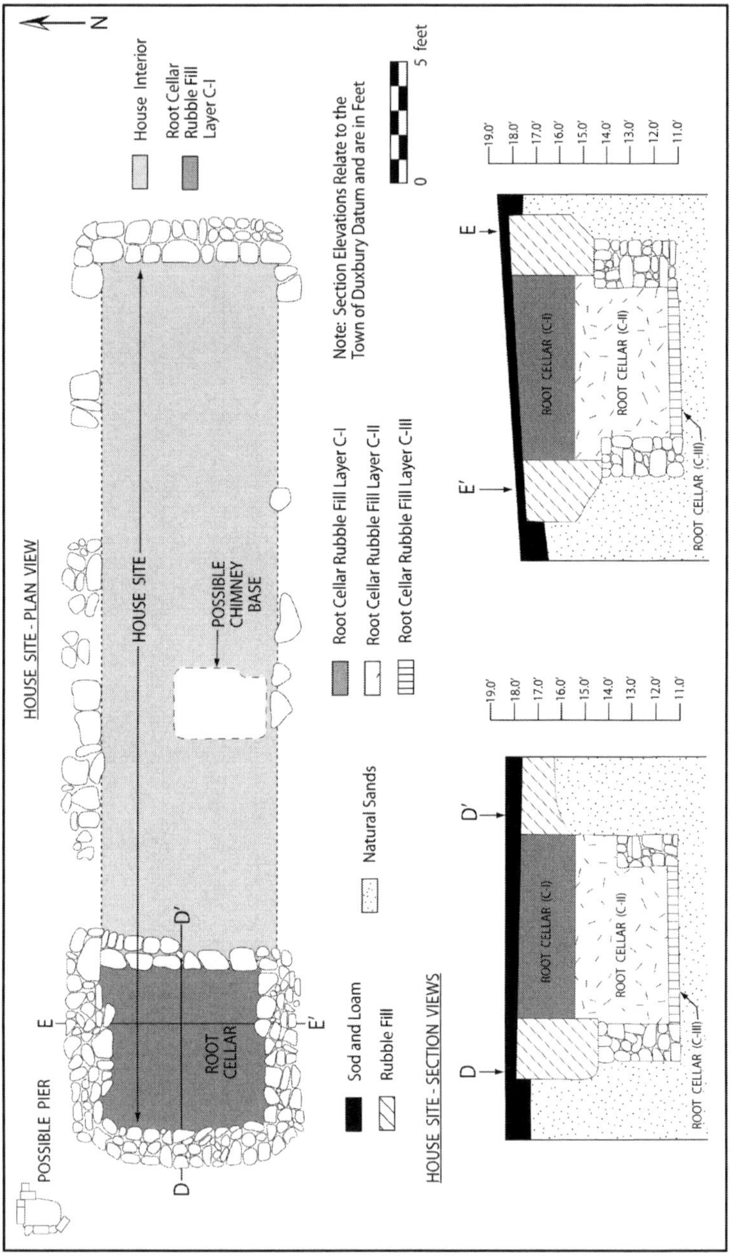

Figure 5.4. House Site Plan of the Alden House with Profiles of the Root Cellar (Robbins 1969, 44–45)

With the exception of the excavation of the root cellar, artifact recording was horizontal only. The lack of recording of vertical depths in the interior foundation and surrounding area is unfortunate and makes it difficult to provide a fine-grained analysis of artifact deposition and associations. On the basis of the similarity of materials in the collection from the surrounding soils, and the considerable distance to other houses in the historic period, it is assumed that the fill in the interior of the foundation was derived from the immediate surrounding area. Filling may have occurred when the area was landscaped in the late nineteenth century, probably earlier. Robbins states, "It was quite evident that the soils and rubble that filled the interior of the Alden house site were of the same nature as the fill removed during the cellar excavation. . . . The Indian items showed that the area around the house site provided the soils and the trash that were used to bury the remains of the house foundation and grade the site after the house had been removed . . . soon after the house disappeared, it would seem, as no stratums [*sic*] of separate deposits were found to indicate the filling took place over a long period" (Robbins 1969, 25).

The Artifact and Faunal Assemblage

Robbins recovered bone and shell along with metal and ceramic artifacts, and a large number (approximately 1,750) of Native American artifacts left by the earliest occupants of the site (Robbins 1969, 41). The majority of the historical artifacts date from the early seventeenth century (Robbins 1969, 29). Most of the ceramic sherds (77 percent) were redware, which was undated (Claire Carlson 2004, personal communication). The second highest frequency ware included large sherds of Iberian storage jars (7 percent). The remaining ceramic wares included delft sherds (temporally problematic dating from ca. 1640 to the nineteenth century), a small number of Bellarmine (ca. 1625–1700), Devon (ca. 1650–1783), Westerwald (ca. 1700–1783), and Buckley (ca. 1720–1783) sherds. Other seventeenth-century artifacts included a snaphance musket lock mechanism, a possibly associated gun fork, knife blades, clothing hooks and buckles (some from armor), a portion of a pike head, diamond-paned window glass and associated lead cames, brass spoon handles and a spoon bowl, scissors, bricks, wattle and daub, and approximately 2,100 nails and nail fragments.

On the basis of the assemblage and background research, Robbins concluded, "The house was built during the first third of the seventeenth century. It is unlikely the house remained standing after the third quarter of the seventeenth century" (Robbins 1969, 39). The archaeological materials in the collection support this. A very small number of nineteenth century artifacts also exist in the collection, including creamware (ca. 1762–1820) and whiteware (ca. 1820–1900), but the few shards are derived from the topsoil outside the foundation.

Native American artifacts were recovered consistently throughout the excavation, as shown in Robbins's artifact charts (Robbins 1969, 51–55). Robbins counted approximately 2,000 Native artifacts, but those remaining in the collection numbered 1,758. Temporally diagnostic projectile points are mostly of the Levanna style (1,000 to 400 years ago), and a few points are made of English flint. The Native American artifacts were recovered from the interior of the foundation and the area surrounding it. Their presence in the fill with European artifacts suggests to Robbins that "it is quite likely that a high percentage of the clam and the oyster (*sic*) shells, and the animal bones found at the early Alden home site had their origin with the Indian habitation" (Robbins 1969, 40). Since this is a secondary rather than a primary deposition context (Joukowsky 1980, 152) with no clear associations, Robbins's point is well taken. The lack of temporal control over such an assemblage precludes certain conclusions regarding the data. For example, the question of whether the Aldens included deer and other wild species in their diet *cannot be answered with certainty* because of *known Native* exploitation of these species. Individual bones may be submitted for AMS radiocarbon dating at a future time. The optimum AMS standard deviation is ± thirty years with a range of sixty years. Depending on the time of deposition, this may be sufficient to separate an early historic from a late pre-Colonial occupation (A. Cherkinsky, November 28, 2005, personal communication). However, this may not provide evidence regarding which ethnic group used or deposited the bones.

Methods

The bones were analyzed using the facilities and reference collections of the Zooarchaeology Laboratory of the Peabody Museum, Harvard University.

Identifications were made to the lowest taxonomic level permitted by preservation and fragmentation. Sometimes species cannot be identified with certainty due to taphonomic factors. Several of the bones and shell are identified with the prefix "cf." from the Latin *confere*, meaning that bone fragment most closely "compares with" that taxon rather than with any other (Largy 1995, 66; Reitz and Wing 1999, 37). Taxonomic nomenclature for marine shell follows Weiss (1995). The data for all taxonomic classes are summarized in Table 5.1.

Table 5.1. Vertebrate Taxa From The Alden House Site

Taxon	NISP	Total Wt. (g)
Domestic Taxa		
Mammal		
Bos Taurus (cattle)	14	278.5
Sus scrofa (pig)	29	90.6
Ovis/Capra (sheep/goat)	1	2.2
Total	44	371.3
Bird		
Gallus gallus (chicken)	1	0.1
Wild Taxa		
Mammal		
Odocoileus (white-tailed deer)	7	10.7
Rattus sp.(rat)	1	0.1
Total	8	10.8
Bird		
Phalacrocorax auritus (cormorant)	1	0.3
cf. *Ardea alba* (great egret)	1	3.6
Branta Canadensis (Canada goose	1	3.2
Anser sp. (goose)	1	1.3
cf. *Mergus sp.* (merganser)	1	1.7
Corvus brachyrhynchos (crow)	10*	4.9
Larus sp. (Gull)	2	1.1
Aves (bird)	12	3.7
Total	29	19.8
Other Mammal		
Artiodactyla (even-toed)	18	46.6
Large Mammal	8	33.6
Medium/Large Mammal	29	99.3
Medium Mammal	31	31.9
Small/Medium Mammal	2	1.7
Small Mammal	19	3.9
Unidentified Mammal	31	9.1
Total	138	226.1
Bird/Mammal	12	2.7

*Several of these are from the same individual

Preservation

In general, the condition of the bones is good with differential degradation. The degradation and damage to the bone, however, sometimes interfere with identification, making it difficult to assign a family or genus. Identifiable elements often preserved in archaeological sites are carpals and tarsals, which are foot bones from the fore and hind limbs. These elements resist breakage because of their denser structure.

The shell assemblage as a whole is more degraded. Since this is a fill context, the possibility of differing conditions within the fill may account for some of the taphonomic variability.

Recovery

Field recovery methods affected the final faunal assemblage and may affect identifications as well. Robbins describes excavation methods as follows: "The soils were carefully removed from each of the 2 1/2 ft. sq. grid boxes and were taken beyond the house site where sifting trays had been set up . . . local persons did much of the slow, but *intriguing work* of screening the excavated soils, recovering all the artifacts they contained, even to the small fragments of brick" (Robbins 1969, 24, emphasis added). Robbins does not mention the size of mesh used in the sifting trays. Local citizens, presumably without previous experience, were collecting artifacts from the sifters. Both factors may introduce a bias in the recovery. There is also an issue of some attrition in the number of artifacts from the collection over the years. Larger mesh screens allow bones of fish and other small vertebrates to pass through. Untrained eyes may not recognize small bones or consider small fragments important enough to keep. In fact, a number of bones exhibit modern breakage, but very few bones could be mended in the laboratory, suggesting that fragments of these bones were discarded. Partial loss of elements also affects identification. However, smaller elements of bird and small mammal tooth fragments were recovered. Meadow (1980) discusses in great detail the deposition of animal bones, their preservation, and their recovery.

Results

The assemblage is made up of both animal bone and marine shell. Two taxonomic classes of bone and seven taxa of shell are represented in all.

The bones are predominantly mammal with a fair representation of bird. No fish, reptile (turtle/snake), or amphibians are identified. Although seven taxa of marine mollusks are identified in this assemblage, only two taxa are ubiquitous. The remaining five taxa are represented by only one specimen each. These are discussed later.

Robbins catalogued a "total of 247 bones" (Robbins 1969, 41). The final count for this assemblage is 235 bones after culling out non-bone materials (two stones from Unit C-I) and mending several elements broken during or subsequent to excavation. In addition, Robbins's catalogue listed several calcined bone fragments as shell, and these were added to his final bone count.

Analysis of shell is incomplete. The assemblage includes sixty-five lots of shell. Due to funding limitations, only thirty-eight lots (58 percent), a total of 351 shell fragments, were analyzed. Twenty-seven lots (42 percent) remain to be analyzed, should additional funding become available.

Mammal bone. Both wild (cervidae) and domestic (bovidae and suidae) taxa are identified in this sample. In these families, a number of elements, when fragmented, strongly resemble each other, especially those of cervid (deer) and bovid (sheep/goat). Heavy damage and degradation may prevent this basic separation between the two families. In many cases, elements of young suids (pigs) also may resemble the other two families, making necessary the broader identification to the order artiodactyla (even-toed hoofed mammals) to which all three families belong. Pig is the most numerous domestic taxon. Cattle are next, with sheep/goat barely represented. The white-tailed deer is also represented. The number of pig bones initially seems surprising. However, Jones describes the diet likely eaten by the Aldens as this: "A usual breakfast included rye pudding and bread, or 'ye Indian porridge' (hasty pudding) along with pea or bean soup, or a stew of pork or salt fish. A typical Duxbury dinner . . . was served in the middle of the day and consisted of bean soup, or pork and beans, along with squash, turnips, onions, or other vegetables from the garden" (in Robbins 1969, 9).

Bird. Bird taxa are predominantly wild species. Only one bone, a proximal carpometacarpus (wing bone) of a chicken (*Gallus*), was identified. Another carpometacarpus, *Anser* sp. (goose), was identified, but whether it is wild or domestic is unclear. Both are in the same taxon. The wild taxa represented are double-crested cormorant (*Phalacrocorax auritus*), a likely merganser (cf. *Mergus* sp.), Canada goose (*Branta Canadensis*), common crow (*Corvus* [*brachyrhynchos*]), a likely great egret (cf. *Ardea alba*), and unspecified seagulls (*Larus* sp.). Numerous wing and foot bones of crow were identified. Except for the sternum, these bones were well preserved. More than one individual was represented. All of these species range along the southern New England coast today and may have been more numerous in Alden's day.

Shell. Seven taxa of marine mollusks are represented in the sample (58 percent) analyzed to date. The greatest percentage is northern quahog (*Mercenaria mercenaria*), although soft-shell clam (*Mya arenaria*) is also strongly represented. Four taxa represented by one specimen each are ocean quahog (*Arctica islandica*), a deep-water species, Atlantic jackknife/razor clam (*Ensis directus*), mussel family (Mytilidae), and one fragment of questionable eastern oyster (*Crassostrea virginica*). Two gastropods are also represented—one identified as whelk (*Busycon* sp.) and the other unidentified.

The shells show differential degradation. Mr. Graf offered his impression that many of the fragments appeared to be reduced to a small size, possibly by being water worn. In his opinion, they resembled the salt water-worn remains present on any ocean beach. The authors concur with his observation. Robbins's suggestion is that much of the shell may have been collected and left by Natives living at the site before John and Priscilla Alden moved to that location. Note that Robbins referred to the "clams and oysters" when, in fact, only one oyster fragment has been identified. It is unlikely that the Aldens would have overlooked this food source in their efforts to provide for their many children.

Conclusion

This analysis provides a glimpse into an assemblage of faunal remains from the earliest Colonial times. Even with unclear stratigraphic context, the identification of certain species provides information about which animals the Aldens' or their Native American predecessors or contemporaries were exploiting for food or other purposes. The quantification of these finds is also useful.

The lack of temporal control over this assemblage limits interpretation. Sample size is also a limiting factor. The processing of meat and disposal patterns may skew the data and not truly represent the importance of a particular taxon to subsistence (Chaplin 1971). In this regard, the many factors that ultimately determine "the nature of a faunal sample and its eventual published representation" have been cogently discussed by Meadow (1980).

Even with limitations, this assemblage is exciting and has the potential to provide additional data about the size of early domestic species during Colonial times and perhaps other new information as well. The collection clearly warrants further study.

While this analysis is already somewhat complete, it is our plan to revisit the collection in the future, should additional funding become available, for a more detailed analysis of the domestic species and the birds represented in the collection. Therefore, to paraphrase Robbins (1969, 5), this analysis is "not intended to be the final word on the subject" and should be considered a preliminary report subject to revision.

Acknowledgments

The authors wish to thank Dr. Richard H. Meadow, director of the Zooarchaeology Laboratory, Peabody Museum, for his support and assistance with this project. We especially would like to acknowledge Mr. Dan Graf, then curatorial assistant in the Malacology Department, Harvard Museum of Natural History, who provided work space and other hospitality, and Mr. Richard Johnson, research associate, for his interest. Both provided valuable assistance.

Works Cited

Chaplin, Raymond E. 1971. *The Study of Animal Bones from Archaeological Sites.* London: Seminar Press.

Jones, Evan. 1969. John Alden and the Beginning of Duxbury. In *Pilgrim John Alden's Progress: Archaeological Excavations in Duxbury*, ed. Roland Wells Robbins, 8–9. Plymouth, MA: The Pilgrim Society.

Joukowsky, Martha. 1980. *Field Archaeology.* Englewood Cliffs, NJ: Prentice Hall.

Largy, Tonya Baroody. 1995. Bone from Concord Shell Heap, Concord, Massachusetts. *Bulletin of the Massachusetts Archaeological Society* 56(2): 64–70.

Linebaugh, Donald W. 1996. *The Road to Ruins and Restoration: Roland W. Robbins and the Professionalization of Historical Archaeology.* Unpublished PhD dissertation, American Studies Program, College of William and Mary, Williamsburg, Virginia.

Linebaugh, Donald W. 2000. Forging a Career: Roland W. Robbins and Iron Industry Sites in the Northeastern U.S. Industrial *Archeology* 26 (1): 5–36.

Linebaugh, Donald W. 2005. *The Man Who Found Thoreau: Roland W. Robbins and the Rise of Historical Archaeology in America.* Durham: University of New Hampshire Press.

Meadow, Richard H. 1980. Animal Bones: Problems for the Archaeologist Together with Some Possible Solutions. *Paleorient* 6: 65–77.

Mulholland, Mitchell T. 1999. An Interdisciplinary Study of the John Alden Houses, 1627 and 1653, Duxbury, Massachusetts: Archaeology and Architecture. In *The Archaeological Northeast*, ed. Mary Ann Levine, Kenneth

Sassaman, and Michael S. Nassaney, 235–48. Westport, CT: Bergin and Garvey.

Reitz, Elizabeth J., and Elizabeth S. Wing. 1999. *Zooarchaeology*. Cambridge: Cambridge University Press.

Robbins, Roland Wells. 1960. *John Alden—1st House in Duxbury. Unpublished Daily Log of Excavations at the John Alden House, Duxbury, Massachusetts (1960–1970). Papers of Roland Wells Robbins.* Lincoln, MA: Henley Library.

Robbins, Roland Wells. 1969. *Pilgrim John Alden's Progress: Archaeological Excavations in Duxbury.* Plymouth, MA: The Pilgrim Society.

Weiss, Howard M. 1995. Marine Animals of Southern New England and New York. State Biological and Natural History Survey of Connecticut. Department of Environmental Protection. *Bulletin* 115.

6

The "Indian Planting Fields" in Concord, Massachusetts

Influence of New Techniques on Archaeological Explanatory Models

Shirley Blancke

In the 1990s the Concord Cemetery Committee started plans to expand the Sleepy Hollow Cemetery in Concord, Massachusetts. The field that would become the extension was an area where collectors had picked up Native American artifacts since the end of the nineteenth century and was thought to be the site where Indian planting fields existed at the founding of the town in 1635. These "planting fields," together with a weir, were mentioned in a 1637 deed as given in exchange for wampum, tools, and clothing by the Native people of the Musketaquid River to the Concord founding fathers (Shattuck 1835, 6). Concord was the earliest English community founded inland from Boston. This field, then, promised to be a place where remains of Native American settlement such as wigwams, corn storage pits, and graves might be found. This chapter describes two features, a Late Archaic fire pit, and a fifteenth-century A.D. Late Woodland living floor, together with the role played by soil micromorphology in determining what they were. In addition, thin-section analysis identified two unusual lithic types, mylonite and amphibolite.

In expanding the town cemetery there was, ironically, a real danger of destroying Native American graves protected by law. The cemetery committee consulted Blancke and decided to contract for an archaeological survey. A survey also raised the real possibility of finding evidence of Concord's Native past with respect to shelter and agriculture, specifically wigwams and maize. Over a three-year period, 1997–1999, an archaeological survey and excavation were conducted in the field into which the Sleepy Hollow Cemetery was to expand. Although the chances of finding maize preserved in a planting field might be slight, there was some reason to think that the edge of the site might yield habitation loci where maize might be found. No maize was in fact recovered. The prospect of finding Native maize was of particular interest to Betty Little, who was specializing in the technology of accurately dating early Native maize samples, and she subsequently demonstrated a clustering of radiocarbon dates for maize in New England around cal A.D. 1300–1500 (Little 2002).

Site Background

The expansion field is southwest of the Great Meadows Wildlife Sanctuary, which has natural resources that were a magnet for Native life starting at the end of the Pleistocene. Thirty years ago a long, narrow, 6-inch Late Paleo-Indian spear point of the Ste. Anne/Varney type was found sticking down vertically in the mud at the river's edge, where it may have snapped from its shaft in the course of fishing or hunting (Bradley 2007; Concord Museum 2007). The name "Musketaquid" was first applied to the river on a 1634 map made by the English settler William Wood (Wood 1977[1634]) and means a place of reeds or grasses in the Algonquian language. The sanctuary is currently an area of man-made ponds created out of former swampland and water meadow on the south side of the Concord River and immediately abutting it. It is an area rich in wildlife, with turtles, muskrats, otters, and many other species, particularly birds, which attracts bird-watchers from many miles around. Large numbers of Native American artifacts have been collected from fields surrounding the sanctuary. The expansion field was part of an area named "Cranefields" or "The Great Fields" in some nineteenth-century maps (Walcott 1885, in Wheeler 1967, 28; Gleason 1906).

The Concord Cemetery Committee planned to create a rolling landscape reminiscent of the Mt. Auburn Cemetery in Cambridge, Massachusetts, by grading the flat expansion field. Nothing was visible above ground to indicate the existence of any past history, neither a Native past suggested by the artifacts, nor anything more recent. Three archaeological sites had been recorded for the general area in the Massachusetts Historical Commission's site files identified by artifacts in Benjamin Smith's collection at the Concord Museum, but only one had been excavated previously by Blancke (1987, 1988). The field had also been plowed since the seventeenth century and was acquired in 1853 by the trustees of the Middlesex Agricultural Society. This society, founded in 1794, held cattle shows in Concord from 1820 onward, erecting stock pens and an exhibition shed in the field (see Figure 6.1).

The environs of the expansion field have been known to local archaeological collectors for over 100 years, resulting in thousands of artifacts being picked up before there was any awareness that this practice denudes a nonrenewable resource, archaeological sites. The practice appears to have been started by Henry David Thoreau, who is the earliest known Concord collector (Blancke 1995). Several important collections

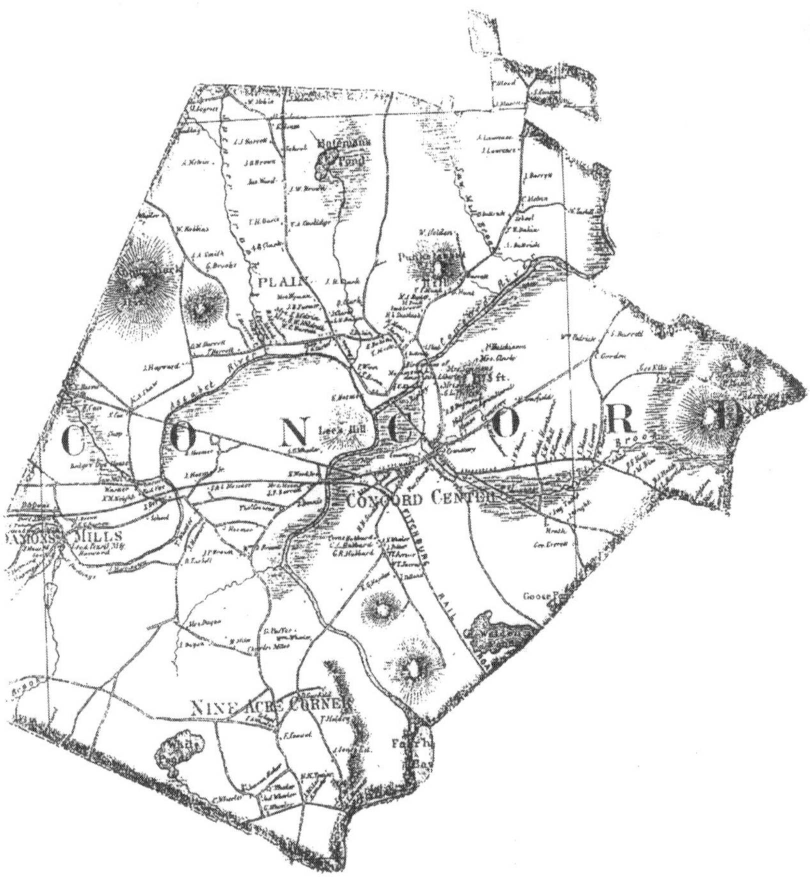

Figure 6.1. Walling's 1856 Map of Concord "Middlesex Agricultural House" is in the center between the large "C" and "O" of Concord.

in the Concord Museum were donated by men who carefully numbered each artifact and recorded their find spots in notebooks. This degree of recording was unusual and, happily, the practice rendered the collections of value for archaeological research. Adams Tolman's collection made at the end of the nineteenth century contains artifacts from the cemetery expansion area as well as Benjamin Smith's twentieth-century material (Johnson and Mahlstedt 1984). The Dee family, who owned much of the land, also collected artifacts in this area (Blancke 1981).

In the spring of 1997, the Public Archaeology Laboratory (PAL) of Pawtucket, Rhode Island, conducted a town-funded intensive survey that tested some areas of the field judged to be archaeologically sensitive—that is, most likely to have intact archaeological sites (Waller and Ritchie 1997). The most sensitive area was on the west side next to a water source, now a swampy area with a small pond, but formerly a stream. On that side, PAL's survey found traces of features, but the degree of information was not enough to allow the town to know if there were graves or anything else that should be avoided. Blancke considered that it would be desirable to test more of the area, and since town funding for further research was not available, she offered to organize a dig with volunteers (Blancke 1998, 1999, 2003). It seemed possible from PAL's results that loci where people might have lived on a short-term basis to tend a planting field could occur on the west edge of the field. The subsequent discovery of a small Late Woodland living floor in that area, even without finding maize, suggests a fit with Elizabeth Chilton's model of mobile farmers that she was developing at that time (Chilton 1999, 2008). A large burned tree root that occurred in the field was radiocarbon dated in case it provided evidence for early field clearing, but it proved to be of the twentieth century (Blancke 2003).

Overview of the Excavations

When the volunteer surveys started, it was hoped that the initial test pits would uncover features beyond what the PAL survey had uncovered. At the Sleepy Hollow site, six features were encountered, although they were seriously impacted over the centuries by plowing. Two of these turned out to be of particular interest, and they are the focus of this chapter. The features were explored further through the opening of adjacent meter squares.

Only seventeen artifacts apart from lithic waste flakes and cores were recovered in the course of excavation and included diagnostic projectile points. Projectile points from the field included spear and dart points of hunters and gatherers of the Archaic period and points and potsherds of later Woodland peoples (a few of these diagnostic projectile points are shown in Figure 6.2). As well as projectile points and pottery, other kinds of artifacts excavated were knives, scrapers, perforators, and

Figure 6.2. Projectile Points and Potsherds from Sleepy Hollow Expansion Site by Type (Top, left to right: Small Stemmed I; Fishtail, Adena-like. Middle, left to right: Fox Creek Stemmed base, untyped stemmed point of brown chert, two sherds. Bottom, left to right: Neville variant, Atlantic, Fox Creek Stemmed)

gouge fragments. A fair quantity of chipping debris provided important information.

In addition, artifacts from the Benjamin Smith collection reinforced and augmented that data. In that collection there were thirty-four diagnostic points that represented six Precontact periods: Middle, Late, and Terminal Archaic, and Early, Middle, and Late Woodland. There were also twenty-four other tools, mainly knives and scrapers, including abraders, perforators, and single examples of an axe, a gouge, a plummet, grooved stone, and an ulu fragment. Further, the weight of bifaces, bifacial fragments, and debitage that included flakes, chunks and cores totaled over 9 kilograms (Blancke 1987).

Recovery of over 1,000 stone flakes and pieces of chipping debris from test pits in the plow zone allowed an analysis of the varieties of stone preferred in making artifacts, some brought long distances, and conclusions to be drawn about manufacturing. Most of the materials used were volcanics from the Boston basin consisting of gray, black, and rarely purple rhyolites, and also a black hornfels likely brought from New Hampshire. Less utilized were local gray argillite, quartzite, and white quartz.

Chipping waste from the excavations, combined with a great deal of chipping debris in the Benjamin Smith collection, demonstrated that the area must have been an extensive manufacturing location for producing stone artifacts in Precontact times. The quantity of stone manufacturing debris from this site made it unusual but not unique among Concord sites. Chipping debris was lightly scattered in the plow zone throughout the field (four to twenty-four flakes per square meter), except for a dense cluster in one place with a Middle Archaic point (Waller and Ritchie 1997). Also found in the plow zone was historical trash, such as ceramic fragments and part of an eighteenth-century Bristol clay pipe bowl with an identifiable molded design (Blancke 2003).

The test pits, as well as containing artifacts, provided information about the geology of the field. They showed that the loam was relatively shallow (with a depth of 20–40 cm) underlain in the northern part of the site by fine gravel, while in the southern part a layer of yellow silty sand was interspersed between loam and gravel. These deposits were laid down during the period of glacial Lake Concord long before human colonization. In a few pits lenses of orange, iron-stained sand suggested stagnant water, and the human occupation site during its earliest periods might have been at the edge of a drying glacial lake.

After the completion of the three seasons of survey and excavation, specialized microscope techniques were employed to identify plant and organic remains in the soil as well as the types of stone used for artifacts. Two unusual local stones only recently recognized, mylonite and amphibolite, were identified by thin-section lithography (Calogero and Philpotts, in Blancke 2003; Largy and Ritchie 2002). These techniques added significantly to the interpretation of the site.

Two Features

The Fire Pit

One of the two more interesting features discovered was what appeared to be a modest-size fire pit. It turned out to be the oldest feature on the site, belonging to the Late Archaic period. The pit was a well-defined oval of darkened soil with a heavy accumulation of charcoal and reddened sand clearly visible in the top of the yellow sandy subsoil. The loam overlying it was 22–24 cm deep. The pit was 80 cm wide in a north-south direction and 70 cm east to west, but only 10 cm deep, the upper portion of it having been destroyed when the loam was plowed. No artifacts were found in the pit. A radiocarbon date obtained for the pit was 3820 ± 85 B.P. (GX-24954, wood charcoal, $\delta^{13}C = -26.1$ percent). Calibrations made by the Geochron Laboratories at 2σ, using two methods (Stuiver and Pearson 1993; Stuiver et al., 1998), summarized here, produced the following ranges: cal B.C. 2471–1970 (method A), and cal B.C. 2471–2012 (method B, $p = .99$). Both show an early date of cal B.C. 2471, with a good probability of the date falling within the latter half of the third millennium B.C.

While the appearance of this bowl-shaped feature of reddened and charcoal-blackened soil immediately suggested a fire, it was not obvious that it had been used for cooking, since no visible bone or plant remains were recovered. Only a micromorphological analysis of the soil was able to provide evidence indicating that it probably was a cooking fire. A microscopic examination of a soil sample showed that a fragment of bone lay in a black greasy layer that also contained some animal organ and tissue fragments (Volmar 2000, 4, 5, 9).

The fire pit contained plenty of charcoal that was identified by microscope as oak, probably white, with one fragment resembling strongly the red oak group. Many samples had narrow rings of "stressed" wood, showing trees reacting to drought conditions (Largy, in Blancke 1999). The stressed oak appeared to support data from pollen and charcoal in Walden Pond and other areas that there was a relatively brief dry, warm climatic interlude approximately 4,000 years before the present (Winkler 1993). The oak wood of this fire contrasted with the conifer found in the feature described later, the "black platform."

No other features were found within a radius of 2 meters around the edge of the fire pit, and no artifacts were recovered from the top of the subsoil, but the quantity of chipping debris in the plow zone was at the higher end of the density range for the field (eleven to twenty-four flakes per sq. m), suggesting that some manufacturing activity took place there. This conclusion was reinforced by the occurrence of a core of black rhyolite, as well as two large flakes, one of black rhyolite and the other hornfels. This was one of only two places in the field where cores were found. The only other place in the field where they were found was in the loam over the other main feature, the "black platform."

An analysis of chipping waste (flakes and chunks) found in the vicinity of the fire pit indicated the types of stone that were likely to have been used in the Late Archaic period. The debris consisted mainly of hornfels and black and gray rhyolites, with a few other stone types (gray argillite, gray quartzite, and white quartz). The more recently identified stone types were also represented by a small chunk and flake of what appeared to be amphibolite and one chunk of mylonite (Blancke 2003).

The "Black Platform"

The other major feature presented a puzzle to be solved. During the first season's test-pit digging, traces of an extensive blackened area or "black platform" were uncovered whose purpose or function was far from clear. The platform was located about 50 meters to the north of the fire pit, on the edge of a bank above the swamp. It was eventually determined to be roughly oval in shape, about 7.5 m long by 4 m wide, but less than 2 cm thick. When approximately 40 cm of loam were removed, this black feature was very visible at the top of the yellow subsoil (see Figure 6.3). Plow marks in the black platform indicated that this feature was impacted by the plow, but unlike the fire pit, traces of it still remained in the plow zone. Three levels of brown loam were apparent in the profiles of trenches that cut through the plow zone. These darkened in tone from the surface down, with the darkest bottom level resting on the black platform. This bottom level was 2–4 cm thick and dark and greasy in texture, intermixed with flecks of charcoal. It represented a disturbed upper level of the feature.

Two radiocarbon ages were obtained on charred wood from the black platform. The calibrated ages for both fell within the first half of

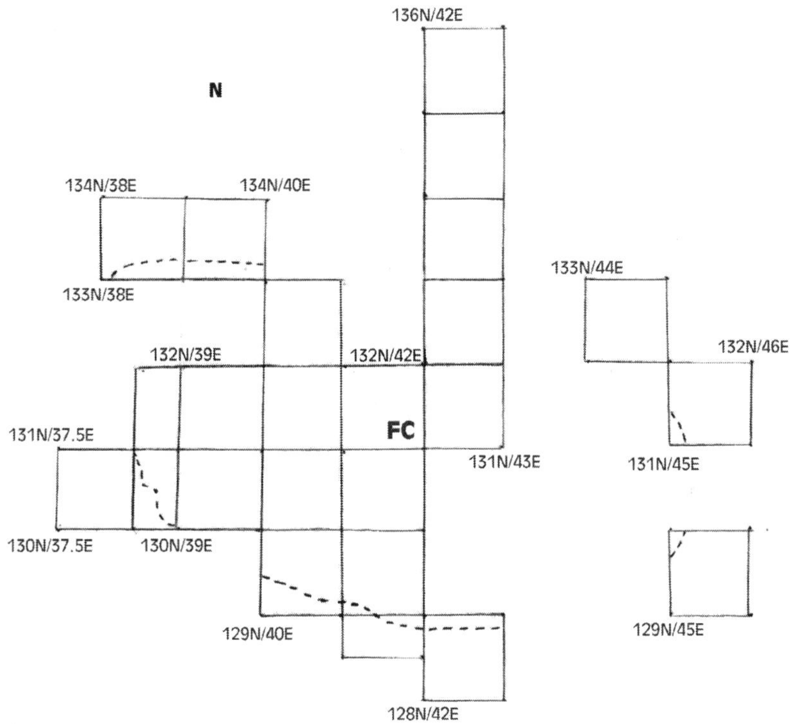

Figure 6.3. Plan of the "Black Platform" (Living Floor) at the Sleepy Hollow Expansion Site (FC = Fire Center). The dotted line represents where the edge of the blackened area was found. The grid consists of meter squares.

the fifteenth century A.D., with cal A.D. 1406 for the fire at the center, and cal A.D. 1431 at its edge. The sample at the center of the fire (131N/41E) had an age of 550 ± 50 B.P. (GX-25983, wood charcoal, $\delta^{13}C = -26.1$ percent). The sample from the edge of the black platform (131N/38.5E) gave an age of 470 ± 60 B.P. (GX-26646, wood charcoal, $\delta^{13}C = -26.6$ percent). Calibrated ranges made by the Geochron Laboratories at 2σ, using two methods (Stuiver and Pearson 1993; Stuiver et al. 1998), are summarized here as follows: For the fire at the center: cal A.D. 1300–1441 (method A), and cal A.D. 1305–1366 (p = .46), 1384–1436 (p = .54) (method B). The center fire ranges may be seen to extend from the early fourteenth century to the mid-fifteenth century A.D., with the fifteenth century slightly more probable in method B. For the edge of the platform, the calibrated ranges were: cal A.D.

1398–1499 (method A), and 1383–1520 (p = .87) (method B). These ranges fall squarely in the fifteenth century. (Ranges from the fourteenth to the seventeenth centuries that had low probability under method B have been omitted.) These dates indicated that the feature belonged to the very end of the Late Woodland period, probably before European contact took place. Thus it fell within the time frame of Native agriculture, in particular, the cultivation of maize after about 1000 A.D., and its location on the edge of an area historically known as Indian planting fields raised the hope of finding ancient maize that might be datable (Little 2002; Chilton 2008).

At the end of the second season's digging, the black platform was thought to be circular in shape from two test pits that caught its edge north and south and a transect that appeared to cover most of its east-west diameter. This highly visible area in the top of sandy subsoil was blackened by what appeared to be charcoal dust with some reddened soil, but there was very little actual charcoal. Also recovered were some small balls of what appeared to be greasy dirt. Under the microscope, they had no special features and were described as "organic concretions" (Largy, in Blancke 1999).

The third season's digging showed that the shape of the blackened area was not circular but an ill-defined oval that gave the impression of charcoal dust scattered in an elongated oval shape from a central fire. The only remnants of a possible fire were very small fragments of charred wood (not charcoal) in the center of the feature (see Figure 6.3, FC) No other visible finds were made, and it was a disappointment that no plant materials such as carbonized maize or other foods were evident. No seasonality could be determined. The wood was identified as conifer, comprising pine, spruce, larch, or tamarack. This showed a difference from the Late Archaic fire pit that contained oak, but pine species have been dominant in the area since the end of the Pleistocene, varying in frequency with changes in the climate (Winkler 1993).

The northeast curve of the feature could not be traced in charcoal-mottled soil that contained small trimming flakes but no clear edge separating dark platform from yellow subsoil (see Figure 6.3). This area may have been dug previously by the PAL survey team in 1997, as it was the approximate location where a concentration of hornfels chipping flakes as well as a Middle Archaic projectile point were found (Stark type made of argillite; see Waller and Ritchie 1997, 53). In the feature's center (FC), near the wood fragments and on the platform layer in the top of the subsoil, a small leaf-shaped point made of brown chert was uncovered (see Figures 6.4a, b). If this is a projectile point, then it presents a puzzle, because one would expect the Late Woodland date of

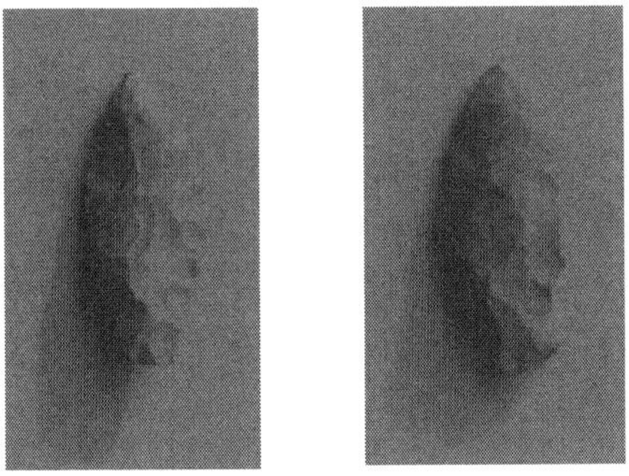

Figure 6.4a, 6.4b. Obverse and Reverse of the Brown Chert Point from the Living Floor (Length 2.2 cm)

the black platform to imply an association with the Levanna point type, a single example of which is in the Benjamin Smith collection from the site (Blancke 1987). The point could be a highly resharpened knife or scraper, worked out to a very small size. Moreover, because of traces of plow furrows seen in the platform, it may have landed on the platform accidentally and may not belong to it. The point was made of a chert, probably from New York State, and since no chert chipping debris was recovered, it was probably not manufactured at the site.

Also of woodland date and likely connected originally with the platform were two tiny potsherds retrieved from the plow zone over the black platform in previous seasons. Both were tempered with grit, and in one case the grit contained white quartz. Both the inner and outer surfaces of one sherd were dark, with one surface decorated with incised lines. The other undecorated sherd had a dark exterior with a red interior surface. Other artifacts from the loam in the vicinity were a black rhyolite teardrop-shaped scraper, the tip of a gouge, and other fragments of knives, scrapers, and points.

The areas of the black platform and fire pit were the only locations in the field where the excavations uncovered stone cores, indicating manufacturing. Near the platform two were found: a small pyramidal core of gray quartzite, and a small rough core or chunk of gray argillite, together with a flake that fit it. In addition, a large gray quartzite flake with a worked edge was recovered. Occurring uniquely in this location in the loam were seven pieces of chipping waste of purple rhyolite from the Lynn volcanics, an unusual lithic to be found in Concord. Otherwise, as at the fire pit, the chipping debris consisted primarily of hornfels and the gray and black rhyolites, with a lesser quantity of gray argillite, gray quartzite, and white quartz. Thirteen large flakes (2–4 cm wide) were made of purple rhyolite, argillite, gray quartzite, and gray or black rhyolite, and a possible perforator base was identified as amphibolite. This amphibolite, together with mylonite, at the site was identified by thin-section analysis (Calogero and Philpotts, in Blancke 2003).

What Was the "Black Platform"?

By the end of the second digging season it was still not at all clear what the black platform was, but because of certain aspects of the site and its more recent history, a number of possibilities were considered, and five "models" were proposed. The goals of the third season were to test these out as well as obtain radiocarbon dates for the feature. Testing the models required finding the platform's edges and exploring a substantial part of the interior to see where other features such as fires might be within it. There was also the real possibility that post molds might be found at its edge whose differing patterns might suggest certain possibilities (Blancke 1999). Dating the feature would also narrow the possibilities. The proposed alternatives for the black platform were the following:

- It was an area where brush was cleared from the field and burned.
- It was a roasting platform or pit.
- It was an area where canoes were made.
- It was a Native house floor (wigwam).
- It was an area where animals were penned.
- It was the floor of a shed or tent at the nineteenth-century agricultural fair.

Each of these models required a certain pattern of features to be identified in the ground. The first three models depended on differing positions for fires, while for the remaining three it was expected that post molds would be located in different patterns.

The first possibility that it was the site of a brush fire was suggested by the fact that a pile of brush had been dumped recently at the side of the field near the feature, so it seemed possible that it might have been an area where brush had been burned in the past. The implications of that alternative and for the possibility that it was a roasting platform or pit were that one might expect to find a large amount of charcoal and possibly wood fragments spread out in a broad area of irregular shape.

The site's proximity to the river and the fact that two fragments of stone gouges were found in the loam and on the surface near the black platform suggested that it could have been an area where canoes were made in the past. Ethnographic experiments at Plimoth Plantation to make dug-out canoes in the ancient manner, using fire and gouges to hollow out the log, indicated that an oval area of wood chippings and shavings with charcoal dust would surround the canoe, and charcoal would be found at the edge of this area from a small fire kept to replenish coals for burning out the canoe. The charcoal dust and "organic concretions" of the black platform might have been the remains of wood chippings, so if it proved to be oval with a fire somewhere at its edge, then this was a possible model.

For the feature to be a Native house floor (a wigwam or living floor), the boundary of the area would have had to be oval or circular, and one might expect to find post molds at the edges caused by the stakes that would have formed the lattice-style framework to support mats or bark. The center should have the remains of a fire. This could account for charcoal dust spread over a wider area.

The occurrence of historical trash in the plow zone suggested that the black platform feature might relate to some activity by Concord townspeople that took place in the last 350 years. Based on an eighteenth-century clay pipe find, it could have been an eighteenth-century animal pen, or it could have been a pen for the nineteenth-century agricultural fair that a document described as having been built in the field. In either case, one might expect the area to have had straight sides and post molds for a rectangular pen. The same document referred to the positioning of lumber to build a shed (see Figure 6.3). If the black layer were the floor of such a shed, then it would have had straight sides, and one might perhaps find some remains of lumber. On the other hand, if a tent had been erected for the agricultural fair, then it could have had either straight or oval sides and posts supporting it at different locations, so that post molds could be in a variety of locations. An exploration of the edges of the "platform" and some of its interior could answer most of these questions.

Evaluating the Alternatives

Each of these models had its criteria that needed to be found in the ground. The wigwam, pens, and tent or shed models all required different configurations of post molds or foundation trenches to be identified.

After the third season, no such features were apparent, not even a single post mold, so that all of these models were eliminated, although the platform's oval shape and charred wood fragments at the center, suggesting a fire, could indicate a wigwam floor. The canoe-making model required an oval area of wood chips and shavings and charcoal dust with a fire at its edge. The "platform" was oval, but the only obvious remains of a fire were not at the edge but at the center, and no chips or shavings were apparent, so that model was also eliminated. The most likely model, then, appeared to be the first, the brush fire for field clearance, or second, the roasting platform, except that there seemed to be too little charcoal and too few wood fragments either at the level of the feature or in the darkened loam immediately above it to indicate an extensive occurrence or use of fire.

The final decision on which model fit the data best hinged on a micromorphological soil test of the platform. The test showed microscopic organic remains that were most consistent with a living floor, perhaps a wigwam floor (Volmar 2000). The wigwam or Native house floor model had been eliminated because there was no evidence of post molds, but it now appeared that a living floor of some kind had been uncovered (Blancke 1999; Volmar and Blancke 2002). The "organic concretions" and greasy layer at the base of the loam profile fit this explanation. Initially it was thought that it might have been an uncovered floor, but subsequently it was learned that it is not unusual for wigwam floors in New England to show no evidence of post molds that may be obliterated by the plow. The soil sample pointed to a living floor, whether open or covered over.

With the possibility that it was in fact a wigwam floor, the radiocarbon dating of the feature became of particular interest. Two charcoal samples were taken, one from the central point where charred wood suggested a fire, and the other from the edge of the blackened area. When the dates were calibrated, there was a high probability that the feature belonged in the first half of the fifteenth century, or between 1400 and 1450 A.D. The dates indicate the living floor likely was created at the end of the Late Woodland period.

Sleepy Hollow Historical Sequence and Cultural Conclusions

Three seasons of excavation uncovered traces of a long history of Native American stone working at Sleepy Hollow expansion field, part of an area traditionally thought to be Indian planting fields at the time of the founding of the town of Concord. Recovered radiocarbon dates and diagnostic artifacts indicated a Native American presence from about 7,000 years ago until the fifteenth century A.D. The two main features just described come from almost each end of this span, except that the makers of the 4,500-year-old Late Archaic fire pit were preceded by Middle Archaic people represented only by projectile points. The living floor is at the latest end of the time span.

In addition to these two features where the presence of cores and large flakes suggested tool manufacturing, other smaller features suggested tool making on a smaller scale. The excavations uncovered two small fire pits on the edges of the field, in the southern part and on the west side near the brook. Small quantities of chipping debris beside the fires suggested that some small-scale manufacturing took place there. Chipping waste in the loam showed that the main stone manufacturing area where the bulk of the stone manufacturing took place in the Middle and Late Archaic periods was in the middle of the west side of the field in the general location of the Late Archaic fire pit. Collections material indicated that there was yet another small tool-making station on the east edge of the field.

The quantity of chipping debris in Benjamin Smith's collection in the Concord Museum indicated, however, that much more tool manufacturing occurred at the site than the excavations demonstrated. Many kilograms of chipping waste indicated that the field was a widespread workshop area with a number of different stations where artifacts were made at different time periods. The waste included not only flakes but also an unusually large number of cores (twenty-seven), representing mostly the predominant gray and black rhyolites and hornfels but also white quartz, quartzite, argillite, and mylonite.

Diagnostic artifacts from the collections also made it possible to determine in what periods certain types of stone were being worked. The Middle and Late Archaic periods, ranging from 7,500 to 3,000 years ago, saw the use of the greatest variety of stone types in the manufacture of artifacts, the same types represented by the aforementioned cores, with the addition of purple rhyolite. The stone sources that are known were accessible by the Sudbury, Assabet, Concord, and Merrimack rivers leading to the seacoast. These were hornfels from the Ossipee Mountains in New Hampshire, rhyolites from the Marblehead-Saugus area, and mylonite from Sudbury. The lack of cortex on most flakes indicated that cores were shaped at the source before being brought back.

Apart from the Late Archaic period, the only other period with significant feature remains, that is, the living floor, possibly a small wigwam floor, was the latter part of the Late Woodland period. No artifacts were found associated with the living floor, however, unless the small stemmed brown chert artifact really belonged there. The potsherds from the loam probably belonged to it, and perhaps the gouge fragments. It is known from seventeenth-century written sources that in the succeeding Contact period most artifacts were made of perishable materials rather than stone. From the collections, the only major stone type that seemed to have been used in the Woodland periods was black rhyolite, although mylonite and a gray quartzite may also have been utilized. A few Woodland artifacts of exotic materials were on the site, in particular, New York State cherts that implied a far-flung trading network typical of this era. Archaeological sites datable to the fifteenth century are rare in Massachusetts, so the identification of a living floor from that period is of intrinsic interest.

Acknowledgments

Betty Little's characteristic enthusiasm and interest focused on the radiocarbon dating at this site particularly because the site had potential for finding corn in an archaeological context. I especially want to thank those who undertook the microscope analyses for this project: Michael Volmar of Fruitlands Museum for the soil micromorphology, Tonya Largy of the Harvard Zooarchaeology Laboratory for the wood, and Barbara Calogero and Anthony Philpotts of the University of Connecticut, Storrs, for the lithics. Thanks are due also to David Wood of the Concord Museum who identified the clay pipe and historic period potsherds. Throughout the work, Thurston Handley for the Concord Cemetery Committee, Sara Wilbur for the Concord Historical Commission, and David Turocy of the Concord Public Works Department were very supportive. The Concord Historical Commission provided funding for radiocarbon dates and an intern supervisor, and the Concord Public Works Department has marked the positions of the late Archaic fire pit and Woodland living floor with aluminum pins at ground level to preserve them within the new expansion area for Sleepy Hollow Cemetery.

Works Cited

Blancke, Shirley. 1981. *Survey of Pre-Contact Sites and Collections in Concord: Final Report.* On file. Boston: Massachusetts Historical Commission.

Blancke, Shirley. 1987. *Archaeological Site Examination of the Bedford Street Housing Asparagus Farm Area, Concord, Massachusetts.* On file. Boston: Massachusetts Historical Commission.

Blancke, Shirley. 1988. *Bedford Street Survey, Concord, Massachusetts (Site 19-MD-100, Survey No. 2)*. On file. Boston: Massachusetts Historical Commission.

Blancke, Shirley. 1995. Concord Shell Heap and Field at Clamshell Bluff: Introduction and History. *Bulletin of the Massachusetts Archaeological Society* 56(2): 29–34.

Blancke, Shirley. 1998. *Volunteer Intensive Archaeological Survey of the Sleepy Hollow North Cemetery Expansion: Final Report, Concord, Massachusetts.* On file. Boston: Massachusetts Historical Commission.

Blancke, Shirley. 1999. *Archaeological Data Recovery at Sleepy Hollow North Cemetery Expansion: Final Report, Phase 1, Concord, Massachusetts.* On file. Boston: Massachusetts Historical Commission.

Blancke, Shirley. 2003. *Archaeological Data Recovery at Sleepy Hollow North Cemetery Expansion: Final Report, Phase 2, Concord, Massachusetts.* On file. Boston: Massachusetts Historical Commission.

Bradley, James W. 2007. Paleo-Indian Sites and Finds in the Lower Merrimac River Drainage. *Bulletin of the Massachusetts Archaeological Society* 68(1): 12–20.

Chilton, E. S. 1999. Mobile Farmers of Pre-Contact Southern New England: The Archaeological and Ethnohistorical Evidence. In *Current Northeast Ethnobotany*, New York State Museum Bulletin 494, ed. J. P. Hart 157–76. Albany: The New York State Museum.

Chilton, E. S. 2008. So Little Maize, So Much Time: Understanding Maize Adoption in New England. In *Current Northeast Paleoethnobotany II*, New York State Museum Bulletin 512, ed. J. P. Hart, 53–58. Albany: New York State Museum.

Concord Museum. 2007. In Our Collection. *Concord Museum Newsletter* (Fall): 3.

Gleason, Herbert. 1906. Map of Concord, Mass. In *Special Collections*, Concord Free Public Library, Concord, MA.

Johnson, Eric S., and Thomas F. Mahlstedt. 1984. Report on the Benjamin Smith Archaeological Collection, Concord, MA. *Bulletin of the Massachusetts Archaeological Society* 45(2): 51–66.

Largy, Tonya Baroody, and Duncan Ritchie. 2002. Local Lithic Materials in Archaic Technologies: Mylonite and Amphibolite from the Castle Hill Site, Wayland, Massachusetts. *Bulletin of the Massachusetts Archaeological Society* 63(1, 2): 51–65.

Little, E. A. 2002. Kautantowit's Legacy: Calibrated Dates on Prehistoric Maize in New England. *American Antiquity* 67: 109–18.

Ritchie, Duncan, Marsha K. King, Christy Vogt, and Patricia Fragola. 1990. Archaeological Investigations of Minute Man National Historical Park. Vol. 2., *An Estimation Approach to Prehistoric Sites.* Boston, MA: National Park Service.

Shattuck, Lemuel. 1835. *History of the Town of Concord.* Boston, MA: Russell, Odiorne, and Company.

Stuiver, M., and Gordon W. Pearson. 1993. High-Precision Bidecadal Calibration of the Radiocarbon Time Scale, AD 1950–500 BC and 2500–6000 BC. *Radiocarbon* 35(1): 1–23.

Stuiver, M., and P. J. Reimer, E. Bard, J. W. Beck, G. S. Burr, K. A. Hughen, B. Kromer, G. McCormac, J. van der Plicht, and M. Spurk. 1998. INTCAL98 Radiocarbon Age Calibration, 24,000–0 ca; BP. *Radiocarbon* 40(3): 1041–83.

Volmar, Michael A. 2000. *Sleepy Hollow Expansion Archaeological Site, Concord, Massachusetts: Soil Micromorphology Report.* On file. Boston: Massachusetts Historical Commission.

Volmar, Michael A., and Shirley Blancke. 2002. Landscape Interpretation on the Microscopic Scale: Case Studies in Southern New England. In *A Lasting Impression: Coastal, Lithic, and Ceramic Research in New England Archaeology*, ed. Jordan E. Kerber, 125–37. CT: Praeger.

Waller, Joseph N., and Duncan Ritchie. 1997. *Intensive Archaeological Survey of the Sleepy Hollow North Cemetery Expansion, Concord, Massachusetts.* Public Archaeology Laboratory (PAL) Report No. 818, Pawtucket, RI.

Wheeler, Ruth. 1967. *Climate for Freedom.* Concord, MA: Concord Antiquarian Society.

Winkler, Marjorie Green. 1993. Changes at Walden Pond during the Last 600 Years: Microfossil Analyses of Walden Pond Sediments. In *Thoreau's World and Ours: A Natural Legacy*, ed. Edmund A. Schofield and Robert C. Barron, 199–211. Golden, CO: North American Press.

Wood, William. 1977[1634]. *New England's Prospect.* Amherst: University of Massachusetts Press.

7

Wampum Use in Southern New England

The Paradox of Bead Production without the Use of Political Belts

Marshall Joseph Becker

Between 1600 and 1620, marine shell beads of a standardized size and shape, specifically called "wampum" (from *wampompeag*, the general Algonquian term for white shell beads), emerged as a commodity produced by foraging peoples living along the shores of Long Island Sound. Wampum use spread rapidly in the Northeast, but for purposes that were far from uniform among the Native cultures. Detailed studies of the archaeological and historical records for each specific tribe reveal clues to variations in patterns of use, which include ornamental, diplomatic, and ecclesiastical functions. A general summary of recent findings, presented here, reflects the discovery that the major Native producers of wampum all lived in a region distinct from the principal area of diplomatic wampum use.

Native demand for wampum as a commodity influenced Colonial trading patterns as well as tribal dynamics over a wide area. Despite southern New England being the principal area of Native wampum production, by 1640 diplomatic uses of strings and belts were limited to a very specific part of the Northeast identified here as the "Core" (Becker 2005b, 2007b), defined here as the territories of the three great Native horticultural confederacies: the Huron, the Five Nations Iroquois, and the Susquehannock. The Core area peoples all lived in inland areas and utilized palisaded villages as a major adaptation linked with maize horticulture. The "longhouses" typical of Core area villages provided safe storage and protection for maize as well as for the increasing quantities of wampum used in diplomacy.

The territories of the peoples immediately surrounding the Core formed a "Periphery" within which uses of wampum for diplomatic purposes were infrequent and primarily involved political interactions with peoples in the Core. Western New England lay within the Periphery, including the areas of western New England occupied by the Mahican, Sokoki, and other peoples living between the Hudson and Connecticut rivers. Eastern New England lay beyond the Periphery, forming a region in which wampum use was focused on decorative functions, except during infrequent trips to interact with peoples in the Core. These people, including the French allied "Eastern Indians" and the peoples of southern New England, never became involved in the use of wampum in diplomatic contexts (Becker 2005b). Since the Native peoples of southern New England were central to nearly all early wampum production, we find an interesting paradox. Why did the peoples in the wampum-producing areas never develop the complex diplomatic protocols of wampum prestation (formal presentation of strings or belts of wampum with the expectation of a reciprocal action) most commonly associated with Native uses of this commodity?

Southern New England: The Periphery and Beyond

In New England, as well as in other areas along the eastern seaboard of North America, the histories of the individual Native cultures are increasingly better understood. Several of these "groups" or tribes maintained their identities, and often some of their traditional boundaries, well into the nineteenth century. Each of these Native peoples used a specific and unique set of strategies for cultural survival (Bonner and Herbster 2005; cf. Becker 1987, 2001). The tendency to assume that the several Indian cultures of one region shared similar political, social, and material systems robs each of these Native peoples of their specific histories and identities and distorts our ability to recognize the differences. Examination of the differences in the ways that wampum was used within each individual culture helps reveal the integrity of each specific system. This approach continues the efforts of Salwen (1978), Conkey and colleagues (1978), and others to understand the workings of the specific and distinct cultures within this region.

Notable is the nearly complete absence of wampum diplomacy, or use of formal wampum protocols anywhere in New England (Becker 2005b). Wampum bands used in diplomacy in eastern New England are as rare as they are informative (see, e.g., Becker 2005b). The smoking of the "peace pipe," or calumet ceremonialism (Nassaney 2000; Becker 2003), remained the normative means of keeping the "peace" during intertribal meetings in New England, as well as during Native-Colonial meetings (see, e.g., Altham 1963[1623–1625], 35, 58–59). Diplomatic uses for smoking pipes were not specifically noted by Emmanuel Altham of the Plimouth Colony, who sent three examples of these pipes to his relatives in England, but treaty records for the period reveal that the calumet "ritual" was basic to social and political interactions in New England, as it was among many other Native American cultures.

Foragers, Not Farmers

A mobile forager model for coastal New England is in accord with Lynn Ceci's (1979–1980) and E. Little's evidence concerning the limited presence and use of maize among the Native peoples of southern New England (Little and Schoeninger 1995). These peoples appear to have been gardening maize in much the same way that the Lenape of the lower Delaware River Valley, who were oriented toward anadromous fish as a basic food resource (Becker 2006a), gardened maize (Becker 2006b; also see Becker 1999). Chilton's (1999, 2002) overview of subsistence and settlement patterns in Native New England suggests that similar strategies were employed by these peoples. The evidence from wampum use suggests that foraging strategies in New England, as in the Delaware Valley, were not conducive to the conservation, or communal "holding" (storage), of the diplomatic wampum strings and belts that represented essential "treaty" (formal meeting) documents among peoples living within the Core. The rare use of this commodity in diplomatic contexts in New England reflects features relating to social organization and political processes.

The origins and development of wampum as a commodity within this multicultural scenario (see Becker 2002) are of particular interest as they reflect the cultural dynamics among the Native peoples as well as relations that developed with European immigrants. Prior to 2005, I had believed that the use of wampum as a commodity-cum-currency had become a feature of Colonial economic life in the region from New England to as far south as the Delaware River Valley by the 1620s. Given the shortages of small coins in the early English colonies, the monetization of wampum (see Becker 1980) and other commodities (dried fish, tobacco) is easily understood. The use of dried and salted "fish" as a local commodity reflects the focus of the Plymouth colonists and others exploiting the vast fisheries in this region. However, the work *Chronicles of the First Planters of the Colony of Massachusetts Bay, from 1623 to 1636* makes not a single reference to wampum (Young 1970[1846]). Even the *Records of the Colony of New Plymouth in New England* (Schurtleff 1968[1855]) suggests an *absence* of wampum in this colony during the period circa 1620–1640. In the *Records* the first appearance of debts to be paid, on March 25, 1633, stipulates that payment be made only "in money, merchantable beaver, or fish, at the ordinary rates accustomed." Elsewhere we find payments that were to be made in land, "sutes of apPell" (suits of apparel, see Becker 2005a), as well as the usual "money or corne" (Schurtleff 1968[1855], vol. 1, 9, 15). Wampum *may* be first indicated, late in the 1630s, in a reference "Concerning the trade of beaver, corne, & beads, &c, wth the Indians . . ." (Schurtleff 1968[1855], vol. 1, 54, from the original page 107). The importance of wampum as a trading commodity may have focused its use on the wholesale pelt trade, directing wampum into the hands of the major Native pelt brokers, who lived far from the principal Colonial procurers of this commodity in the Long Island Sound area.

In 1638, the instructions for Johann Printz (Johnson 1930), based on Peter Minuit's information relating to trade in the Northeast, involved making a stop to purchase wampum, recognized as an essential commodity for purchasing peltry from Native peoples. By the 1650s, wampum had become an essential commodity throughout much of the Northeast. In a letter dated February 22, 1650, Cornelis van Tienhoven (O'Callaghan 1856, vol. 1, 360; cf. Nelson 1894, 36, n. 3) describes continuing English encroachments on Dutch lands and trade. Noted here is the *Crumme gouw* area of Long Island, the "considerable inland sea," where "The Greatest part of the Wampum, for which furs are traded, is manufactured there by the Natives." Van Tienhoven, on March 4, 1650, observed that the eastern end of Long Island, now the Gardiners Bay region, was "well adapted to secure the trade of the Indians in Wampum (the mine [wealth] of New Netherland), therein situate lie the cockles whereof Wampum is made, from which a great profit could be realized by those who would plant a colonie or hamlet at the aforesaid Point" (O'Callaghan 1856, vol. 1, 365–66, original spelling). Despite wampum production being centered in the Long Island Sound area and its use as a currency-commodity, no diplomatic uses for wampum can be documented in this zone. Wampum beads are even absent in the documents recording payments made to Natives for sales of their land (see also Little and Sussek 1981), suggesting that this commodity was still being sold wholesale to merchants into the 1650s.

The Long Island Region

The history of Dutch trade in southern New England and the Manhattan Island region, and Dutch development of the wampum trade, is brilliantly summarized by McBride (1993b, 38–41). McBride also adjusts and incorporates information from L. Ceci's corpus (see, e.g., Ceci 1990) in his delineation of regional cultural dynamics of the early seventeenth century. Neither recognized the specific Native uses of wampum as ornament in this coastal region, as distinct from wampum use within the Core area. Isaack de Rasieres's (1628) letter reporting his sale of wampum to the English at Plymouth, during September–October 1627, provides an interesting account of an unnamed Native group in an area near Fort Amsterdam. In the 1620s, de Rasieres was secretary general of the West India Company's outpost in New Netherlands. By the time he wrote this 1628 letter, wampum had been employed for more than a decade among these people, who "support themselves by hunting, and when the spring comes, by fishing" (de Rasieres 1628, 69; Becker 2006b). In the winter these people made "sewan." They "string it, and wear it around the neck and hands; they also make bands of it, which the women wear on the forehead under the hair, and the men around the body; and they are as particular about the stringing and sorting [of sewan] as we can be here about pearls" (de Rasieres 1628, 69–70; cf. Denton 1670, 12, Becker 2005a, 742).

The Native American peoples of eastern Long Island, resident within the area of major wampum production during the Colonial period, used wampum for ornament and tribute payments. Cornelis van Tienhoven's account, noted earlier, and various entries in the "Acts of the Commissioners of the United Colonies" offer important clues. In September 1657 there was a discussion of "The Tribute of Wampam [*sic*] brought in by the Pequoutts [*sic*]" and the use of this tribute to pay various officers of the United Colonies (Pulsifer 1968[1859], vol. 2, 193–94). After these payments were noted, the record indicates that "The Remainder being 14 fathom is left with The Treasurer of the Massachusetts vpon the Collonies account. There was alsoe paied in to the Tresurer of Newhaven by the Mantackett [Montauk?] Sachem [Wyandanck?] 78 fathom which Remaines vpon the accounte of the Collonies" (Pulsifer 1968[1859], vol. 2, 194 [page 113 in the original ms., spelling in original]). Complaints made by the Montauk regarding the Pequot taking shells from their waters, and note of Montauk tribute payments to the governor of Connecticut, are documented elsewhere (Becker 2008b).

Accounts noting wampum use by the Narragansett and among the Pequot provide an indication of differences between peoples in the Core and those in the Periphery. Bradford's (1952, 202–203) recollection of events that took place during the important year 1628 provides an important view of the developments taking place in the early wampum trade, and the beginnings of what became an extensive Native-based industry. In 1628, the "Dutch sent [sold] again unto them" various goods of use to the Plymouth colonists in facilitating trade with the Natives. Of course, the rates made the venture favorable to the Dutch. Not only were the Plymouth colonists benefiting from these purchases, "But that which turned most to their profit, in time, was an entrance into the trade of wampumpeag," which the Dutch noted was in demand at Fort Orange (Albany, New York). The Dutch correctly predicted that wampum would sell well at Kennebec, whose people were linked by trade with those of the Huron confederacy. The English bought £50 worth of wampum, but the quantity received for this vast sum is not noted, nor is the year specified as 1627 or 1628. Bradford notes (1952, 203) that wampum sold poorly for two years, "till the inland people knew of it [being available via the Kennebec], and afterwards they could scarce ever get enough for them."

The "inland people" noted by Bradford were the Huron, whose confederated members constituted the northernmost peoples of the Core area. Their access to wampum was facilitated by Norridgewock and Penobscot intermediaries in present Maine, as well as the peoples along the Connecticut River, such as the Sokoki and the Pequot. All of these people could exchange pelts for wampum at relatively low rates and could exchange these beads for peltry brought in by peoples from the interior:

> And strange it was to see the great alteration it made in a few years among the Indians themselves; for all the Indians of these parts and the Massachusetts had none or very little of it, but the sachems and some special persons that wore a little of it for ornament. Only it was made and kept among the Narragansetts and Pequots, which grew rich and potent by it . . . that it was a commodity of that worth and value. (Bradford [ca. 1628] 1952, 203)

In addition to creating a boom market, these shell beads facilitated economic participation in the "new economy" by most of the coastal peoples who previously had been only marginal players in the pelt trade. This expansion also made possible Native purchase of guns and other armaments, leading to increasingly lethal conflict among the cultures wrestling for control of wampum production. The Pequot, securing guns from both the French and the Dutch, became particularly successful in these wars. The effects of this trade on the Pequot are noted later.

McBride (1993b, 42–43) notes that circa 1626, de Rasieres asked his suppliers at home to supply beads of the wampum type. In 1629, not more than two years after the Dutch began to supply the Plimouth Plantation traders with wampum, Mr. Isaac Allerton, along with Mr. James Sherley, a later immigrant, organized an expedition to buy peltry at Penobscot, the station and people at the mouth of the river of that name, some 80 leagues from Plimouth. The Plimouth colonists already had a trading post on the Kennebec River, where the Caniba (or Kennebec, variously spelled) provided contact with the St. Lawrence peltry routes. The two distinct destinations provide us with an indication that even at this early date the Native peoples along these two major rivers represented independent cultures. The organizers of the Penobscot venture decided to send Edward Ashley as their representative. He immediately made a request "to be supplied with wampumpeag, corn [grain] against winter and other things" (Bradford 1952, 29). McBride indicates that there is no evidence that the Dutch were producing wampum at this early date. Turgeon (2004, 22–24) suggests that wampum may have been produced in Paris circa 1650. Colonial production in North America can be documented by circa 1700 (Lesniak 2003). Several scholars now are researching the important transition of wampum production from Native hand labor to a Colonial proto-industrial process.

The Pequot: A Prelude

Well-documented accounts of the Pequot abound, but their role in dominating the early wampum trade is rarely explored (see Becker 2008a). A few observations on early Narragansett relations with the Pequot help set the stage. The Pequot had grown rich and powerful in the 1630s by brokering wampum that was made by or for them. This wealth enabled the Pequot to expand and/or shift their territorial range in order to take control of several wampum-producing areas along Long Island Sound (see Bradford 1952, 291). The Pequot soon became the focus of enmity for all their neighbors and traditional enemies. The Pequot's wealth and power also made them a target for the Dutch as well as the English, especially in the region of the latter's growing settlements in Connecticut. Despite growing rich, the Pequot never developed the complex diplomatic protocols involving wampum then becoming important among the Native peoples of the Core area. As the English escalated their encroachment into the Dutch sphere, where most of the wampum was being produced, the Pequot enhanced their relationship with the Dutch by selling to them, in 1632, most of present Connecticut (Becker 2008a). The Pequot claimed this large region by right of conquest (cf. McBride 1993b, 41). Over the next thirty years, Dutch control of the coastal area, extending as far south as Delaware Bay, was lost to the English (see O'Callaghan 1897). The change in local control, from a primarily mercantile Dutch trade system to the colonizing English system, inexorably led to political decline among almost all of these Native peoples. The Dutch to English transition was paralleled by changes in power relationships among the Native tribes, most of them having become "tributaries" to the Pequot circa 1625–1635 (McBride 1993b, 46–49). By the 1630s, Pequot power had been sufficiently weakened that the English could demand thousands of fathoms of wampum in tribute or payment for various reasons (see Ceci 1990, 61). The more the English found they could impose on the Pequot, the more eagerly the English found reasons to impose crushing "fines" on these Natives, all to be paid in wampum.

Narragansett

The interesting history of the Narragansett reflects the diversity and separate courses of each of the Native American tribes after 1500. Research directed at distinguishing between the two groups identified as Narragansett and Niantic (see Boissevain 1963, 494–95) requires further effort (cf. Hamilton 1948[1712–1756], 162; also see Boissevain 1968). The data relating to wampum use among these two peoples are considered here, without attempting to decode their specific tribal relationships.

Bradford reported (1952, 291) that by 1634 the Pequot, "puffed up with many victories," turned their aggression on the Narragansett. As part of their strategy the Pequot made overtures to the English colonists in Massachusetts, to whom they "offered much wampum and beaver, etc." for a treaty of peace and friendship (291). Bradford notes that the Plymouth colonists accepted this alliance only reluctantly, and on terms quite favorable to themselves. This offer of wampum was not a "prestation" (gift with an expectation of reciprocity) but a cash payment to be delivered as strings or fathoms (strung), rather than as "belts," which soon after had become the normal items "presented" in diplomatic contexts within the Core area that was developing to the west.

The Pequot continued to suffer loses to Colonial expansion (Washburn 1978, 90), leading to the war of August 1636 to September 1637. To a great extent the Pequot War was intended by the English to take control of the last vestiges of the wampum and pelt trade from the Dutch, as much as to eliminate Pequot power in the region. In a pattern seen throughout the New World, alliances between European traders and/or colonists and the region's less powerful tribes created a force able to topple the dominant local Native polity. The Massachusetts Bay Colony joined with the Connecticut River Colony, as well as with the Mohegan, Narragansett, and those "Long Island" tribes supporting the Narragansett (cf. Grumet 1996, 116; see also Strong 1996), to destroy the Pequot.

The victors, principally the Connecticut River Colony, drew up the Treaty of Hartford (September 21, 1638; see Vaughan 1979, 340–41) to indicate how the spoils, which included a number of Pequot survivors, were to be divided among themselves. The treaty was signed first for the Narragansett with the mark of "Miantinommy," the foremost of their elders (sachems). His mark is followed by the mark of "Poquiam, alias Unkas," for the Mohegan (cf. Johnson 1996). This is only one of several Natives with the name "Uncas" or some variant. The fact that only one representative of each of these two tribes signed this document suggests that each was acting as a true chief at this treaty. However, "Miantinommy," more commonly identified as "Miantonomi," also had been the first of the five Native signatories to an unrestricted deed signed on January 12, 1642, at Shawomet (now Warwick, Rhode Island), selling the land for 144 fathoms of wampum (Vaughan 1979, 348–49), suggesting an egalitarian ownership of lands, as was the case among the foraging Lenape (Kent 1979) and Lenopi (Becker 1998) in the Delaware Valley.

Below the marks of these two Natives we see the signatures of John Haines, Roger Ludlow, and Edward Hopkins. The text of this peace treaty allocated the "200 Peaquots living that are men, besides squawes and paposes," then held as captives, to be assigned as slaves to the conquering Indians. Miantinommy of the Narragansett received eighty Pequot in addition to the eleven that his people already held, and to "Poquime his number," generally interpreted to be eighty. The actual count remains uncertain (Sylvester 1910, vol. 1).

Most significant in the 1638 treaty is the declaration that these slaves "shall no more be called Peaquots but [shall be known as] Narragansetts and Mohegans" (Vaughan 1979, 340–41). Those tribes who, in effect, were what I call "renting" these slaves were instructed to make annual payments in wampum to the English at set rates for these people.

Payment for males was set at a fathom for each adult, half a fathom for "every youth," and "one hand" for every male "papoose" (Vaughan 1979, 340–41). The payments were "to be paid at Killing time of Corn at Connecticut yearly" (340–41), thus it was to the financial advantage of the colonists to preserve the cultural identity of these individual Pequot at the same time that the English, or perhaps only their Native allies, wished to exterminate the Pequot as a distinct culture. Despite these events, the Pequot soon reemerged as a viable people, having been liberated by the Connecticut Colony in 1650 and provided with two independent reservations. One of the two 1650 reservation tracts was provided to those former Pequot who had been slaves of the Narragansett, and the other to those Pequot slaves freed from the Mohegan. This latter group is believed to have been the ancestors of those people who received the Mashantucket tract in 1666 (McBride 1993a, 64).

Land sales from the victorious Narragansett to various colonists had begun at an early date and continued for more than a century. Throughout this period the Narragansett, as all Native peoples in this region, adapted their foraging lifestyles through various modes of adjustment, such as amplifying their maize and other gardening activities (cf. Becker 1999, 2006b) to coexist with the radically different political and economic situations imported by European immigrants. Roger Williams pointed out at a very early date that the Narragansett had several ornamental uses for wampum, but the documents also reflect Native receipt of wampum in payment for land:

> *Obs*. They hang these strings of money about their necks and wrists; as also upon upon [*sic*] the necks and wrists of their wives and children.
>
> Máchequoce. | A Girdle: Which they make curiously of one[,] two, three, foure, or five inches thicknesses and more, of this money which (sometimes to the value of ten pounds or more) they weare about their middle and as a scarfe about the shoulders and breasts. Yea the Princes make rich Caps and Aprons (or small breeches) of these Beads thus curiously strung into many formes and figures: their blacke and white finely mixt to-gether. (Williams 1971[1643], 149, spelling in original)

In addition to suggesting status differences among the Narragansett, as indicated by the use of different amounts of wampum, Williams (1971[1643], 152) also notes that the Natives "store up shells in Summer against Winter whereof to make their money." Although the girdles or bands described by Williams appear to represent the kinds of wampum bands then used in diplomatic contexts in the Core area, not a single case of wampum protocols can be found in the extensive documentary records from southern New England.

By 1643 the loosely united English colonies, excluding Roger Williams's Providence Plantation, were creating increased economic pressures on the Narragansett, then allied with Williams. The Narragansett had declared war on the Mohegan, who had recently been their allies, living along the Connecticut River and still "led" by "Poquiam, alias Unkas." The important leader of the Narragansett, Miantonomi, was captured in 1643, leading his people to offer an indemnity of "several packages of wampum" valued at £40 (Jennings 1976, 266–68). Uncas accepted the wampum, but the Mohegan rendered Miantonomi to the English. Bradford (1952, 337) states that in 1644 the English commissioners holding Miantonomi told the Narragansett that there was (or had been?) no agreement on the ransom, nor had any wampum been paid. The English may have felt free to renege on promises, as by 1644 they were using Mohawk mercenaries to control local Native groups. The English then killed Miantonomi, removing a capable and an important source of Narragansett leadership (Sylvester 1910, vol. 1, 382–99), and a person who may have been an emerging Narragansett "chief."

On August 27, 1645, the Narragansetts signed a treaty with the confederated New England colonies (Bradford 1952, 437–39). In this treaty the "sagamores" of the Narragansett and the Niantic agreed that they "Should pay . . . the full sum of 2000 fathom of good white wampum, or a third part of black wampumpeag, in four payments" within two years. In this 1645 treaty, it is also noted (Bradford 1952, 439) that the Narragansett were to continue to make payments for Pequot slaves allocated to them under the terms of the 1638 Treaty of Hartford. Bradford states that the Narragansett were to pay the colony a fathom of white wampum for every Pequot man, a half fathom for each youth [male], and a hand [measure] for each male child. The thirty women allocated to the Narragansett are not mentioned in Bradford's account. Perhaps the assumption was made by the colonists that the women would intermarry and be absorbed by the Narragansett. However, if these groups used matrilineal descent, as I suspect, then an interesting problem of cultural identity would have been generated by the patrilineal colonists.

These years of struggle to control this part of New England are often identified as the period of the wampum wars (see Salwen 1978). What are often represented as large-scale military conflicts, however, were only episodic events marking the slow and grinding process of cultures in conflict. As noted earlier, this extremely complex process can be revealed only through study of the hundreds of documents recording the intricate story of each of the cultures and the many Native and Colonial personalities involved. Among the dozens of surviving land deeds is one from 1646 that is particularly revealing of Native power and Native methods of negotiation that were so frustrating to colonists trying to focus on a modern cash economy. For one of these Native land sales we have, in addition to the text of the deed, some discussion of the important negotiations that preceded the drafting of the sale document (location now uncertain).

The discussion cited here regards a deed to land at Wapewasick, near Portsmouth, sold on October 7, 1646, by Ousamequin to Gregory Dextor, Roger Williams, and two other named colonists. As was the rule, the metes and bounds of this tract are noted, with its location relative to adjacent and previously sold parcels of land. The purchasers then

> offered him but fifteen fathom of white wampum (it being a time when white wampum only was current; and which we knew he only would accept). But he desired to have commodities and wampum, and at last we agreed upon ten fathom of white wampum, four coates of English cloth, six of the best English howes and English axes, and twelve great knives. (Bartlett 1968[1856–1865], vol. 1, 33–34, spelling in original)

The goods listed as "commodities" had a value in excess of five fathoms of wampum, indicating that Ousamequin had achieved a considerable increase in the purchase price that he was to be paid. Then the party went to buy the required goods, wherein Ousamequin selected what he wanted from among the many items available until he was satisfied. But at that point "he begged two coats" in addition to the four agreed upon, and these two more were granted. Then Ousamequin continued to make further demands, and ultimately the purchasers "layed out, y[e] valew of aboutt forty fathom of wampum" for the land, including "a coate to his councellor which he desired" (Bartlett 1968, vol. 1, 34) or nearly triple the amount of the original agreement. Native bargaining power was obviously much stronger than modern myth might have one believe.

De Forest (1853, 246–47) reviews the evidence for the reemergence of various Pequot groups by 1655. De Forest (citing Hazard II, 308–81) records a gathering in September 1655 at which Natives came from several groups carrying tribute to the New Haven Colony.

Paucatuc brought 58 fathoms of wampum, Wecapaug 37, and Uncas 143 in payment of two years' debt. The total value is given as £301 1s 6d. Tributaries that were behind in payments included "Long Island" (36 fathoms due) and others. Other accounts of payments made provide names and amounts that may suggest population dynamics (see DeForest 1853 and his sources). Most important at this 1655 gathering is the Pequot request for commissioners and laws by which they should live. Cashawashet, also known as Hermon Garret, was appointed governor to the Pequots at Paucatuc and Wecapaug, and Cassasinamon (the first Native known to bear this name) was appointed governor at "Nameag or New London." Native assistants also were named. In effect, the acculturation process, as indicated by the use of English names and political forms, was already well under way in this region by 1655.

By 1676, during Metacom's War (King Philip's War) the Pequot people had reemerged as a recognized and an independent population (or possibly two populations), firmly allied with the English of the Connecticut Colony. Following that conflict the Pequot became important allies of the colonists in the defense of the region against Mohawk incursions, and they maintained this alliance with Europeans thereafter (McBride 1993a, 71). Wampum continued to flow to the Five Nations peoples along established trade routes, but Native production in southern New England appears to have gone into decline by the end of the seventeenth century. As the Native population entered into the Colonial economic mainstream, hand production of individual wampum beads was replaced by early industrial processes. Wampum was still being produced by the Pequot into the 1750s, but in very limited quantities. The huge demand for wampum in the Core area after 1750, for use in treaties, further stimulated the complex Colonial cottage industry involving wampum production that had emerged in Albany, New York (see Lesniak 2003), and possibly in the area of Paterson, New Jersey. The shift in the center of commercial production of wampum to colonists living in Albany, well up the Hudson River, also relates to the early "industrial production" of these shell beads. These shifts were part of the significant changes in wampum production taking place after 1700, which accelerated in the decades after 1740 (summarized in Becker 2002). McBride's (2005) demonstration that these were not years of rapid change for New England's Pequot but reflected the long process of gradual cultural change by which these people adapted to shifting economic and social patterns in this region is revealed in the general decline in Native wampum production.

The ornamental use of wampum bands with various designs woven into them, and also the use of glass and metal beads, rapidly increased after 1709, a date by which the Narragansett and Niantic may have merged (cf. Lechford 1642, 50–52). The D. Gookin account (1792, but written by 1674) on Native uses of wampum as decoration reflects earlier Narragansett patterns of use (see also Becker 2005a, 777, n. 8, 775). Wampum use in Narragansett land sales became normative after 1700 (Becker 1980; Gookin 1792[1674], 152; Marten 1970, 11). As the importance of this commodity in the Core area increased toward the middle of the eighteenth century, the ornamental use for wampum in southern New England also appears to have changed, probably declining in direct proportion to acculturative processes.

Discussion and Conclusions

Early accounts of decorative wampum in southern New England, used on Native clothing and artifacts, reflect the observation by Thomas Morton in 1627 (see Morton 1637, 28–31). This was the same year in which the Dutch introduced wampum to the English in New England. Morton's detailed description of the clothing worn by people presumed to have been the Massachusett is the most thorough early account of the ways skins were used prior to the adoption of European cloth (Becker 2005b). Nowhere in his account is any mention made of wampum ornamentation, reflecting the delay between the first purchases by the English of wampum from the Dutch in 1627 and 1628 and the very rapid acceleration in local Native demand indicated at a later date by William Bradford. By the 1630s, Native use of wampum was spreading rapidly throughout northeastern North America, but the use to which this commodity was put varied significantly among the many Native cultures of the region.

The complex integration of the multitude of cultural traits within a culture may be viewed through the study of any subset or combination of them. A focus on differences in wampum use among specific peoples in southern New England enables us to explore differences among these cultures. Production of this commodity offered them access to European goods (cf. Appadurai 1986; Kopytoff 1986). In southern New England, after 1630, wampum became a commodity used for ornamentation, to pay ransoms and tribute as well as wergild (indemnity given to relatives as payment for a death), and for arranging marriages (cf. Becker 2005b) or other services of value. In addition to textual evidence, decorative uses for wampum in southern New England are documented in both the iconographic and archaeological record (Becker 2007a, 2008b; cf. Beauchamp 1901, 356–65).

The Native producers of wampum were, in effect, "minting" the small change that soon became an essential part of the region's economy. Of considerable note is that in southern New England, where the Native production was concentrated, these beads were rarely if ever used in diplomatic contexts. Within the Core area and the Periphery, even short strings of wampum served to fulfill the requirements of wampum prestation in diplomatic contexts (see Richter 2001 for Iroquois wampum protocols). The documentary record reveals quite clearly that peoples beyond the Periphery almost never engaged in wampum diplomacy when in their homeland (Becker 2005c).

Specific aspects of culture, and the limited distribution of identifying traits, have been examined by Mary Helms (1988, 4). Cook and Crang (1996, 132) discuss the nature of a "cultural mosaic" within an area, noting that it is made up "of bounded cultural regions or areas" (cf. Friedman 1994). Cook and Crang specifically examine food (a bulk commodity) and habits regarding varied uses of comestibles from a distributional point of view. The study of the distribution and use of wampum as a commodity provides a parallel example. Turgeon (2004, fn. 82) speculates that geographical as well as cultural differences led the peoples of the Core area to employ wampum in diplomatic contexts because of its rarity, and therefore value (cf. Helms 1988, 4). This interpretation suggests that diplomatic uses would be even more common at greater distances from the sources, which is definitely not the case! The people in the Core area used huge quantities of wampum secured through trade, but to the west of the Core area wampum diplomacy was absent until groups from the Core area became active in those parts.

The significant variable in the diplomatic uses for wampum appears to be the presence of horticultural villages, with the northern horticulturalists ("middle-range" societies, or sedentary peoples without true chiefs) being the only users of wampum for political interactions. The foraging cultures living in and beyond the Periphery had lower absolute populations, did not live in relatively permanent villages, and had no relatively durable and protected structures in which to preserve quantities of wampum. More significantly, the redistributive aspects of their social structure did not enable large quantities of diplomatic wampum to be stored or held by a single person or kin group. That these foraging peoples (Becker 2006b) were marginal players in the pelt trade is of less significance than their egalitarian social structure. The peoples of the Core area developed various "offices" or differentiated roles to play in each society, including that of a relatively formal "keeper" of the diplomatic wampum. When this role emerged among the Five Nations confederates is not known, nor do we know when the Onondaga became designated as keepers of the belts of the confederacy.

By 1806, when Louis and Clark returned from their tour of the Louisiana Purchase, or America's new frontier, the widespread use of wampum as a currency was ending, and its political uses had become vestigial. The historical and archaeological evidence from among the Narragansett and their neighbors indicates that ornamental uses for wampum were well established in this region by the 1630s. At the same time diplomatic uses for wampum were evolving in the Core area, where they were well established by 1640. Wampum diplomacy in some areas lasted until circa 1815. As a generic commodity, wampum circulated from circa 1620 into the 1830s (Becker 2002, 2006b). In New England, various acculturative processes reduced decorative uses for wampum among Native-descent peoples after 1800, and wampum soon faded as a cultural identifier, only to reemerge in the twenty-first century as a "cultural" symbol.

The evolution of wampum bead technology and wampum uses after 1620 and the many variations in decorative and political uses to which these shell artifacts were put offer an interesting aspect of the process of culture change following culture contact (see Silliman 2005). Also predictable is the continued use of the ancient calumet ritual among the Native peoples of New England. Even after wampum diplomacy became important in the Core area, the calumet ceremony survived. In the Periphery, calumet ceremonialism was much more commonly found as the only means by which intercultural dealings were conducted. Nassaney's (2000) survey of ritual tobacco use and its relationship with gender in southeastern New England indicates continuities in these Native diplomatic traditions (cf. Becker 2003, 2005c).

An extremely important finding of this research is that the popular myth that wampum bands or strings were "sacred objects" (see Salisbury 1982, 149) or "a spiritually charged material" (Romero 2006, 289) is not supported by any evidence, prior to Handsome Lake's revitalization activities circa 1800. These ideas appear to be based entirely on modern recreations or speculations regarding past beliefs. While this view of wampum may be frequently repeated in the twenty-first century, there is no evidence to support the idea that wampum bands or strings had been used for rituals anywhere in southern New England, or elsewhere in the Periphery, prior to the reinvention of various Native ethnic identities in the period after 1950.

Acknowledgments

This chapter is dedicated to Charles C. Willoughby and Elizabeth Little, scholars of brilliance and insight.

Sincere thanks to M. L. Rainey for her kind invitation to focus my research on wampum on the Native peoples of southern New England

and to use this study to carry forward research that was important to Elizabeth Little. Thanks also to Irene Axelrod (Peabody Essex Museum), Dr. James W. Bradley, Stephen Cook (head curator, Mashantucket Pequot Museum and Research Center), Dr. Philip Crang (Royal Holloway, University of London), Dr. Ilaria Bonoldi (Cremona), Professor William Engelbrecht, T. Rose Holdcraft, Dr. Ann Marie Plane, Professor Timothy Shannon, Professor Richard Swain and his entire staff, Tamar Diana Wilson, and many others for their very kind efforts.

Special thanks to Professor Kevin McBride for providing indications of the extent and excellent quality of the archaeological recovery and conservation efforts relating to the Long Pond site. His important publications offer an introduction to this landmark research, and we look forward to many more works on this subject. Special thanks also to Professor Elizabeth Chilton and Julie Woods for their important editorial guidance, to Jonathan Lainey for his encouragement and support of my renewed interest in the study of wampum and its uses, to William Turnbaugh and Michael Nassaney for their generous sharing of data, to Kelly McVeigh for important computer support, and to Christopher Mazzoli, whose help in focusing this research was essential to completing this study.

This chapter is part of a research program focusing on the origins and variations in the uses of wampum among the many Native peoples who incorporated this commodity into their daily lives. This phase of the program was generously supported by F. P. and M. E. Gillon. The encouragement and support of this research by the tax laws of the Congress of the United States of America is deeply appreciated. The ideas presented here as well as any errors of interpretation or in presentation are entirely the responsibility of the author.

Works Cited

Altham, Emmanuel. 1963[1623–1625]. Emmanuel Altham Letters. In *Three Visitors to Early Plymouth: Letters about the Pilgrim Settlement in New England during Its First Seven Years*, ed. Sydney V. James Jr., 29–62. Plymouth, MA: Plimoth Plantation.

Appadurai, Arjun. 1986. Introduction: Commodities and the Politics of Value. In *The Social Life of Things: Commodities in Cultural Perspective*, ed. A. Appadurai, 3–63. Cambridge: Cambridge University Press.

Bartlett, John Russell, trans. and ed. 1968[1856–1865]. *Records of the Colony of Rhode Island and Providence Plantations in New England*. 10 vols. Reissued by AMS Press, 1968. Originally published 1856–1865, Providence, RI: A. C. Greene and Brother. See also Library of American Civilization 20169-20175.

Beauchamp, William M. 1901. Wampum and Shell Articles Used by the New York Indians. *Bulletin of the New York State Museum* 41:8. Albany: State University of New York.

Becker, Marshall Joseph. 1980. Wampum: The Development of an Early American Currency. *Bulletin, Archaeological Society of New Jersey* 36: 1–11.

Becker, Marshall Joseph. 1987. The Moravian Mission in the Forks of the Delaware: Reconstructing the Migration and Settlement Patterns of the Jersey Lenape during the Eighteenth Century through Documents in the Moravian Archives. In *The American Indians and the Moravians* 21/22: 83–172. Special Issue. Unitas Fratrum.

Becker, Marshall Joseph. 1998. Mehoxy of the Cohansey Band of South Jersey Indians: His Life as a Reflection of Symbiotic Relations with Colonists in Southern New Jersey and the Lower Counties of Pennsylvania. *Bulletin of the Archaeological Society of New Jersey* 53: 40–68.

Becker, Marshall Joseph. 1999. Cash Cropping by Lenape Foragers: Preliminary Notes on Native Maize Sales to Swedish Colonists and Cultural Stability during the Early Colonial Period. *Bulletin of the Archaeological Society of New Jersey* 54: 45–68.

Becker, Marshall Joseph. 2001. The Vatican Wampum Belt: An 1831 Example of an "Ecclesiastical-Convert" Belt and a Typology and Chronology of Wampum Belt Use. *Bollettino-Monumenti, Musei e Gallerie Pontificie* 21: 363–411.

Becker, Marshall Joseph. 2002. A Wampum Belt Chronology: Origins to Modern Times. *Northeast Anthropology* 63: 49–70.

Becker, Marshall Joseph. 2003. Calumet Smoke, Wampum Beads and Bird Quills: The Meanings and Materials Used by Natives in Economic Interactions with Europeans in Colonial America. *Bulletin of the Archaeological Society of New Jersey* 58: 19–41.

Becker, Marshall Joseph. 2005a. Matchcoats: Cultural Conservatism and Change. *Ethnohistory* 52(4): 727–87.

Becker, Marshall Joseph. 2005b. Penobscot Wampum Belt Use during the 1722–1727 Conflict in Maine. In *Papers of the Thirty-Sixth Algonquian Conference*, ed. H. C. Wolfart, 25–31. Winnipeg: University of Manitoba.

Becker, Marshall Joseph. 2005c. Wampum Used by Lenape and Swedes in Colonial America: A Tale of Sex and Violence Involving "Decorative" Belts of Wampum. *Newsletter of the Archaeological Society of New Jersey* 208 (March): 1–4.

Becker, Marshall Joseph. 2006a. Anadromous Fish and the Lenape. *Pennsylvania Archaeologist* 76(2): 28–40.

Becker, Marshall Joseph. 2006b. Foragers in Southern New England: Correlating Social Systems, Maize Production, and Wampum Use. *Bulletin of the Archaeological Society of Connecticut* 68: 75–107.

Becker, Marshall Joseph. 2007a. Unique Huron Ornamental Bands: Wampum Cuffs. *Material Culture Review* 66: 59–67.

Becker, Marshall Joseph. 2007b. Wampum Held by the Oneida Indian Nation, Inc., of New York: Research Relating to Wampum Cuffs and Belts. *The*

Bulletin. Journal of the New York State Archaeological Association 123: 1–18.

Becker, Marshall Joseph. 2008a. Small Wampum Bands Used by Native Americans in the Northeast: Functions and Recycling. *Material Culture* 40(1): 1–17.

Becker, Marshall Joseph. 2008b. Wampum in Southern New England: Archaeological and Historical Documentation. Manuscript on file, Becker Archives, West Chester University of Pennsylvania, West Chester, Pennsylvania.

Boissevain, Ethel. 1963. Detribalization and Group Identity: The Narragansett Indian Case. *Transactions of the New York Academy of Sciences*, 2d ser., vol. 25(5): 493–502.

Boissevain, Ethel. 1968. From Pagan to Protestant: A Case History and Comparative Analysis of Conversion in Colonial New England. *The Bulletin: New Jersey Academy of Science* 13(1): 66–70.

Bonner, Jennifer, and Holly Herbster. 2005. *"Documenting" the Past: Massachusetts "Praying Indians" in the Eighteenth Century.* Paper presented at the Annual Meeting of the Eastern States Archaeological Federation, Williamsburg, Virginia, November.

Bradford, William. 1952. *Of Plymouth Plantation 1620–1647.* New ed. by Samuel Eliot Morison. New York: Alfred A. Knopf.

Ceci, Lynn. 1979–1980. Maize Cultivation in Coastal New York: The Archaeological, Agronomical, and Documentary Evidence. *North American Archaeologist* 1(1): 45–74.

Ceci, Lynn. 1990. Native Wampum as a Peripheral Resource in the Seventeenth-Century World-System. In *The Pequots in Southern New England: The Fall and Rise of an American Indian Nation*, ed. Laurence M. Hauptman and James D. Wherry, 48–63. Norman: University of Oklahoma Press.

Chilton, Elizabeth. 1999. Meaningful Materials and Material Meanings: An Introduction. In *Material Meanings: Critical Approaches to the Interpretation of Material Culture*, ed. Elizabeth S. Chilton, 1–6. Salt Lake City: University of Utah Press.

Chilton, Elizabeth. 2002. "Towns They Have None": Diverse Subsistence and Settlement Strategies in Native New England. In *Northeast Subsistence-Settlement Change: A.D. 700–A.D. 1300*, ed. J. Hart and C. Reith, 289–300. *New York State Museum Bulletin* 496. Albany: New York State Museum.

Conkey, Laura E., Ethel Boissevain, and Ives Goddard. 1978. Indians of Southern New England and Long Island: Late Period. In *Handbook of North American Indians: Northeast*, vol. 15, ed. Bruce G. Trigger, 177–89. Washington, DC: Smithsonian Institution Press.

Cook, Ian, and Philip Crang. 1996. The World on a Plate: Culinary Culture, Displacement, and Geographical Knowledge. *Journal of Material Culture* 1(2): 131–53.

DeForest, John William. 1853. *History of the Indians of Connecticut from the Earliest Known Period to 1850.* Library of American Civilization 14673. Hartford, CT: W. J. Hammersley, Library of American Civilization 14673.

Denton, Daniel. 1670. *Brief Description of New-York, formerly Called New-Netherlands.* London: [printed for] John Hancock (Microfilm edition: Early American Books [Wing] 414: 6).

De Rasieres, Isaack. 1628. Letter. In *Three Visitors to Early Plymouth: Letters about the Pilgrim Settlement in New England during Its First Seven Years*, ed. Sydney V. James Jr., 63–80. Plymouth, MA: Plimoth Plantation.

Friedman, Jonathan. 1994. *Cultural Identity and Global Process.* London: Sage.

Gookin, Daniel. 1792[1674]. Historical Collections of the Indians in New England. Boston: Massachusetts Historical Society. Detached from the *Collections of the Massachusetts Historical Society for the Year 1792*, vol. 1, 142–288. Library of American Civilization 40051.

Grumet, Robert S. 1996. Suscaneman and the Matinecock Lands, 1653–1703. In *Northeastern Indian Lives 1632–1816*, ed. R. S. Grumet, 116–39. Amherst: University of Massachusetts Press.

Hamilton, Alexander. 1948 [1712–1756]. *Gentleman's Progress: The Itinerarium of Dr. Alexander Hamilton, 1744*, ed. Dr. Carl Bridenbaugh. Chapel Hill: University of North Carolina Press.

Helms, Mary W. 1988. *Ulysses' Sail: An Ethnographic Odyssey of Power, Knowledge, and Geographical Distance.* Princeton, NJ: Princeton University Press.

Jennings, Francis. 1976. *Invasion of America: Indians, Colonialism, and the Cant of Conquest.* New York: Norton.

Johnson, Amandus. 1930. *The Instruction for Johan Printz.* Translated and edited by A. Johnson. Philadelphia, PA: The Swedish Colonial Society.

Johnson, Eric S. 1996. Uncas and the Politics of Contact. In *Northeastern Indian Lives 1632–1816*, ed. R. S. Grumet, 29–47. Amherst: University of Massachusetts Press.

Kent, Donald. 1979. Early American Indian Documents: Treaties and Laws, 1607–1789. In *Pennsylvania and Delaware Treaties 1629–1737, vol. 1*, series ed. Alden Vaughan. Washington, DC: University Publications of America.

Kopytoff, Igor. 1986. The Cultural Biography of Things: Commoditization as Process. In *The Social Life of Things: Commodities in Cultural Perspective*, ed. Arjun Appadurai, 64–91. Cambridge: Cambridge University Press.

Lechford, Thomas. 1642. "Concerning the Indians, or Nations." In *Plain Dealing, or, Nevvs from New-England*, 49–53. London: American Culture Series, reel 5, no. 34.

Lesniak, Matthew. 2003. New Evidence of Wampum Use and Production from Albany, New York. In *People, Places and Material Things: Historical Archaeology of Albany, New York*, ed. Charles L. Fisher, 129–34. Albany: New York State Museum, Bulletin 499.

Little, Elizabeth A., and Margaret J. Schoeninger. 1995. The Late Woodland Diet on Nantucket Island and the Problem of Maize in Coastal New England. *American Antiquity* 60(2): 351–68.

Little, Elizabeth A., and Marie Sussek. 1981. Index to Mary Starbuck's Account Book with the Indians [1683–1766, in the Peter Foulger Museum,

Nantucket]. *Nantucket Algonquian Studies* 5. Nantucket, MA: Nantucket Historical Association.

Marten, Catherine. 1970. The Wampanogs in the Seventeenth Century: An Ethnohistorical Study. *Occasional Papers in Old Colony Studies* 2. Fall River, MA: R. E. Smith, for the Plimouth Plantation Inc.

McBride, Kevin A. 1993a. "Ancient and Crazie": Pequot Lifeways during the Historic Period. In *Algonkians of New England: Past and Present* (The Dublin Seminar for New England Folklife Annual Proceedings [for] 1991), ed. Peter Benes, 63–75. Boston, MA: Boston University.

McBride, Kevin A. 1993b. Source and Mother of the Fur Trade: Native-Dutch Relations in Eastern New Netherland. In *Enduring Traditions: The Native Peoples of New England*, ed. Laurie Weinstein, 31–51. Westport, CT: Greenwood Press.

McBride, Kevin A. 2005. *Pequot Adaptations to European Techniques.* Paper presented at the Annual Meeting of the Eastern States Archaeological Federation, Williamsburg, Virginia.

Morton, Thomas, of Clifford's Inn (1564–1659). 1637. Book I: Natives. In *New English Canaan, or New Canaan*, 11–58. London: Printed for Charles Greene and sold in Pauls Church-yard, 2d ed., from the first of 1627). Microform, Early English Books, STC I, unit 51, reel 1754, no. 12 (item 18203).

Nassaney, Michael S. 2000. Archaeology and Oral Tradition in Tandem: Interpreting Native American Ritual, Ideology, and Gender Relations in Contact-Period Southeastern New England. In *Interpretations of Native North American Life: Material Contributions to Ethnohistory*, ed. Eric S. Johnson and Michael S. Nassaney, 412–31. Gainesville: University Press of Florida.

Nelson, William. 1894. *The Indians of New Jersey: Their Origin and Development.* Paterson, NJ: The Press Printing and Publishing.

O'Callaghan, Edmund Bailey, compiler and ed. 1856. Documents Relative to the Colonial History of the State of New-York, vol. 1, *Holland Documents.* Albany, NY: Weed, Parsons and Company.

O'Callaghan, Edmund Bailey. 1897. Record of New Amsterdam from 1653–1674 anno Domini. 7 vols. Edited by Berthold Fernow. New York: Knickerbocker Press.

Pulsifer, David, ed. 1968[1859]. *Records of the Colony of New Plymouth in New England: Acts of the Commissioner of the United Colonies of New England*, vol. 2: 1653–1679. New York: AMS Press.

Richter, Daniel K. 2001. *Facing East from Indian Country: A Native History of Early America.* Cambridge, MA: Harvard University Press.

Romero, R. Todd. 2006. "Ranging Foresters" and "Women-Like Men": Physical Accomplishments, Spiritual Power, and Indian Masculinity in Early Seventeenth Century New England. *Ethnohistory* 53(2): 281–329.

Salisbury, Neal. 1982. *Manitou and Providence: Indians, Europeans, and the Making of New England 1500–1643.* New York: Oxford University Press.

Salwen, Bert. 1978. Indians of Southern New England and Long Island: Early Period. In *Northeast: Handbook of North American Indians,* vol. 15, ed. Bruce G. Trigger, 160–76. Washington, DC: Smithsonian Institution.

Schurtleff, Nathaniel B., ed. 1968[1855]. *Records of the Colony of New Plymouth in New England. Court Orders.* 11 vols. Vol. 1: 1633–1640; Vol. 3: 1651–1661. New York: AMS Press, reprint. Originally published in 1855, Boston, MA: William White.

Silliman, Stephen W. 2005. Culture Contact or Colonialism? Challenges in the Archaeology of Native North America. *American Antiquity* 70(1): 55–74.

Strong, John A. 1996. Wyandanch: Sachem of the Montauks. In *Northeastern Indian Lives 1632–1816*, ed. R. S. Grumet, 48–73. Amherst: University of Massachusetts Press.

Sylvester, Herbert Milton. 1910. *Indian Wars of New England.* 3 vols. Boston, MA: W. B. Clark.

Turgeon, Laurier. 2004. Beads, Bodices, and Regimes of Value: From France to North America, c. 1500–c. 1650. In *The Archaeology of Contact in Settler Societies*, ed. Tim Murray, 19–47. Cambridge: Cambridge University Press.

Vaughan, Alden. 1979. *New England Frontier: Puritans and Indians, 1620–1675.* 2d ed., 1965. New York: Norton.

Washburn, W. W. 1978. Seventeenth-Century Indian Wars. In *Northeast: Handbook of North American Indians*, vol. 15, ed. Bruce G. Trigger, 89–101. Washington, DC: Smithsonian Institution.

Williams, Roger. 1971[1643]. *A Key to the Language of America*. London: Menton Scholar Press. Originally published in 1643, London: Gregory Dexter.

Young, Alexander, collector. 1970[1846]. *Chronicles of the First Planters of the Colony of Massachusetts Bay, from 1623 to 1636.* Boston, MA: Da Capo Press, reprint. Originally published 1846, Boston, MA: Charles C. Little and James Brown.

8

The Origin and Spread of Maize (*Zea Mays*) in New England

Elizabeth S. Chilton

The adoption and practice of maize horticulture by Native Americans in Precontact New England are both poorly understood and hotly debated. While some archaeologists argue that the adoption of maize had a major transformative effect on Native groups, the extant archaeological evidence supports a model of mobile farming and the continuation of hunting and gathering by Native peoples. At the source of the maize debate is the lack of an accurate chronology for the adoption of maize. While associated radiocarbon dates from wood charcoal associated with maize have led archaeologists to believe that maize was adopted at the beginning of the Late Woodland period (A.D. 1000–1600), the results of accelerator mass spectrometer radiocarbon dates directly on maize indicate that it became prevalent only after A.D. 1250. These results are consistent with other studies that have demonstrated the problem with relying on wood charcoal for radiocarbon dates, since wood charcoal (and the wood it came from) may be considerably older than the archaeological deposit in which it is found. Sorting out the maize chronology in New England is important for understanding the relationship between the adoption of maize horticulture and the origins of social complexity in the region and beyond.

I examine in this chapter when and in what manner maize (*Zea mays*) was introduced to New England's Native peoples and what effects the production of maize had on the region's populations. Betty Little, like many of us working in the region, was intrigued by the challenge of determining when maize first arrived in New England. The poor preservation of maize kernels in the archaeological record presents a special challenge. Little applied her knowledge of archaeological science to the problem, focusing primarily on stable isotope analysis (Medaglia et al. 1990; Little and Schoeninger 1995) and the radiocarbon dating of maize samples (Little 1994, 1997, 1999, 2002). The latter has proven to be particularly complex, as I discuss later.

The timing of the adoption of maize by Native peoples is more than simply academic curiosity: it has important implications for understanding the relationship among sedentism, farming, and social complexity in the region and beyond. New England archaeologists have both pondered and debated the role of maize horticulture in the region. In this chapter I review the current data and possible interpretations. I conclude with the implications of the maize chronology for understanding the adoption of farming more broadly.

The Origins of *Zea Mays*

Maize was first domesticated in Mesoamerica. The earliest evidence of domesticated maize was recovered in the Tehuacan Valley in Mexico and dates to about 5,500 years ago (calibrated; Long et al. 1989). The process of domestication likely took thousands of years, so this early maize represents the end result of a long process of domestication (Smith 1998). The archaeological record in Mesoamerica shows a long period of increasing sedentism in the region prior to the domestication of maize, so it is likely that the origin of maize represents a mutual process of domestication, so to speak, by and of humans and plants. The wild precursor or progenitor of maize was teosinte, which is a type of wild grass (for a discussion of this process, see Piperno and Pearsall 1993). Grass seeds are not usually considered choice foods by hunter-gatherers; this suggests that at the time there was a need for the production of surplus food, at least during certain seasons.

Over time, maize made its way to North and South America. This was a complicated and an uneven process. Not all societies in the Americas adopted maize farming: the decision to adopt maize, and the process that unfolded, was different for each group, and was largely dependent on preexisting subsistence and mobility, ecological setting, and historical factors. We should not think of the adoption of maize as an obvious or easy choice, since it involves a great deal of labor, risk, and change to both seasonal scheduling and associated ideology.

As maize spread out from its origin point in Mesoamerica, some groups and individuals experimented with its biology in order to create varieties that would grow in new and different climates and ecological settings. For example, in the American Southwest, the earliest maize dates to about 3,600 years ago and was likely from the Chapalote series of twelve-to-fourteen-rowed popcorns (Upham et al. 1987). Maiz de Ocho (eight-rowed maize) first appeared in the Southwest approximately 3,200 years ago (Upham et al. 1987). Maiz de Ocho represents a hybrid between earlier twelve-to-fourteen-rowed maize and teosinte, and it may have originated in the Southwest (Upham et al. 1987). It is this eight-rowed maize that spread across eastern North America approximately 900 years ago (Upham et al. 1987).

Maize was certainly not the first domesticated plant in eastern North America, since there is clear evidence for the domestication of indigenous (or local) plants in eastern North America approximately 4,000 years ago. These include goosefoot (*chenopodium*), sumpweed or knotweed (*Iva annua*), and sunflower (*helianthus*) (Smith 1992). All of these would have been exploited for their starchy, oily seeds, and all of them would have required intensive cooking and preparation to make them both palatable and digestible, which is why we see the appearance of cooking pots (stone and ceramic) coincident with this subsistence shift (Braun 1983). These are all plants—weeds, really—that were and continue to be collected by hunter-gatherers. However, in some parts of eastern North America (e.g., the Midwest and Southeast), these plants were so intensively collected and propagated so as to become domesticated (see Smith 1992). The archaeobotanical evidence for domestication includes such things as increased seed size and a thinner seed coat (to facilitate processing). Like the domestication of maize, the domestication of these indigenous cultigens was clearly the end result of a long process of increasing sedentism, intensive collection, and domestication. Thus the process likely started by about 6000 B.P., during the Late Archaic period.

The degree to which these indigenous weedy plants were domesticated in New England is not known. There is only one site that has produced a *chenopodium* seed that *may* represent a domesticated variety (George and Dewar 1999). It is clear that we need more and better use of flotation techniques on Late Archaic and Early Woodland sites—and careful archaeobotanical analyses—in order to determine whether New England peoples domesticated these plants. There is, however, circumstantial evidence for intensive collection and, perhaps, domestication. For example, the use of soapstone bowls beginning around 3500 B.P., followed by the appearance of the region's first ceramics, represents a major change in cooking technology and, thus, subsistence. If we think of "pots as tools" (Braun 1983), then pottery clearly represented a revolution in cooking technology. Also, the appearance of what appear to be food storage pits during the Late Archaic period may provide evidence of the production of food surplus for the first time in the region's history (McBride 1978; McBride and Dewar 1987; Pagoulatos 1988). Since it is clear from the number of Late Archaic archaeological sites in New England that the population was higher during this period than ever before (Keegan and Noble 1999), it makes sense that Native peoples sought alternative foods and techniques of exploitation as a means to support the growing population. These subsistence changes are coincident with changes in forest composition, which included a decline in hemlock and a subsequent increase in nut-bearing trees (Foster 1999). Here again there is a clear relationship among sedentism, subsistence, and environmental change that has yet to be fully explored.

The Arrival of Maize in New England

One might use several techniques to determine the appearance of maize horticulture in a particular region. The first, and most common, is to obtain radiocarbon dates on the maize kernels themselves or wood charcoal that is found in association with maize (discussed later). Other methods of determining the date of the arrival of maize include the following: (1) stable isotope analyses of human bone (e.g., Medaglia, Little, and Schoeninger 1990; Little and Schoeninger 1995); (2) analysis of pottery residue (Hart et al. 2003; Reber 2001; Schulenberg 2003); (3) pollen analysis or other paleoecological analyses of landscape change (McAndrews 1988; McLauchlan 2003); and (4) artifactual and/or settlement pattern evidence for subsistence changes (although this cannot be used in the absence of other techniques). Please note that in the remainder of this chapter I refer only to calibrated radiocarbon dates, that is, dates that have been converted from radiocarbon years to calendar years (for more discussion of this in a regional context, see Little 1997, 2002).

The earliest evidence for maize in eastern North America comes from the Holding site, Illinois, and dates to about 2000 B.P. (Riley et al. 1994). In the lower Great Lakes, radiocarbon dating of maize remains, and stable isotopes analyses indicate the consumption of maize by about A.D. 500 (Crawford et al. 1997). In New York, phytolith evidence in pottery residue supports the presence of maize in the region by the early seventh century A.D. (Hart et al. 2003), as do stable isotope analyses of human bone collagen (Vogel and Van Der Merwe 1977). Stable isotope analyses of bone collagen from sites in southern Ontario and New York indicate that maize was a dietary staple in these regions by A.D. 1000 (Katzenberg et al. 1995; Schwarcz et al. 1985).

So what is the evidence for New England? While associated wood charcoal dates indicate that maize horticulture was practiced in New England by A.D. 1000, associated wood charcoal dates tend to be older than direct dates on cultigens (see Figure 8.1; see Table 8.1). The difference between a "direct date" and an "associated date" is that a direct date is a radiocarbon age determination of the maize kernel or other cultigen itself. An associated date (usually wood charcoal or shell) is not as reliable, since the exact association between the wood/shell and the maize cannot be determined (e.g., see a discussion of the "old wood effect" by Schiffer [1986]). On the basis of several direct radiocarbon dates for maize, it appears that maize horticulture may not have become prevalent in the region until about A.D. 1250 (see Tables 8.1–8.3).

Almost all of the sites with direct dates have been dated using accelerator mass spectrometry (AMS) (see Table 8.1), which requires

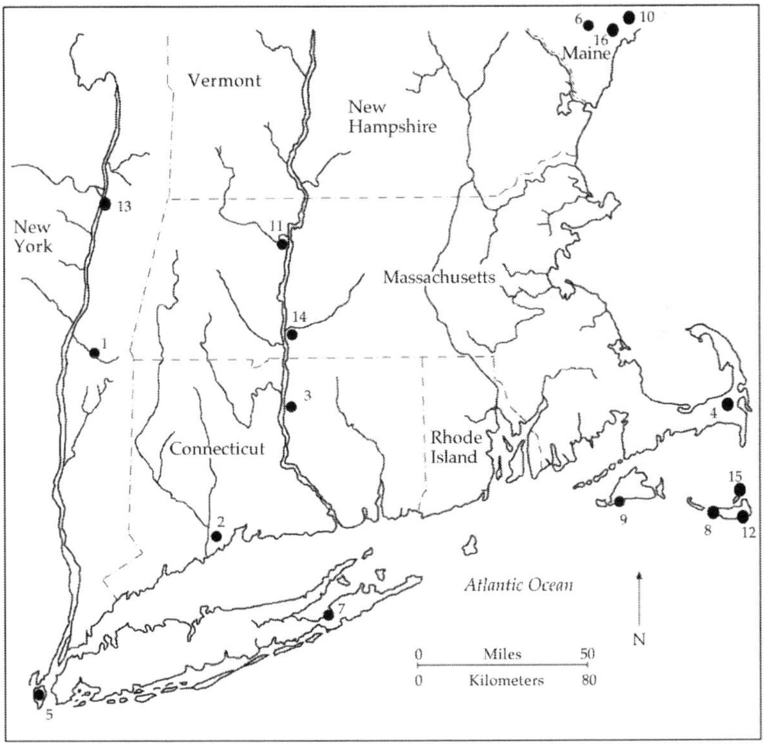

Figure 8.1. Location of Sites with Direct Dates on Maize (see Table 8.1 for a key to sites)

Table 8.1. Sites with direct radiocarbon dates on pre-Contact and early Contact period maize, prior to Pilot Project (see Figure 1 for site locations).

#	Site	Lab #	^{14}C yrs B.P.	95.4 % (2s) Calibrated Age (A.D.) and Probability (*p*)	Citation
1	211-1-1	B84970	850±60	1039–1142 (*p*=0.335, 1150–1277 (*p*=0.665)	Cassedy and Webb (1999)
	211-1-1	B84969	810±50	1058–1087 (*p*=0.0396), 1121–1138 (*p*=0.026), 1156–1291 (*p*=0.936)	Cassedy and Webb (1999)
	211-1-1	B84971	390±50	1435–1533 (*p*=0.590), 1541–1636 (*p*=0.410	Cassedy and Webb (1999)
2	294A-25-2	B84973	690±60	1224–1231 (*p*=0.014), 1238–1334 (*p*=0.587), 1336–1401 (*p*=0.399)	Cassedy and Webb (1999)
	294A-25-2	B84972	310±60	1446–1669 (*p*=0.979), 1781–1796 (*p*=0.021)	Cassedy and Webb (1999)
3	Burnham Shepard	B27676[1]	620±70	1279–1428 (*p*=1.00)	Bendremer and Dewar (1994)
4	19BN811	GX19319	620±59	1284–1415 (*p*=1.000)	Little (1994)
5	Bowman's Brook	B15769[1]	610±60	1287–1420 (*p*=1.000)	Ceci (1990)
6	Little Ossipee North	B102060	570±40	1302–1370 (*p*=0.595), 1380–1428 (*p*=0.405)	Asch Sidell (1999)
7	Sebonac	B15788	555±85	1278–1491 (*p*=0.997), 1603–1608 (*p*=0.003)	Ceci (1990)

8	Ramp Pasture-1, 19NT30	GX22044	500±60	1301–1371 (p=0.216), 1379–1494 (p=0.767), 1502–1507 (p=0.004), 1601–1613 (p=0.012)	Little (2002)
9	Lucy Vincent Beach	GX26424	500±40	1327–1346 (p=0.075), 1393–1468 (p=0.925)	Chilton and Doucette (2002)
10	Permaquid	B141592	440±40	1409–1517 (p=0.946), 1597–1619 (p=0.054)	Spiess and Cranmer (2001)
11	Pine Hill	GX21994	400±60	1426–1637 (p=1.000)	Chilton et al. (2000)
12	19NT50, Polpis	B123998	400±30	1436–1521 (p=0.824), 1580–1626 (p=0.176)	D. Cox *p*.c. in Little (2002)
13	Goldkrest	GX22651	380±50	1439–1533 (p=0.546), 1539–1636 (p=0.454)	Little (1999)
14	Indian Crossing	GX27629	310±40	1482–1654 (p=1.000)	Chilton (2002)
15	19NT166	B123997	290±40	1485–1664 (p=0.995), 1784–1787 (p=0.005)	D. Cox *p*.c. in Little (2002)
16	Norridgewock	B104792	130±40	1673–1778 (p=0.405), 1800–1942 (p=0.577), 1945–1951 (p=0.018)	Petersen and Cowie (2002)

[1]conventional radiocarbon method; not AMS

Note: All dates are d[13]C corrected. Calibration by CALIB 4.4 (Stuiver and Reimer 1993) using calibration dataset by Stuiver et al. (1998). Method B was used for calibration, since the probability ranges are now accepted as the best representation of the calibrated ages ((Bowman 1990); Reimer, personal communication 2003)

Table 8.2. Examples of New England sites where there is a lack of match between direct maize dates and associated word charcoal dates.

Site/Location	Maize*	Associated Wood Charcoal*
211-1-1, NY (Cassedy and Webb 1999)	390±50	1100±70
Lucy Vincent Beach, Martha's Vineyard, MA (Chilton and Doucette 2002)	500±40	1100±80
Ram Pasture, Nantucket, MA (Little 2002)	500±60	1010±100
Little Ossipee North, ME (Asch Sidell 1999)	600±40	1010±60
Bowman's Brook, Long Island, NY (Ceci 1990)	610±60	920±70

*Uncalibrated age in radiocarbon years before present (BP), $d^{13}C$-corrected.

significantly less carbon than standard radiocarbon dating, thus making possible the dating of a single maize kernel (minimum of 2 mg, as opposed to 2 g for conventional radiocarbon dating). Because it costs more than conventional radiocarbon dating, and because archaeologists resist destroying cultigen samples for fear of losing important data for future researchers, AMS is not a common method of dating cultigens. Consequently, most archaeologists prefer to date cultigens using associated wood charcoal, even though associated wood charcoal dates have been shown to be unreliable for dating. Using AMS, John Hart and Margaret Scarry (Hart and Scarry 1999) have demonstrated that beans—another Mesoamerican domesticate—did not arrive in the Northeast until approximately cal A.D. 1300, 200–300 years more recent than previously reported, associated wood charcoal dates. Similarly, Little (2002) reports that in several other cases radiocarbon dates for maize are often 200–300 years younger than associated wood or shell dates (see Table 8.2).

Thus the direct dating of maize indicates that the archaeological visibility of maize increases significantly during the period A.D. 1300–1600, whereas the earliest dates for wood charcoal associated with

Table 8.3. Samples analyzed and dated as part of this study

State	Site	Lab #	Sample size/Type	^{14}C yrs B.P.	95.4% (2s) Cal Age (A.D.)	Probability	Citation
CT	6HT116	Not dated	unidentifiable				Jordan, personal communication in Bendremer and Dewar (1994)
CT	Burnham-Shepard	GX30218	9 kernals	280±30	1493–1501 1515–1599 1616–1665 1784–1790	0.011 0.556 0.423 0.009	Bendremer and Dewar (1994)
CT	Kasheta	GX30219	1 kernal frag	360±30	1452–1530 1546–1635	0.471 0.529	Bendremer and Dewar (1994)
CT	Tubbs	Not dated	Hickory nut fragments				Russell (1947)
NH	Campbell	Not dated	unidentifiable				Bunker (1988)
NH	Hunter	GX30220	Cob fragments and 60 kernals	370±30	1445–1527 1552–1632	0.551 0.449	Sargent (n.d.)

(continued on next page)

Table 8.3. *(Continued)*

State	Site	Lab #	Sample size/Type	^{14}C yrs B.P.	95.4% (2s) Cal Age (A.D.)	Probability	Citation
NH	Ingalls	GX30221	6 kernals	680±40	1269–1329 1343–1395	0.547 0.453	Boisvert (1994)
		GX30222	2 kernals	740±30	1223–1232 1237–1298	0.032 0.968	
		GX30223	1 kernal	960±30	1019–1159	1.000	
		GX30224	4 kernals	580±30	1303–1369 1382–1416	0.667 0.333	
		GX30225	1 kernal	600±30	1300–1372 1378–1406	0.749 0.251	
		GX30226	4 bean halves	290±30	1493–1504 1508–1600 1615–1660	0.023 0.643 0.334	
		Not dated	Several possible beans				
NY	Selden Island	Not dated	Not maize				McBride (1984)

Note: All dates as AMS dates and are d^{13}C corrected. Calibration by CALIB 4.4 (Stuiver and Reimer 1993) using calibration dataset by Stuiver et al (1998). Method B was used for calibration, since the probability ranges are now accepted as the best representation of the calibrated ages (Bowman 1990: 46–49; Reimer, personal communication 2003) maize are in the range of A.D. 1000. A possible explanation for the lack of agreement between direct and associated dates is that the wood charcoal found in association with cultigens may have been from "old wood" or an inner ring of a tree, which produces an older radiocarbon date, or, that post-depositional bioturbation or stratigraphic mixing is not detectable by the excavators. Regardless of the interpretation of this phenomenon, we now know that "direct AMS dating is the only technique available to firmly establish the age of potentially early maize" (Hart and Means 2002). The direct dating of cultigens using AMS is critical for establishing an accurate chronology for the adoption and spread of maize horticulture in the region and, more broadly, in the Americas (Fritz 1994, 1990; Long et al. 1989).

It is important to note that the earliest radiocarbon date for archaeological maize in a region does not necessarily indicate when maize was first introduced (Hart 1999). Maize may have been grown in New England long before we have evidence for it. The recovery of maize depends on the use of proper recovery techniques (i.e., flotation), the intensity of sampling, the intensity of maize use at the site, and whether or not it was burned before it entered the archaeological record (Hart 1999; Hart and Means 2002). Thus radiocarbon dates on maize give archaeologists a latest possible date for maize adoption and need to be interpreted within the context of other subsistence and settlement data.

Maize Dating Project

As an example of what can be gleaned from careful archaeobotanical analysis and AMS dating, in this section I discuss a research project that I undertook a few years ago to try to contribute to our understanding of the maize chronology. I have published on this project elsewhere (Chilton 2005), so I provide only a summary here. I deeply regret that Betty Little did not live to see the results of this research, although we discussed it several times. The purpose of the project was to (1) take an inventory of existing collections of maize in New England, (2) to have a sample of these collections identified/verified by an archaeobotanist, and (3) to obtain AMS dates on selected samples. This was similar to a project undertaken by Little and published in 2002, except that while her work was primarily focused on coastal New England, my project concentrated on the interior.

With the aid of a faculty research grant from the University of Massachusetts Amherst, and the assistance of Niels Rinehart, a graduate student research assistant, I was able to obtain fourteen botanical samples from eight archaeological sites that were reported to have maize (see Table 8.3). Dr. Lucinda McWeeney analyzed these samples and determined that eight of them included maize and one included beans. Samples from Campbell (Bunker 1988), 6HT116 (Jordan, personal communication, in Bendremer and Dewar 1994), and Selden Island (McBride 1984) were not identified as maize, indicating that the original identifications were incorrect. Some of the samples from the Ingalls site (Boisvert 1994), which were all thought by the excavators to be maize, were identified as beans.

Nine AMS dates were obtained for samples positively identified as maize or beans. These dates produced some interesting results. First, similar to what was reported by Betty Little (2002), most of the dates fell within the period A.D. 1300–1600 (see Table 8.3; see Figure 8.2). This date range supports the hypothesis that maize prevalence increased after A.D. 1250 (Little 2002). Second, the Ingalls site in New Hampshire produced a very early date for maize: cal A.D. 1019–1159 (p = 1.0, 2 sigma calibration by CALIB 4.4 [71] using calibration data set by Stuiver et al. 1998). This date represents the earliest date on maize east of New York State. The early presence of maize in New Hampshire leaves open the possibility that maize horticulture was introduced by people and communication from the north via the St. Lawrence and Connecticut rivers, rather than the more common view that maize spread from west to east (e.g., Bendremer and Dewar 1994). I would not wish to push too hard on this suggestion of a northern route, given that we have only one early date from New Hampshire. Clearly, more dates are needed to clarify the direction of entry of maize into New England, although the site location is consistent with Little's (2002) observations about the riverine and coastal position of the earliest maize sites. Third, and finally, the AMS date on maize obtained for the Burnham-Shepard site is 400 radiocarbon years younger than a previous direct date reported by Bendremer and Dewar (1994; also see Tables 8.2 and 8.3). Thus even when a direct date is obtained for maize from an archaeological site, it cannot be assumed that this date reflects the age of all maize samples from the site.

The results of this project demonstrate three important considerations for maize research: (1) Not all maize reported in the literature is, in fact, maize, since not all reported maize samples have been analyzed by a professional archaeobotanist; (2) Not all occurrences of maize are in the published literature; and (3) The earliest appearance of maize across New England may not, in fact, demonstrate a clear west-to-east trend.

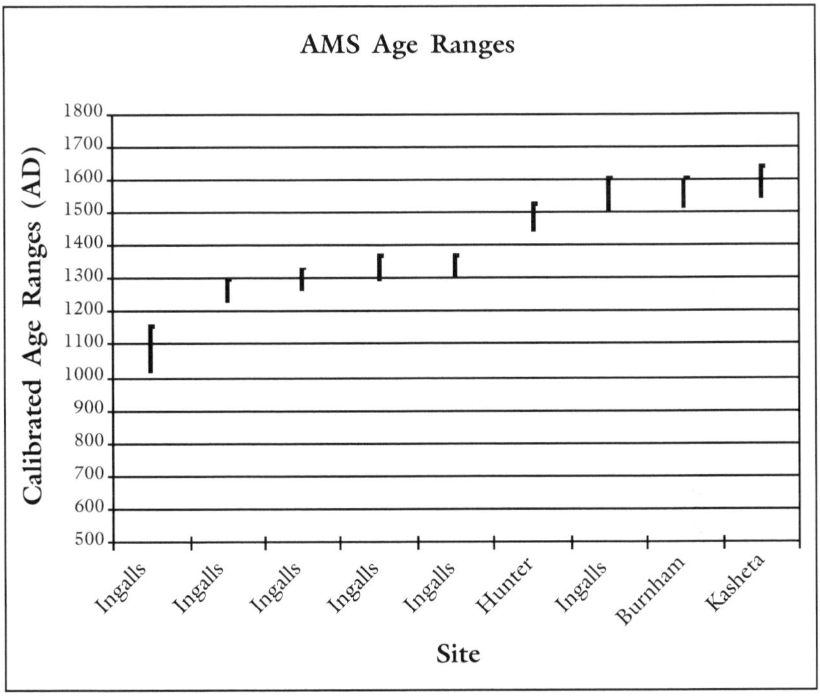

Figure 8.2. AMS Age Ranges for Cultigen Samples in the Present Study

The Maize Debate: Putting the Dates into Context

For quite some time, New England archaeologists have bemoaned the invisibility of Late Woodland period villages (Luedtke 1988; Thorbahn 1988). What does it mean that we now have a handful of dates for maize in the vicinity of A.D. 1000 and several more for circa 1300 A.D.? What does it mean to have 100 (half a cob) or even 1,000 kernels (about five cobs) of maize on an archaeological site?

I have outlined the so-called "maize debate" in detail elsewhere (Chilton 1999, 2002, 2005). Suffice it to say that a few regional archaeologists believe(d) that the adoption of maize was a non-event (McBride and Dewar 1987), while others believe that it was the major transformative event in Precontact Native history (Bendremer 1999; Petersen and Cowie 2002). Still others, myself included, believe that while maize adoption was clearly an important event in Native history, at present there is no evidence for sedentary, year-round farming villages in New England (Dincauze 1990). Likewise, in my opinion, there is no evidence for intensive maize horticulture until after European colonization.

At the heart of the maize debate is a general disagreement over how to interpret the evidence at hand. Certainly most of us agree that we need more data on settlement patterns, we need more and more careful flotation, and we need more funds for archaeobotanical analysis and radiocarbon dating. Despite what we need for the future, it is important to assess the data we currently have at hand.

The most important bodies of evidence that we have for interpreting degrees of sedentism and overall economy are settlement patterns, that is, the patterning of structures and features within an archaeological site and the distribution of sites across the landscape in time and space. Settlement pattern data are not plentiful for New England. This is in part due to historic disturbance, amateur digging, the scarcity of regional surveys, and geomorphological processes (Chilton 1999). Hasenstab (1999) underscores this last point, arguing that village sites are simply "hard to find" in New England because of their hypothesized location on stratified alluvial floodplains. There is little evidence for structures, much less villages, in Late Woodland New England. While it is true that we simply may not have yet found such evidence, we must proceed *on the basis of the data we now have on hand.* We may change our interpretations later in light of new data, and this is how any science—even social science—must proceed.

So what is the current evidence for settlement patterns during the Late Woodland period? For the New England coast, as Ceci (1979–1980) and Luedtke (1988) suggested, there is no evidence for settled village life prior to European contact. There *is* evidence for year-round or nearly year-round habitation in some protected harbors on the coast beginning in the Late Archaic period (Bernstein et al. 1997; Bernstein 1993, 1999; Gwynne 1982), but this coastal sedentism is not a process that appears to be associated with the adoption of horticulture. Instead, it is likely that the year-round availability of both marine and terrestrial resources in these areas was the impetus for increasing sedentism. This sedentism may have paved the way for the adoption of horticulture (maize, as well as indigenous plants), rather than the other way around. As Little and Schoeninger (1995, 364) put it: "The modest recoveries of maize and lack of evidence for land clearing [on the coast] . . . argue that maize was probably grown in small gardens near houses with southern exposures."

For the New England interior, identifying postmolds on any archaeological site is rare; postmolds tend to be small and relatively shallow and are often disturbed by the typically deep and extensive

New England plow zone. Rarely do these postmolds form a pattern that can be used to identify structure size or shape. For the most part, postmold patterns seem to indicate short-term wigwam-type structures, and the overlapping nature of these structures and features, as well as a general lack of well-defined middens, indicates repeated seasonal use of site locations over time (Chilton et al. 2000). There is evidence for fairly large—though not necessarily year-round—Late Woodland sites in the lower Connecticut Valley, but these lack published settlement pattern data, making them difficult to evaluate (Lavin 1988). Occasionally there is evidence for large structures or "longhouses" in New England, but these are rare occurrences, and they seem to represent multiseasonal and potentially multicomponent sites (e.g., the Goldkrest site in New York [Largy et al. 1999] and the Tracy Farm site in Maine [Cowie 2000]).

Implications of a Chronology for Maize Horticulture in New England

Our understanding of the lifeways and social choices of Precontact Native people in the region depends on an accurate chronology for the adoption of maize. For example, if maize horticulture was adopted by A.D. 1000 or earlier, then why is there no evidence for sedentism and intensive horticulture until after European contact? Alternatively, if maize became prevalent only after A.D. 1300, then we must revise models that suggest that the adoption of maize was the source of major subsistence and settlement changes at the start of the Late Woodland period, circa A.D. 1000 (e.g., Petersen and Cowie 2002). Little (2002) argued that the increased use of old shell or alluvial limestone for fertilizer increased both the yield and the preservation of maize and beans post A.D. 1250 (and, therefore, its archaeological visibility). While a consideration of soil chemistry with respect to both growing conditions and preservation is both brilliant and essential, I do not think this explanation can completely account for such a consistent sweep of AMS dates during the period A.D. 1300–1500 across such diverse environmental zones. Little and I discussed this a few times, and it was clearly a problem she wanted to continue to pursue. I find it likely that maize became more prevalent in New England by A.D. 1300 because of cultural choices and/or possibly as a result of the Medieval Warm period, which may have improved the environmental conditions for the growing of maize. Ultimately, as (Demeritt 1991) put it, the adoption of agriculture "involve[d] cultural and aesthetic considerations as well as material ones." Thus archaeologists need to turn to cultural models to understand subsistence choices, particularly with respect to the adoption of horticulture.

The timing and intensity of maize horticulture in Precontact New England have important implications beyond the region. According to Bragdon (1996), the "theoretical issues that have emerged in recent analyses of southern New England native society [make] this region one of intense interest, particularly to those concerned with the origins of, and relations between, agriculture, sedentism, and social inequality, and their ideological and cosmological correlates." It is clear that we cannot make assumptions about what happened in New England after the adoption of maize on the basis of what happened in other times and places (e.g., the Iroquois). Likewise, we cannot base our assumptions about the importance of maize on the number of kernels found on archaeological sites (Chilton 1999). Instead, we need (1) an accurate and detailed chronology for the adoption of maize and other tropical cultigens, (2) an accurate chronology for other major subsistence changes over the last 2,000 to 3,000 years, (3) an understanding of important environment changes that may have affected (or were the cause of) subsistence choices during the Late Woodland period, and (4) a clear understanding of settlement and social changes (e.g., changes in level of sedentism, social boundaries, movement of peoples, etc.).

Based on the evidence we have now, Precontact New England provides us with an important example of a society that is at once complex but not necessarily socially stratified, committed to horticulture but not sedentary. Thus regional archaeologists have much to contribute to worldwide discussions on the causes and effects of farming.

Betty Little was one of the very few archaeologists who have been able to bring New England's maize question to a national audience. She was one of a small number of regional archaeologists to be published in *American Antiquity*—and she worked very hard to get her work published there. She was determined to put New England on the national and international map in discussions of the origins of agriculture. Her energy, excitement, and hard work challenged us all to take up the cause.

Acknowledgments

This research was supported by a Faculty Research Grant from the University of Massachusetts in 2002–2003. Niels Rinehart, a graduate student at the University of Massachusetts Amherst, was the research assistant for the duration of this project. Nick Bellantoni (State Archaeologist of Connecticut) and Dick Boisvert (State Archaeologist of New Hampshire) were exceptionally generous with their time and assistance.

A special thank-you goes to Michael O. Sugerman for his editorial and computer assistance. And, of course, I am forever grateful to Betty for inspiration.

Works Cited

Asch Sidell, Nancy. 1999. Prehistoric Plant Use in Maize: Paleoindian to Contact Period. In *Current Northeast Paleoethnobotany*, ed. J. P. Hart, 191–223. Albany: *New York State Museum Bulletin* 494.

Bendremer, Jeffrey C. 1999. Changing Strategies in the Pre- and Post-Contact Subsistence Systems of Southern New England: Archaeological and Ethnohistorical Evidence. In *Current Northeast Paleoethnobotany*, ed. J. P. Hart, 133–56. Albany: *New York State Museum Bulletin* 494.

Bendremer, Jeffrey C., and Robert E. Dewar. 1994. The Advent of Maize Horticulture in New England. In *Corn and Culture in the Prehistoric New World*, ed. S. Johannessen and C. Hastorf, 369–93. Boulder, CO: Westview Press.

Bernstein, D. J., M. J. Lenardi, D. Merwin, and S. Zipp. 1997. *Archaeological Investigation on the Solomon Property, Mount Sinai, Town of Brookhaven, Suffolk County, New York*. Institute for Long Island Archaeology, Department of Anthropology, State University of New York, Stony Brook.

Bernstein, David J. 1993. *Prehistoric Subsistence on the Southern New England Coast*. San Diego, CA: Academic Press.

Bernstein, David J. 1999. Prehistoric Use of Plant Foods on Long Island and Block Island Sounds. In *Current Northeast Paleoethnobotany*, ed. J. P. Hart, 101–20. Albany: *New York State Museum Bulletin* 494.

Boisvert, Richard A. 1994. 1994 Scrap Field School, Ingalls Site, North Havehill. *New Hampshire Archaeological Society Newsletter* 10(2): 5–6.

Bowman, S. 1990. *Radiocarbon Dating*. London: British Museum Press.

Bragdon, Kathleen J. 1996. *Native Peoples of Southern New England*. Norman: University of Oklahoma Press.

Braun, David. 1983. Pots as Tools. In *Archaeological Hammers and Theories*, ed. J. A. Moore and A. S. Keene, 107–34. New York: Academic Press.

Bunker, Victoria. 1988. Two Woodland Components in Litchfield, New Hampshire. *The New Hampshire Archaeologist* 29(1): 1–48.

Cassedy, Daniel, and Paul Webb. 1999. New Data on the Chronology of Maize Horticulture in Eastern New York and Southern New England. In *Current Northeast Paleoethnobotany*, ed. J. P. Hart, 85–99. Albany: *New York State Museum Bulletin* 494.

Ceci, Lynn. 1979–1980. Maize Cultivation in Coastal New York: The Archaeological, Agronomical, and Documentary Evidence. *North American Archaeologist* 1(1): 45–74.

Ceci, Lynn. 1990. Radiocarbon Dating "Village" Sites in Coastal New York: Settlement Pattern Change in the Middle to Late Woodland. *Man in the Northeast* 39: 1–28.

Chilton, Elizabeth S. 1999. Mobile Farmers of Pre-Contact Southern New England: The Archaeological and Ethnohistorical Evidence. In *Current Northeast Ethnobotany*, ed. J. P. Hart, 157–76. Albany: *New York State Museum Bulletin* 494.

Chilton, Elizabeth S. 2002. "Towns They Have None": Diverse Subsistence and Settlement Strategies in Native New England. In *Northeast Subsistence-Settlement Change: A.D. 700–1300*, ed. J. P. Hart and C. B. Rieth, 265–88.Albany: *New York State Museum Bulletin* 496.

Chilton, Elizabeth. 2005. Farming and Social Complexity in the Northeast. In *North American Archaeology*, ed. T. P. and D. D. Loran, 138–60. Malden, MA: Blackwell Studies in Global Archaeology.

Chilton, Elizabeth S., and Dianna L. Doucette. 2002. Archaeological Investigations at the Lucy Vincent Beach Site (19-DK-148): Preliminary Results and Interpretations. In *A Lasting Impression: Coastal, Lithic, and Ceramic Research in New England Archaeology*, ed. J. E. Kerber, 41–70. Westport, CT: Praeger.

Chilton, Elizabeth S., Tonya Baroody Largy, and Kathryn Curran. 2000. Evidence for Prehistoric Maize Horticulture at the Pine Hill Site, Deerfield, Massachusetts. *Northeast Anthropology* (59): 23–46.

Cowie, Ellen. R. 2000. Archaeological Investigations at the Tracy Farm Site (69.11 ME) in the Central Kennebec River Drainage, Somerset County, Maine (revised from 9/99). 2 vols. Farmington: Archaeological Research Center, University of Maine. Submitted to CRM. Copies available from 3071 I and II.

Crawford, Gary W., David G. Smith, and Vandy E. Bowyer. 1997. Dating the Entry of Corn (*Zea Mays*) into the Lower Great Lakes Region. *American Antiquity* 62(1): 112–19.

Demeritt, David. 1991. Agriculture, Climate, and Cultural Adaptation in the Prehistoric Northeast. *Archaeology of Eastern North America* 19: 183–202.

Dincauze, Dena F. 1990. A Capsule Prehistory of Southern New England. In *The Pequots in Southern New England*, ed. L. M. Hauptman and J. D. Wherry, 19–32. The Civilization of the American Indian series, vol. 198. Norman: University Oklahoma Press.

Foster, David R. 1999. *Hemlock's Future in the Context of Its History: An Ecological Perspective*. Paper presented at the Symposium on Sustainable Management of Hemlock Ecosystems in Eastern North America, Durham, New Hampshire.

Fritz, Gayle. 1994. Are the First American Farmers Getting Younger? *Current Anthropology* 35(3): 305–309.

Fritz, Gayle J. 1990. Multiple Pathways to Farming in Precontact Eastern North America. *Journal of World Prehistory* 4: 387–435.

George, David, and Robert E. Dewar. 1999. Chenopodium in Connecticut Prehistory: Wild, Weedy, Cultivated, or Domesticated? In *Current Northeast Ethnobotany*, ed. J. P. Hart, 121–32. Albany: *New York State Museum Bulletin* 494.

Gwynne, Margaret A. 1982. *The Late Archaic Archaeology of Mount Sinai Harbor, New York: Human Ecology, Economy, and Residence Patterns on the*

Southern New England Coast. PhD dissertation, State University of New York, Stony Brook.

Hart, John P. 1999. Maize Agriculture Evolution in the Eastern Woodlands of North America: A Darwinian Perspective. *Journal of Archaeological Method and Theory* 6(2): 137–80.

Hart, John P., and Bernard K. Means. 2002. Maize and Villages: A Summary and Critical Assessment of Current Northeast Early Late Prehistoric Evidence. In *Northeast Subsistence-Settlement Change: A.D. 700–1300*, ed. J. P. Hart and C. B. Rieth, 345–58. Albany: *New York State Museum Bulletin* 496.

Hart, John P., and C. Margaret Scarry. 1999. The Age of Common Beans (*Phaseolus vulgaris*) in the Northeastern United States. *American Antiquity* 64(4): 653–58.

Hart, John P., Robert G. Thompson, and Hetty Jo Brumbach. 2003. Phytolith Evidence for Early Maize (*Zea Mays*) in the Northern Finger Lakes Region of New York. *American Antiquity* 68(4): 619–40.

Hasenstab, Robert J. 1999. Fishing, Farming, and Finding the Village Sites: Centering Late Woodland New England Algonquians. In *The Archaeological Northeast*, ed. K. E. S. Mary Ann Levine and Michael S. Nassaney, 139–53. Westport, CT: Bergin and Garvey.

Katzenberg, M. Anne, Henry P. Schwarcz, Martin Knyf, and F. Jerome Melbye. 1995. Stable Isotope Evidence for Maize Horticulture and Paleodiet in Southern Ontario. *American Antiquity* 60(2): 335–50.

Keegan, William F., and Kristen Noble, eds. 1999. *The Archaeology of Connecticut: The Human Era—11,000 Years Ago to the Present*. Storrs, CT: Bibliopola Press.

Largy, Tonya B., Lucianne Lavin, Marina E. Mozzi, and Kathleen Furgerson. 1999. Corncobs and Buttercups: Plant Remains from the Goldkrest Site. In *Current Northeast Paleoethnobotany*, ed. J. P. Hart, 69–84. Albany: *New York State Museum Bulletin* 494.

Lavin, Lucianne. 1988. The Morgan Site: Rocky Hill, Connecticut. *Bulletin of the Archaeological Society of Connecticut* 51: 7–22.

Little, Elizabeth A. 1994. Radiocarbon Ages of Shell and Charcoal, in a Pit Feature at Myrick's Pond, Brewster, MA. *Bulletin of the Massachusetts Archaeological Society* 55(2): 74–77.

Little, Elizabeth A. 1997. Radiocarbon Ages: How to Report. *Bulletin of the Massachusetts Archaeological Society* 58(2): 64–65.

Little, Elizabeth A. 1999. Maize Notes. *Nantucket Archaeological Study* 17. Nantucket Historical Association.

Little, Elizabeth A. 2002. Kautantouwit's Legacy: Calibrated Dates on Prehistoric Maize in New England. *American Antiquity* 67(1): 109–18.

Little, Elizabeth A., and Margaret J. Schoeninger. 1995. The Late Woodland Diet on Nantucket Island and the Problem of Maize in Coastal New England. *American Antiquity* 60(2): 351–68.

Long, Austin, D. J. Donahue, A. J. T. Jull, L. J. Toolin, and B. F. Benz. 1989. First Direct AMS Dates on Early Maize from Tehuac·n, Mexico. *Radiocarbon* 31(3): 1035–40.

Luedtke, Barbara E. 1988. Where Are the Late Woodland Villages in Eastern Massachusetts? *Bulletin of the Massachusetts Archaeological Society* 49(2): 58–65.

McAndrews, John H. 1988. Human Disturbance of North American Forests and Grasslands: The Fossil Pollen Record. In *Vegetation History*, ed. B. Huntley and I. Thompson Webb, 673–95.

McBride, Kevin A. 1978. Archaic Subsistence in the Lower Connecticut River Valley: Evidence from Woodchuck Knoll. *Man in the Northeast* 15–16: 124–32.

McBride, Kevin A. 1984. *Prehistory of the Lower Connecticut River Valley.* Unpublished PhD dissertation, University of Connecticut, Storrs.

McBride, Kevin A., and Robert E. Dewar. 1987. Agriculture and Cultural Evolution: Causes and Effects in the Lower Connecticut River Valley. In *Emergent Horticultural Economies of the Eastern Woodlands*, ed. W. F. Keegan, 305–28. Center for Archaeological Investigations, Occasional Papers, vol. 7. Carbondale: Southern Illinois University Press.

McLauchlan, Kendra. 2003. Plant Cultivation and Forest Clearance by Prehistoric North Americans: Pollen Evidence from Fort Ancient, Ohio, USA. *The Holocene* 13(4): 557–66.

Medaglia, Christian C., Elizabeth A. Little, and Margaret J. Schoeninger. 1990. Late Woodland Diet on Nantucket Island: A Study Using Stable Isotope Ratios. *Bulletin of the Massachusetts Archaeological Society* 51(2): 49–60.

Pagoulatos, Peter. 1988. Terminal Archaic Settlement and Subsistence in the Connecticut River Valley. Man in the Northeast 35: 71–93.

Petersen, James B., and Ellen R. Cowie. 2002. From Hunter-Gatherer Camp to Horticultural Village: Late Prehistoric Indigenous Subsistence and Settlement in New England. In *Northeast Subsistence-Settlement Change: A.D. 700–1300*, ed. J. P. Hart and C. B. Rieth, 265–88. Albany: *New York State Museum Bulletin* 496.

Piperno, Dolores R., and Deborah M. Pearsall. 1993. Phytoliths in the Reproductive Structures of Maize and Teosinte: Implications for the Study of Maize Evolution. *Journal of Archaeological Science* 20(3): 337–62.

Reber, Eleanora A. 2001. *Maize Detection in Absorbed Pottery Residues: Development and Archaeological Application.* PhD, Harvard University, Boston, Massachusetts.

Riley, Thomas J., Gregory R. Walz, Charles J. Bareis, Andrew C. Fortier, and Kathryn E. Parker. 1994. Accelerator Mass Spectrometry (AMS) Dates Confirm Early Zea Mays in the Mississippi River Valley. *American Antiquity* 59(3): 490–98.

Russell, Lyent W. 1947. Indian Burials at Niantic Connecticut. *Bulletin of the Archaeological Society of Connecticut* 21: 39–43.

Sargent, Howard. n.d. The Hunter Site: An Introductory Statement. Howard Sargent Museum.

Schiffer, M. B. 1986. Radiocarbon Dating and the “Old Wood” Problem: The Case of the Hohokam Chronology. *Journal of Archaeological Science* 13: 13–30.

Schulenberg, Janet. 2003. *Interpreting Stable Carbon Isotope Values from AMS Dates on Food Residue*. Paper presented at the Society for American Archaeology, Mikwaukee, Wisconsin.

Schwarcz, Henry P., F. Jerome Melbye, M. Anne Katzenberg, and M. Khye. 1985. Stable Isotopes in Human Skeletons of Southern Ontario: Reconstructing Paleodiet. *Journal of Archaeological Science* 12: 187–206.

Smith, Bruce D. 1992. *Rivers of Change: Essays on Early Agriculture in Eastern North America*. 1st ed. Washington, DC, and London: Smithsonian Institution Press.

Smith, Bruce D. 1998. *The Emergence of Agriculture. Scientific American Library Series 54*. New York: Scientific American Library.

Stuiver, Minze, and Paula J. Reimer. 1993. Extended 14C Database and Revised CALIB 3.0 14C Age Calibration Program. *Radiocarbon* 35(1): 215–30.

Stuiver, Minze, Paula J. Reimer, Edouard Bard, J. Warren Beck, G. S. Burr, Konrad A. Hughen, Bernd Kromer, Gerry McCormac, Johannes van der Plicht, and Marco Spurk. 1998. INTCAL98 Radiocarbon Age Calibration, 24,000-0 Cal BP. *Radiocarbon* 40(3): 1041–83.

Thorbahn, Peter F. 1988. Where Are All the Late Woodland Villages in Southern New England? *Bulletin of the Massachusetts Archaeological Society* 49(2): 46–57.

Upham, Steadman, Richard S. MacNeish, Walter C. Galinat, and Christopher M. Stevenson. 1987. Evidence Concerning the Origin of Maiz de Ocho. *American Anthropologist* 89(2): 410–19.

Vogel, John C., and N. J. Van Der Merwe. 1977. Isotopic Evidence for Early Maize Cultivation in New York State. *American Antiquity* 42(2): 238–42.

9

Limestone, Shell, and the Archaeological Visibility of Maize and Beans in New England

A Fertilizer Hypothesis

Elizabeth Alden Little

As of 2002, nine calibrated radiocarbon dates were obtained directly on maize kernels and ten dates on associated charcoal or shell from features in alluvial floodplains or coastal shell deposits in New England (Little 1999b, 2002). Four charcoal or shell samples from three coastal features are older than the associated maize kernels by 150 to 400 years. By contrast, four out of six pairs of dates on maize and associated charcoal from floodplains match surprisingly well. The simultaneous increase in the archaeological visibility of radiocarbon-dated maize and beans on the coast and floodplains, and a documented movement of people to the coasts and rivers, supports a hypothesis that by cal A.D. 1290 to 1390, New Englanders had learned to use old saltwater shell midden on coasts and limestone or freshwater mussel shells on alluvial floodplains to increase the yields of beans and maize. As a by-product, this fertilizer increased the preservation of cultigens in New England's acid soils. The river valleys and coasts provide the warmest climates in New England, and it is important to note that the onset of the Little Ice Age in New England coincides with the increase in the archaeological visibility of maize.

Background

Archaeologists often obtain only one radiocarbon date from a single feature, because dates are costly and the process destroys the material dated. In other words, one assumes that young branches, not old dead trees or heartwood, were used for firewood, and that the contents of small pits with maize kernels, shell, and charcoal had been cooked, charred, eaten, and deposited at roughly the same time. Poor matches between dates in a feature are known as the "old wood problem" (Schiffer 1986).

By accelerator mass spectrometer (AMS) dating we can date as little as a single kernel of maize. In 1993 Alan Strauss offered me an opportunity to participate in the first AMS ^{14}C dating directly on maize in Massachusetts. We also dated by ^{14}C decay charcoal and shell associated with the maize in a small pit at Brewster, Cape Cod (Little 1993, 1994; Strauss 1994). Calibration (see the note at the end of this chapter) showed that the ages of the shell and charcoal sample were in excellent agreement, but the maize had a less than 5 percent probability of being as old as the charcoal and shell. Comparisons of the three published direct dates on maize kernels with the nine dates on charcoal associated with undated maize from New England showed that most dates on charcoal were older than dates directly on maize (Little 1994).

To amplify these findings, additional pairs of dates directly on maize and, when possible, associated charcoal or shell have been obtained for a total of eighteen maize dates, nine charcoal dates, and one shell date (Little 2002; see Table 9.1 and the note at the end of this chapter; also see Little 1999b, 39).

Results

Despite the small number, all the maize kernel dates fall within the Late Woodland period (after cal A.D. 1000; see Figure 9.1 (page 186); see Table 9.1). Furthermore, there is an interesting difference between the sites on floodplains and those on the coast bordering shellfish habitat (see Figure 9.2 and Figure 9.3, page 187). Of the six floodplain pairs, four have very similar maize and charcoal dates. On the other hand, the four coastal pairs all have substantially older charcoal or shell dates than maize dates. Furthermore, whereas the oldest kernels found on floodplains date to around cal A.D. 1000, the oldest coastal maize kernels date to the cal A.D. fourteenth century. To put these dates into context, the earliest maize AMS dates in Illinois, Tennessee, Ohio, and Southern Ontario are between cal A.D. 1 and cal A.D. 600 (Crawford et al. 1997, 114). While kernels from most of the maize find sites presently known in New England are yet to be dated, it is not too early to discuss the possible implications of these patterns.

Table 9.1. Comparison of Maize (M) Dates with Associated Charcoal (C) or Shell (S) Dates.

Kernel #	Site, Reference	Lab #	$^{14}C \pm \sigma$ Yrs B.P. (δ^{13} C-corrected)	Sample	$\delta^{13}C$, o/oo	Cal A.D. Yrs. $\pm\sigma$
#4	Hudson R., N.Y., floodplain; CNG-TL470; (Little 1999b)	GX-22651-AMS	380±50	M	–9.8	1444(1481) 1627
		GX-22663-AMS	340±50	C	–26.7	1475–1640
#5	Hudson R., N.Y., floodplain; 211-1-1(44); (Cassedy & Webb 1999);	β-84971-AMS	390±50	M	–11.5*	1442(1476) 1622
		β-53452	1100±70	C		887–1017
#8	Nantucket MA, shell midden; 19NT30; (Stockley Letter of 1982 [Little 1999a: 13])	GX-22044-AMS	500±60	M	–10.8	1403(1426) 1443
		M-1502	1010±100	C		902(1020) 1152
#10	Little Ossipee N., ME, floodplain; (Asch Sidell 1999:192,212)	β-102060-AMS	600±40M			1302(1020)
		β-83651	1010±60	C		984(1020) 1148

(continued on next page

Table 9.1. *(Continued)*

Kernel #	Site, Reference	Lab #	$^{14}C \pm \sigma$ Yrs B.P. (δ^{13} C-corrected)	Sample	$\delta^{13}C$, o/oo	Cal A.D. Yrs. $\pm\sigma$
#11	Bowmans Brook, N.Y., shell midden; (Ceci 1990, Little 1999a)	β-15769	610±60	M	–11.64	1297–1406
		β-15770	920±70	C	–26.9	1023–1213
#12	Connecticut R., CT, floodplain; (Bendremer and Dewar 1994)	β27676-AMS	620±70	M		1293–1406
		β-40849	630±70	C		1290–1403
#13a	Brewster, MA, shell midden; 19BN811 (Little 1994, Strauss 1994);	GX-19319-AMS	620±59	M	–10.1	1296–1403
		GX-19564	865±95	C	–26.1	1033–1273
#13b	Brewster, MA, shell midden; 19BN811 (Little 1994, Strauss 1994)	GX-19319-AMS	620±59	M	–10.1	1296–1403
		GX-19319	1150±90	S	+1.6	1045(1174) 1275

#14	Housatonic R., floodplain; 29A, 25-2(9) (Cassedy & Webb 1999)	β-84973-AMS	690±60	M	–11.5*	1278(1293) 1385
		β-52902	710±50	C		1276(1287) 1376
#16	Hudson R., N.Y., floodplain; 211-1-1(32) (Cassedy & Webb 1999)	β-84969-AMS	1050±50	M	–10*	901(997) 1023
		β-53451	1050±60	C		901(997) 1023

Notes. Numbered (#) maize dates ±σ from conventional ^{14}C dates (Little [2002:Table 2]; calibrated by CALIB 4.2 (Stuiver et al. 1993; Stuiver et al. 1998; Stuiver and Reimer 1993); ΔR = –95±45 for marine samples (Little 1993); dates rounded to nearest 10 years; a pair with non-overlapping ±σ not a likely match.

*: $\delta^{13}C$ estimated from lab $\delta^{13}C$correction/16)-25 in ^{14}C yrs B.P. (Taylor 1987:120–123); [a]for provenience information and dating lab reports, see Little (1999a;2002); multiple intercepts omitted (–).

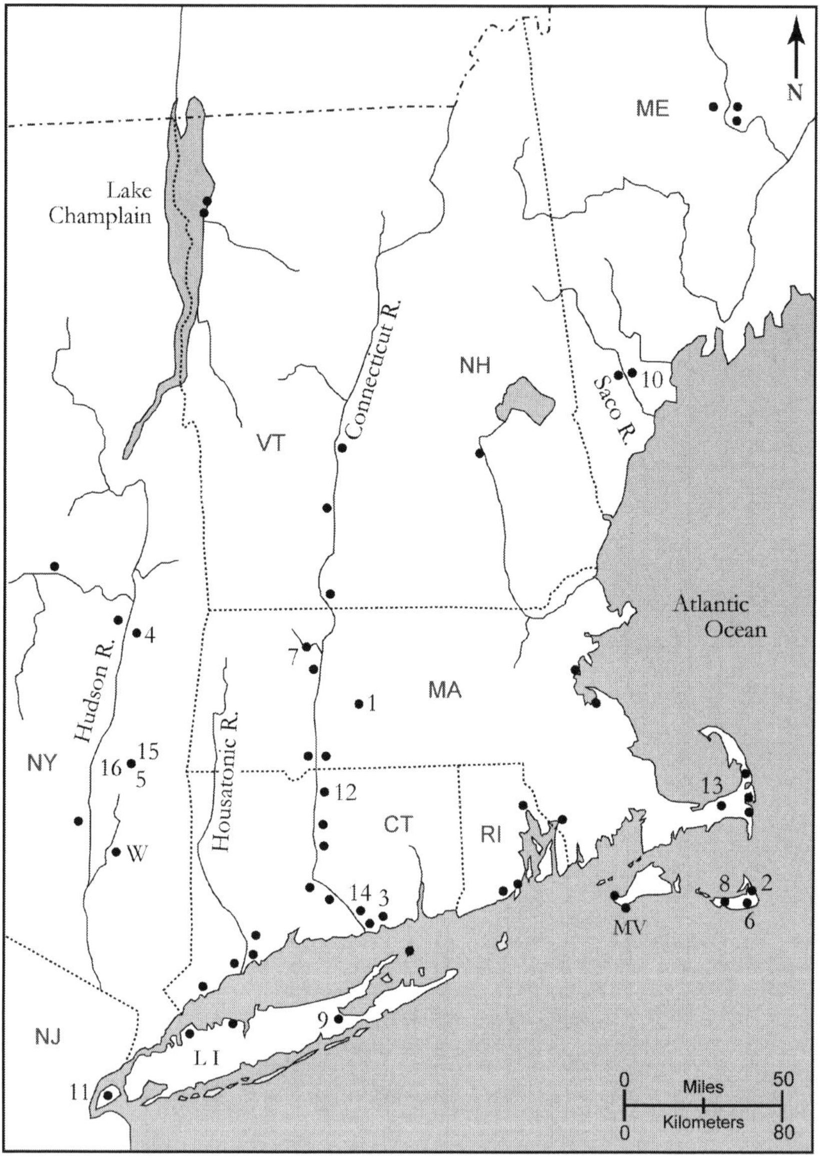

Figure 9.1. Sites of Maize Finds in New England to the Hudson River (Asch Sidell 1999; Chilton 1999; Heckenberger et al. 1992). Maize is undated, charcoal dated, or directly dated: #1–#16 and W (Little 2002); MV (Little 1999a, 38); base map after Heckenberger et al. (1992) (Note the focus on rivers and coasts.)

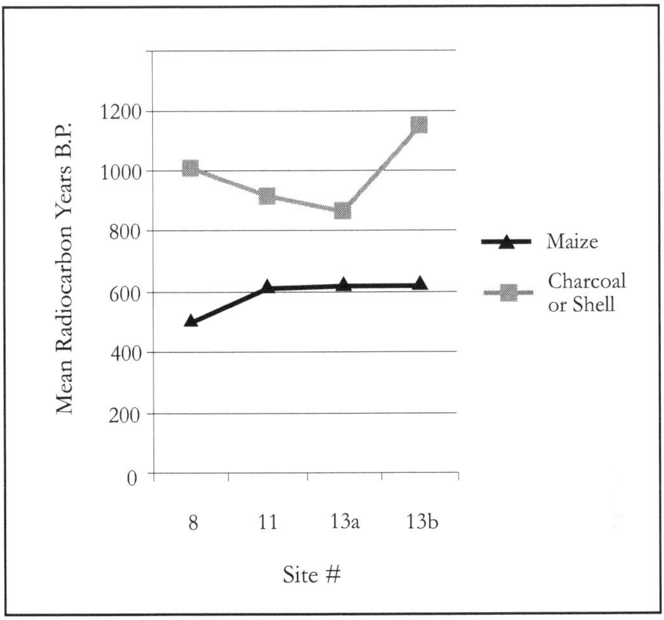

Figure 9.2. Calibrated Dates for Pairs of Maize and Charcoal or Shell from *Coastal* Sites in New England

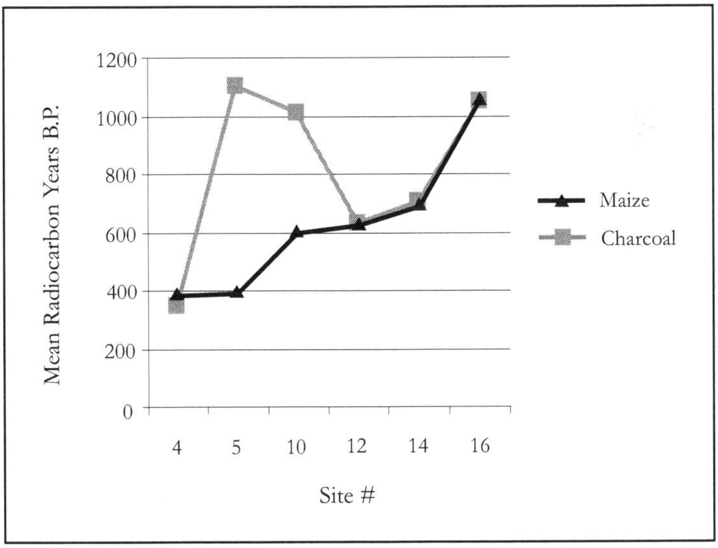

Figure 9.3. Calibrated Dates for Pairs of Maize and Charcoal or Shell from *Floodplain* Sites in New England

Discussion

Shell Middens

New England's coastal shell middens have long been known for the disturbances reflected in their dates, artifact styles, and strata (Ritchie 1969). Therefore, the consistent pairing of coastal maize kernel dates with older midden charcoal and shell dates brings order out of chaos (see Figure 9.2). I have proposed (Little 2002) a hypothesis that by cal A.D. 1300–1400, coastal people had learned by observation, word of mouth, and/or experiment (see Dimmick 1994; Hart 1999) that old shell midden material, including soil, shell, charcoal, bone, and the occasional stone flake (Ceci 1984), could increase the yield of beans and maize in New England's acid soil. That maize appeared later on the coast than on floodplains deserves further exploration.

From Maine to Cape Cod, Champlain in 1605 observed *sigue-noc* (translated as horseshoe crab shells, but see Russell 1970) used in making corn hills, and Lescarbot in 1606 at Saco, Maine, reported that something translated from the French as "shells of fish" was used for fertilizer in corn hills (Dimmick 1994, 247, 248). Howard Russell (1970), an agricultural historian of New England, has argued skillfully in favor of the shells of clams (*Mya arenaria* [soft shell], or quahog (*Mercenaria mercenaria*) for fertilizer; both are found on Nantucket's north shore. Surf clam (*Spisula solidissima*) shells, easily 17.5 cm across, wash up on Nantucket's south shore in numbers after big storms, and one or two often might be found at prehistoric sites at Nantucket's north shore. For hilling corn, they would have been the strongest and largest digging tool.

Shell as fertilizer for corn has been eclipsed by a controversy over William Bradford's 1898[1620–1648, 121) account of Squanto teaching the Pilgrims to put an alewife on every corn hill (Ceci 1975; Nanepashemet 1991). Russell (1976, 388; 1980, 167) considered fish a good fertilizer, but its bone would have provided little lime. My family always threw shells from quahogs and soft-shell clams into a humus pile; I continue the practice with occasionally surprising results (such as giant pumpkins growing in the shade of pines and oaks in Lincoln, Massachusetts). Professor Barbara Luedtke noted the patchy (and puzzling) layer of marine shell that underlies the plow zone on much of the Nantucket Field Station site, which had a neutral pH = 6.3–7.5 (Luedtke 1980). Is this the remains of a field of corn hills? Most of the island has an acid pH of 4.5 to 5.1 (see Table 9.2 and Table 9.3, page 190). Most convincingly, Mrozowski (1994) and Currie (1994)

Table 9.2. Evidence of limestone or shell as fertilizer for maize (See Hasenstab [1994] for increase in yield of maize and beans provided by limestone).

COAST:

Long Island, NY: pH = 3.9–5.5 without lime fertilizer (Ceci 1977:110–119). Ceci (1984) in 1982 found old "failing" trees in an orchard surveyed in 1722, and individually fertilized with prehistoric Indian midden soil including shells, and flint and quartz chips.

Martha's Vinyard Island, MA: Five sites with shell, pH = 8.0. Off-site pH = 6.0–6.5 (Ritchie 1964).

Cape Cod, MA: Myrick's Pond, Brewster, good preservation of botanicals, shell and bone at site; off-site pH = 3.6–6.0; maize kernel #13 (Table 1; Strauss 1994:3,42; Little 1994).

Cape Cod, MA: Sandy's Point, Brewster, good evidence for corn hills with shell; seven charcoal and shell dates: cal A.D. 900 to 1650 (Mrozowski 1994; Currie 1994).

Nantucket Island, MA:

Polpis Harbor: John Swain's Deed to land on which his dwelling house then stood included a Lime Kiln (Nantucket County Deeds Book 4, page 4, 1721), for burning shells for lime. E. Little on site visit (1985) found a few small rocks, widespread shell deposit, and reports of lithic artifacts.

Quaise: University of Massassachusetts Nantucket Field Station in 1978: Overall: pH = 6.3–7.5; evidence for a maize storage feature and widespread small patches of shell up to one km from shore (Luedtke 1980; see Figure 4).

Burial feature: soil pH = 3.0–5.0 (Turchon 1979:37); on bluff near harbor; some eroded shell fragments (Little 1990:10).

Nantucket Elementary School & Teen Center: pH = 4.69–7.13 (Williams and Talmage 1977); center of island; scattered shell; pine woods in 1977.

FLOODPLAINS:

Grand Banks River, S. Ontario: maize dates cal A.D. 500–1000; warm valley, Growing Degree Days:3700; "carbonate bedrock," "calcareous shale" (Crawford et al. 1998:123–137).

Upper New York State: movement of villages to uplands, limestone tills (high pH values), and warmer climates, by cal A. D. 1400 (charcoal) (Hasenstab 1996:19–21).

Hudson River Valley, New York: Greenbush, pH = 6.8 (Largy et al. 1999); maize kernel #4 (Table 1).

Connecticut, Housatonic, Berkshire and Taconic Valleys: Limestone; in 18th century "some of the best land on the continent"; by 1800 in CT, manure needed; in the 20th century, lime (etc.) fertilizer used for tobacco fields (Russell 1976:126–127, 312, 503). See Strauss (1976) and Bidwell and Falconer (1941) for dolomite (limestone with magnesium and calcium).

Connecticut River, Vermont: Skitchewaug; Stratum II: pH = 7–9.5; which accounts for the "exceptional preservation of carbonized" maize and beans (Heckenberger et al. 1992:128–129). The pooled calibrated AMS dates $\pm 2\sigma$ for 3 beans from features is cal A.D. 1280(1297)1390 (Hart and Scarry 1999:656).

Table 9.3. Historic Nantucket corn yields (bushels per acre) and fertilizer.

Nantucket was settled by 27 English Puritans and their families in 1659. At that time there were between 1500 and 2500 Indians (Little 1990), living chiefly on fish, fowl, deer, and corn. There were some trees in wet areas such as the Long Woods, which became increasingly scarce until 1743, after which even firewood was imported (Little 1981). To place the yield data in historic context, see Schroeder (1999) and Bidwell and Falconer (1941).

According to the Nantucket Proprietors' Records of 1664, the Nantucket Indians were permitted by the town to set fires to their land in April (Little 1981). This would have added potassium, calcium, phosphorus, and magnesium and reduced the soil acidity (raised the pH), thereby increasing the maize yield (Heidenreich 1978:380–381).

• Daniel Gookin of Massachusetts in 1675–77 reported 30–40 bushels of corn per year from rich soils in corn hills along the coast and along rivers (Russell 1980:174,142,143).

• Paul Dudley (1724:193–200) of Boston reported to London maize yields of 50 bushels per acre.

• Walter Folger, Jun. (1791:153–155), at Nantucket reported 12 bushels of corn per acre in the common planting ground. Private farms got 20 bushels an acre. In alternate years the fields were planted to rye and oats.

• Zaccheus Macy (1792:158–160) of Nantucket reported: "Since my time [he was born in 1713], we called it only a middling crop, when we got from eighteen to twenty bushels from an acre. But now when we get from twelve to fourteen bushels from an acre, we esteem it a tolerable crop". Wood was entirely gone.

• James Freeman (1807:19–38) reported that in 1801 there were 1,350 acres of tillage land at Nantucket. He wrote that the water in wells was "generally hard" (low Ph). Wood had been in short supply since about 1707, and was gone except for some protected white cedar for whaleboats at Coskata.

• K. H. Langlois, Jr., USDA (1979:14–15) reported that the island soils are generally a loamy till, low in phosphorous and potash. An application of lime is required to raise the pH above the strongly or very strongly acid pH (4.5–5.1). In 1974 there were 276 acres of cropland, chiefly producing sweet corn, tomatoes, squash, snap beans, cabbage, peas, lettuce, carrots, and flowers, and 768 acres of pasture, woodland, etc.

give archaeological support for both shell and fish bones in clustered Indian corn hills at Brewster, Cape Cod.

Another source of shell would have been rivers. At the Clamshell Bluff Site on the Sudbury River (Massachusetts), fresh water mussels, *Elliptio complanata* (Lightfoot), were collected by prehistoric Concord Indians, and the shells were used for fertilizer by historic Concordians (Blancke 1995; Downs 1995, 55–63; Strayer and Jirka 1997, 51). In the 1850s, live freshwater mussel beds were visited by Thoreau (1962) in Concord and surrounding towns. D. F. Dincauze (2002, personal communication) reports a mussel shell midden on the Deerfield River, J. D. C. Little (2002, personal communication) reports another at a pond in Sterling, Massachusetts, and I picked up a fresh elliptio shell near Farrar Pond, Lincoln, in March 2002. In summary, freshwater mussel shells were and are not uncommon at sites on rivers and streams in New England (Outwater 1996, 117–23; Russell 1980).

Floodplains

Of the six maize sites on floodplains (see Figure 9.2), three on the Hudson, and one each on the Housatonic, the Connecticut, and the Saco rivers, four kernels (#4, 12, 14, and 16) support the classical assumption that dates on maize and on associated charcoal should match, as noted by Bendremer and Dewar (1994) and Cassedy and Webb (1999). The mismatch in pair #5 is not discussed, but Asch Sidell (1999) proposed a geological event to account for the mismatch in pair #10. Chance may be responsible for the close duplication of associated dates for pairs #12, 14, and 16. Or, because matching dates were expected, might matching charcoal dates have been selected from multiple charcoal dates associated with those three kernels? Additional testing is required.

The Limestone Hypothesis

Calcium carbonate is found in shell, coral, and limestone in the form of rocks, marl, sand, and clay. Limestone often includes magnesium carbonate, in which case it may be called dolomite. Both compounds are antacids (OED 1971, 1627, 1692) and are especially strong after burning to lime. Limestone fertilizes nitrogen-fixing bacteria on bean (legume) roots, which in turn will produce the nitrogen required to enhance the yield of maize (Hasenstab 1994, 1996, 21). Henry D. Thoreau reported an outcropping of limestone running southwest to northeast in Lincoln (Massachusetts) and was eloquent about its value to Colonial farmers (Thoreau 1962, vol. 2, 16, vol. 10, 175). Limestone/dolomite is found sporadically throughout New England, and a map of its distribution would be worth comparison with find sites of early maize.

The lack of maize finds in sites away from the coast and river valleys, as well as Mulholland's (1984) and McBride's (1984) report of settlement moves to the coast and river valleys by cal A.D. 1300–1400, supports my limestone hypothesis (Little 2002; see also Pretola and Little's [1988] evidence for a major late woodland population increase at the island of Nantucket). Both coastal and floodplain maize sites for which pH values of the soils are reported show very high (alkaline) values, from 7–9.5, in contrast to most New England soils, which have very low (acidic) pH values of 3.5–7 (see Table 9.2). If alluvial deposits of the Connecticut, Housatonic (Russell 1976, 503), and Hudson River floodplains and/or old shell midden in corn hills on the coast and/or riverbanks are the sources of these high pHs, then the enhancement of the yield of maize and beans would have been substantial and readily noticed.

In addition to increasing the yield of maize and beans, limestone, as an antacid, acts as a preservative for cultigens by reducing soil acidity (Dincauze 2000, 286–87, 334–35; Hasenstab 1994; Heckenberger et al. 1992; Strauss 1994). This, along with drying and charring of the maize (Bendremer et al. 1991; DeNiro and Hastorf 1985; Dincauze 2000, 334–35; Wagner 1987, 25–26), would have greatly increased the archaeological visibility of prehistoric maize and beans for archaeologists today. Indeed, the data of Hart and Scarry (1999) and Little (2002) show that the archaeological visibility of beans increased at the same time as that of maize in New England (see Figure 9.1), and regional archaeologists often note the good preservation of cultigens, when found at all (see Table 9.2).

In a recent report of the mining of very large quantities of gypsum at Mammoth Cave, Kentucky, about 2,200–3,000 years ago, Sims (2001–2002, 24–25) suggests that this may have been used as a soil conditioner. Gypsum is calcium sulfate, and, along with limestone, it was burned to produce a fertilizer in the Connecticut and Hudson River valleys by A.D. 1800 (Bidwell and Falconer 1941[1925], 233–34). John Swain had a limekiln to burn Indian midden shells at Polpis, Nantucket, in 1721 (see Table 9.2).

Wood (1987, 278–85), in a discussion of the addition of bone, ash, charred plant material, and mussel shells to prehistoric Midwestern soils, notes the difficulty of proving the use of fertilizer from soil evidence, because historic farmers have fertilized and worked the same soils for at least two centuries. However, new AMS dates for beans (Hart and Scarry 1999, 656) and maize dates (Little 2002) (see Figure 9.1) from New England suggest that beans could be a good proxy for AMS dates on maize. If so, the Skitchewaug site of Vermont establishes the earliest cultivation of maize and beans in soils of very high pH between approximately cal A.D. 1280 and 1390 (see Table 9.2). We need now to look for sources of soil conditioner/antacid fertilizer.

Climate

The New England climate is highly variable over time (Bradley 2000; Demeritt 1991; Keigwin 1996), and there are local microclimates, such as those in valleys or near lakes (Asch Sidell 1999). Nevertheless, during the Little Ice Age (about 2°C colder than today), the northern limit with the more than 2,000 growing degree days annually required by maize to mature would have been significantly farther south than it is today (Demeritt 1991; also see Figure 9.4).

Bradley (2000) reports a Little Ice Age climate roughly from A.D. 1450 to 1600. Two reports from the early seventeenth century graphically describe a New England cold spell before the arrival of the Pilgrims in 1620. Governor William Bradford of Plymouth reported in 1621 (1898, 126) that "the people were much affraid of ye Tarentins, a people to ye eastward, which used to come in harvest time and take away their corne" (spelling in original). In 1634, William Wood of the Massachusetts Bay Colony reported that the Indians said that the Englishman's God "is a good God that sends them so many things, so much good corn . . . temperate rains, fair seasons, which they likewise are the better for since the arrival of the English; the times and seasons being much altered in seven or eight years, freer from lightning and thunder, long droughts, sudden and tempestuous dashes of rain, and lamentable cold Winters" (Wood 1865, 88).

That the current collection of maize find sites in New England is in the warmest areas, the river valleys, and the coasts (Demeritt 1991) suggests that it could have been the warmth that attracted the maize farmers and the limestone or shell that kept them (see Figure 9.4). For students of climate, cal A.D. 1350–1450 was the beginning of the Little Ice Age, and the Maunder sunspot minimum, generally a cold period, was a strange time to be adopting maize agriculture.

Remaining Questions

Radiocarbon ages on maize, shell, and charcoal may include extraneous contributions from limestone (infinite age) and old alluvial humus

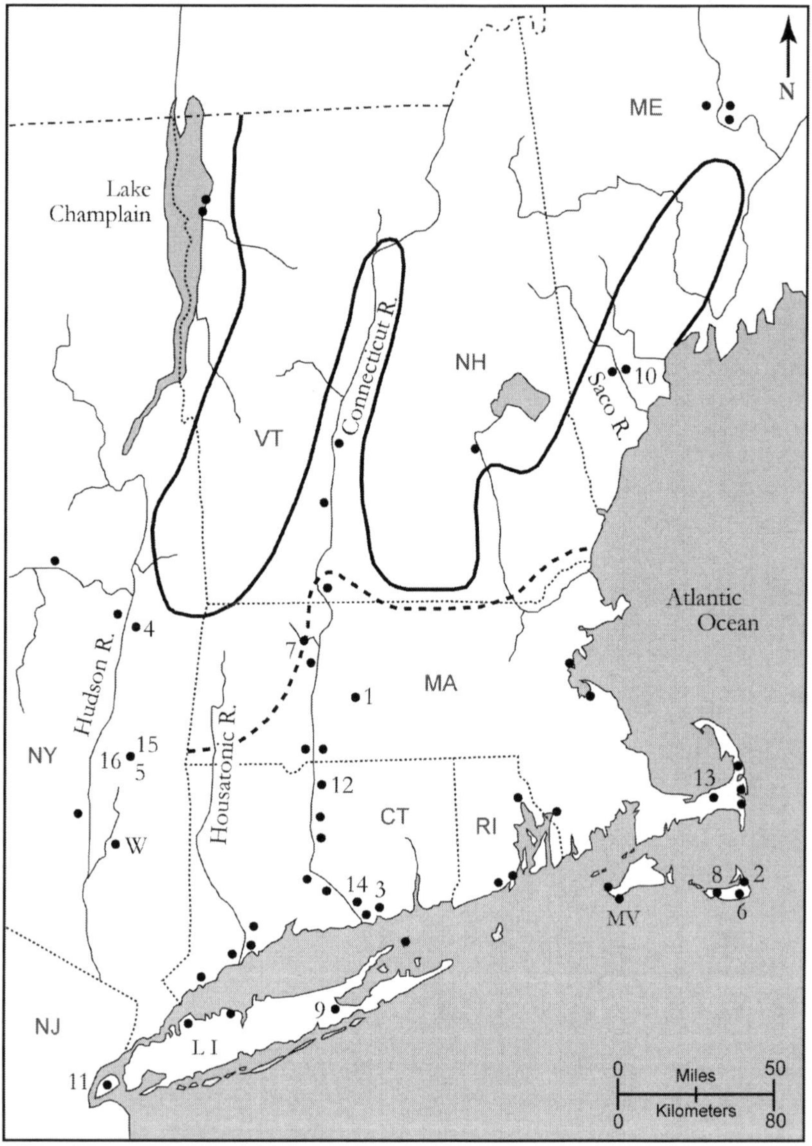

Figure 9.4. Sites of Maize Finds in New England Showing (Heavy Line) Northern Limit of Regions Today with More Than 2,000 Growing Degree Days (Demeritt 1991). For a drop in temperature of 2 degrees C (the Little Ice Age), that line would have moved as far south as the dashed heavy line (Demeritt 1991). Local microclimates would decrease the precision of these boundaries (Asch Sidell 1999). Base map after Heckenberger et al. (1992).

(Haynes 1991; Keith and Anderson 1963; Little 1993; Russell 1976). Although maize subsists on atmospheric CO_2 (Marino and McElroy 1991), old rotting humus on floodplains could be a source of old CO_2 (Little 1993).

What is the source of high pH in prehistoric New England floodplains? We still have only hypotheses. The distribution of sources of limestone (including dolomite), gypsum, and shell needs serious attention.

Summary

Because old shell and old charcoal were used as fertilizers, they are not good proxies for radiocarbon dates on coastal maize. Both floodplains and coastal sites show high pH values at maize find sites, and we find little or no maize and low pH values elsewhere in New England. This may be due to our search techniques. I have proposed the hypothesis that limestone and old marine or freshwater shells increased the archaeological visibility of maize and beans by increasing their yields and preservation so dramatically that a horticultural revolution and movement of sites to the coast and floodplains took place in New England between cal A.D. 1300 and 1400 (Little 2002). Here I have marshaled supporting pieces of data from agricultural history, CRM reports, and other sources, and I invite New England archaeologists to further test this hypothesis.

Acknowledgments

The Nantucket Historical Association, the Nantucket Maria Mitchell Association, the Brewster property owners, N. Asch Sidell, J. Bendremer, D. F. Cassedy, L. Ceci, D. Cox, D. F. Dincauze, R. Hasenstab, T. B. Largy, B. Luedtke, J. Petersen, B. Stockley, A. Strauss, J. Weeks, and R. Will provided maize kernels, AMS maize dates, information relating to maize dates, and encouragement, for which I am grateful.

Note

The introduction of tree-ring calibration, with fractionation and reservoir corrections added to ^{14}C years B.P. opens the possibility of all kinds of errors. The omission of notes stating what corrections have been made and the material dated, especially for maize and shell, where these corrections are large, can lead to errors of hundreds of years. The method for reporting "conventional" (Stuiver and Polach 1977) radiocarbon ages in ^{14}C years B.P. is to normalize (or correct for fractionation) the measured ^{14}C age using the value of $\delta^{13}C$ for the sample material. For AMS dates, the $\delta^{13}C$ correction includes that for fractionation in the measuring procedure. To obtain the $\delta^{13}C$ of the material, one needs to request it from the lab (Little 1994, 1997).

For southern New England shell, in addition to subtracting about 320 years from the age for the $\delta^{13}C$ correction, one needs to add a reservoir age correction ($R = 400 + \Delta R$ years), making the age younger. The local ΔR has been determined from seven pairs of charcoal and shell from deposits in the Cape and Islands and Boston Harbor, as $\Delta R = -95 + 45$ ^{14}C years (Little 1993).

The resulting conventional atmospheric or marine radiocarbon ages are calibrated to calendar years by tree-ring dated marine or atmospheric calibration curves with the software CALIB (Stuiver and Reimer 1993; Stuiver et al. 1998). CALIB gives the one and two sigma (2σ) values, and, in parentheses, the intercepts. It has been revised several times since 1993, and the A.D. 2001 version can be downloaded from http://www.calib.org. Further details can be found in Little (1994, 1997, 1999a, 2002). The results of calibrations in this chapter using CALIB.4.2 are given in Table 9.1.

All the maize, charcoal, and shell dates herein, except the charcoal dates of W. Ritchie, have been confirmed as $\delta^{13}C$-corrected for the material (and for the AMS process when applicable); the correction for charcoal is relatively small. The broad 2σ probability ranges and multiple intercepts of some of the samples are largely the result of wiggles in the calibration curve.

To summarize, large errors can be avoided by noting the material dated and the kind of years one is reporting: A.D., B.C., B.P., Calibrated, ^{14}C years, conventional ($\delta^{13}C$ corrected), or some other kind.

Works Cited

Asch Sidell, N. 1999. Prehistoric Plant Use in Maine: Paleo-Indian to Contact Period. In *Current Northeast Paleoethnobotany*, ed. J. P. Hart, 191–223. Albany: New York State Museum, Bulletin No. 494.

Bendremer, J. C., E. A. Kellogg, and T. B. Largy. 1991. A Grass-Lined Maize Storage Pit and Early Maize Horticulture in Central Connecticut. *North American Archaeologist* 12: 325–49.

Bendremer, J. C. M., and R. E. Dewar. 1994. The Advent of Prehistoric Maize in New England. In *Corn and Culture in the Prehistoric New World*, ed. S. Johannessen and C. A. Hastorf, 369–93. Westview: University of Minnesota.

Bidwell, P. W., and J. I. Falconer. 1941[1925]. *History of Agriculture in the Northern United States, 1620–1860.* Carnegie Institution, Publication #358. New York: Peter Smith.

Blancke, S. 1995. Clamshell Bluff, Concord, Massachusetts. Papers assembled by S. Blancke. *Bulletin of the Massachusetts Archaeological Society* 56: 29–84.

Bradford, W. 1898[1620–1648]. *History "Of Plimoth Plantation."* Boston, MA: Wright and Potter.

Bradley, R. 2000. 1,000 Years of Climate Change. *Science* 288: 153–55.

Cassedy, D. F., and P. Webb. 1999. New Data on the Chronology of Maize Horticulture in Eastern New York and Southern New England. In *Current Northeast Paleoethnobotany*, ed. J. P. Hart, 85–99. Albany: New York State Museum.

Ceci, L. 1975. Fish Fertilizer: A Native North American Practice? *Science* 118: 26–30.

Ceci, L. 1977. *The Effects of European Contact and Trade on the Settlement Pattern of Indians in Coastal New York, 1524–1665: The Archeological and Documentary Evidence*. PhD dissertation, City University of New York. Ann Arbor: University Microfilms, UMI, at the University of Michigan.

Ceci, L. 1984. Shell Midden Deposits as Coastal Resources. *World Archaeology* 16: 62–74.

Ceci, L. 1990. Radiocarbon Dating "Village" Sites in Coastal New York: Settlement Pattern Change in the Middle to Late Woodland. *Man in the Northeast* 39: 1–28.

Chilton, E. S. 1999. Mobile Farmers of Precontact Southern New England: The Archaeological and Ethnohistorical Evidence. In *Current Northeast Paleoethnobotany*, ed. J. P. Hart, 157–76. Albany: New York State Museum, Bulletin No. 494.

Chilton, E. S., T. B. Largy, and K. Curran. 2000. Evidence for Prehistoric Maize Horticulture at the Pine Hill Site, Deerfield, Massachusetts. *Northeast Anthropology* 59: 23–46.

Crawford, G. W., D. G. Smith, and V. E. Bowyer. 1997. Dating the Entry of Corn (*Zea Mays*) into the Lower Great Lakes Region. *American Antiquity* 62: 112–19.

Crawford, G. W., D. G. Smith, J. R. Desloges, and A. M. Davis. 1998. Floodplains and Agricultural Origins: A Case Study in South-Central Ontario, Canada. *Journal of Field Archaeology* 25: 123–37.

Currie, D. R. 1994. Micromorphology of a Native American Cornfield. *Archaeology of Eastern North America* 22: 63–72.

Demeritt, D. 1991. Agriculture, Climate, and Cultural Adaptation in the Prehistoric Northeast. *Archaeology of Eastern North America* 15: 183–202.

DeNiro, M. J., and Hastorf, C. 1985. Alteration of 15N/14N and 13C/12C Ratios of Plant Matter during the Initial Stages of Diagenesis: Studies Utilizing Archaeological Specimens from Peru. *Geochimica et Cosmochimica Acta* 49:1 (January 1985): 97–115.

Dimmick, F. R. 1994. Creative Farmers of the Northeast: A New View of Indian Maize Horticulture. *North American Archaeologist* 15: 235–52.

Dincauze, D. F. 2000. *Environmental Archaeology: Principles and Practice*. Cambridge: Cambridge University Press.

Downs, Elinor F. 1995. Freshwater Bivalves of the Concord Shell Heap. *Bulletin of the Massachusetts Archaeological Society* 56(2): 55–63.

Dudley, P. 1724. Observations on Some of the Plants in New England. *The Philosophical Transactions of the Royal Society*, 193–200.

Folger Jr., W. 1791. A Topographic Description of Nantucket. *Massachusetts Historical Society Collections*, series 1, vol. 3: 153–55.

Freeman, Rev. James. 1807. Notes on Nantucket. *Massachusetts Historical Society Collections*, series 2, vol. 3: 19–38.

Hart, J. P. 1999. Maize Agriculture Evolution in the Eastern Woodlands of North America: A Darwinian Perspective. *Journal of Archaeological Method and Theory* 6: 137–80.

Hart, J. P., and C. M. Scarry. 1999. The Age of Common Beans (*Phaseolus vulgaris*) in the Northeastern United States. *American Antiquity* 64: 653–58.

Hasenstab, R. J. 1994. *The Three Sisters: Staples of the Iroquois*. Paper presented at the Arthur C. Parker Conference, Ethnobiology: Perspectives and Practice in the Northeastern United States and eastern Canada. Rochester, NY: Rochester Museum and Science Center.

Hasenstab, R. J. 1996. Aboriginal Settlement Patterns in Late Woodland Upper New York State. *Journal of Middle Atlantic Archaeology* 12: 17–26.

Haynes Jr., C. V. 1991. More on Meadowcroft Radiocarbon Chronology. Review of Adovasio, Donahue, and Stuckenrath. *The Review of Archaeology* 12(1): 8–14.

Heckenberger, M. J., J. B. Petersen, and N. A. Sidell. 1992. Early Evidence of Maize Agriculture in the Connecticut River Valley of Vermont. *Archaeology of Eastern North America* 20: 125–49.

Heidenreich, C. E. 1978. Huron. In *Northeast*, ed. B. G. Trigger, 368–88. *Handbook of North American Indians* 15, W. C. Sturtevant, general editor, Smithsonian Institution, Washington, DC.

Keigwin, L. D. 1996. The Little Ice Age and Medieval Warm Period in the Sargasso Sea. *Science* 274: 1504–1508.

Keith, M. L., and G. M. Anderson. 1963. Radiocarbon Dating: Fictitious Results with Mollusk Shells. *Science* 141: 634–36.

Langlois, K. H., Jr. 1979. *Soil Survey of Nantucket County, Massachusetts*. United States Department of Agriculture Soil Conservation Service, in cooperation with the Massachusetts Agricultural Experiment Station, Amherst, MA.

Largy, T. R., L. Lavin, M. E. Mozzi, and K. Furgerson. 1999. Corncobs and Buttercups: Plant Remains from the Goldkrest Site. In *Current Northeast Paleoethnobotany*, ed. J. P. Hart, 69–84. Albany: New York State Museum, Bulletin No. 494.

Little, Elizabeth A. 1981. Essay on Nantucket Timber. *Nantucket Algonquian Study #6*. Nantucket, MA: Nantucket Historical Association.

Little, Elizabeth A. 1990. Indian Horse Commons at Nantucket Island, 1660–1760. *Nantucket Alqonquian Study #9*. Nantucket, MA: Nantucket Historical Association.

Little, Elizabeth A. 1993. Radiocarbon Age Calibration at Archaeological Sites of Coastal Massachusetts and Vicinity. *Journal of Archaeological Science* 20: 457–71.

Little, Elizabeth A. 1994. Radiocarbon Ages of Different Materials, Maize, Shell, and Charcoal, in One Pit Feature at Myrick's Pond, Brewster, MA.

Nantucket Archaeological Study, #16. Nantucket, MA: Nantucket Historical Association; Andover, MA: R. S. Peabody Museum of Archaeology.

Little, Elizabeth A. 1997. Radiocarbon Ages: How to Report. *Bulletin of the Massachusetts Archaeological Society* 58: 64–65.

Little, Elizabeth A. 1999a. Maize Age and Istope Values at the Goldkrest Site. Appendix I, 81–82, in Largy et al. 1999.

Little, Elizabeth A. 1999b. Maize Notes. *Nantucket Archaeological Study #17.* Nantucket, MA: Nantucket Historical Association; Andover, MA: R. S. Peabody Museum of Archaeology.

Little, Elizabeth A. 2002. Kautantouwit's Legacy: Calibrated Dates on Prehistoric Maize in New England. *American Antiquity* 67: 109–18.

Long, A., and B. Rippeteau. 1974. Testing Contemporaneity and Averaging Radiocarbon Dates. *American Antiquity* 39: 205–15.

Luedtke, B. 1980. Survey of the University of Massachusetts Nantucket Field Station. In *Widening Horizons*, ed. C. Hoffman, 95–129. Attleboro: Massachusetts Archaeological Society.

Macy, Zaccheus. 1792. Account of Nantucket. *Massachusetts Historical Society Collections,* series 1, vol. 3: 155–61.

Marino, B. D., and M. B. McElroy. 1991. Isotopic Composition of Atmospheric CO_2 Inferred from Carbon in C4 Plant Cellulose. *Nature* 349: 127–31.

McBride, Kevin. 1984. *Prehistory of the Lower Connecticut River Valley.* Unpublished PhD dissertation, University of Connecticut, Storrs.

McWeeney, L. J. 1994. *Archaeological Settlement Patterns and Vegetation Dynamics in Southern New England in the Late Quaternary.* PhD dissertation, Yale University; University of Michigan, Ann Arbor.

Mrozowski, S. A. 1994. The Discovery of a Native American Cornfield on Cape Cod. *Archaeology of Eastern North America* 22: 47–62.

Mulholland, M. T. 1984. *Patterns of Change in Prehistoric Southern New England: A Regional Approach.* PhD, University of Massachusetts Amherst.

Nanepashemet. 1991. It Smells Fishy to Me: An Argument Supporting the Use of Fish Fertilizer by the Native People of Southern New England. In *Algonkians of New England: Past and Present, Annual Proceedings of the Dublin Seminar for New England Folklife* 16: 42–50.

OED. 1971. *The Compact Edition of the Oxford English Dictionary.* New York: OED.

Outwater, A. 1996. *Water: A Natural History.* New York: Basic Books.

Pretola, J., and E. A. Little. 1988. Nantucket: An Archaeological Record from the Far Island. *Connecticut Archaeology Bulletin* 51: 47–68.

Ritchie, William A. 1969. *The Archaeology of Martha's Vineyard.* Garden City, NY: The Natural History Press.

Russell, H. S. 1970. New England Agriculture from Champlain and Others. *Bulletin of the Massachusetts Archaeological Society* 31:1, 2: 11–18.

Russell, H. S. 1976. *A Long, Deep Furrow: Three Centuries of Farming in New England.* Hanover: University Press of New England.

Russell, H. S. 1980. *Indian New England before the Mayflower.* Hanover: University Press of New England.

Schiffer, M. B. 1986. Radiocarbon Dating and the "Old Wood" Problem: The Case of the Hohokam Chronology. *Journal of Archaeological Science* 13: 13–30.

Schroeder, S. 1999. Maize Productivity in the Eastern Woodlands and Great Plains of North America. *American Antiquity* 64: 499–516.

Sims, M. 2001–2002. Archaeologists in Wonderland. *American Archaeology* 5(4): 20–27.

Strauss, Alan. 1976. Lithic Analysis of a Mudstone/"Argillite" Workshop. The Wills Hill Site. *Bulletin of the Massachusetts Archaeological Society* 38: 22–29.

Strauss, Alan. 1994. Intensive Archaeological Survey and Excavation of a Prehistoric Shell Pit Feature at House Lot 37, Bates Lane, in Brewster, Massachusetts. Report on file. Boston: Massachusetts Historical Commission.

Strayer, D. L., and K. J. Jirka. 1997. *The Pearly Mussels of New York State*. Albany: New York State Museum Memoir 26.

Stuiver, M., and H. A. Polach. 1977. Discussion: reporting of ^{14}C data. *Radiocarbon* 19: 355–63.

Stuiver, M., and P. J. Reimer. 1993. Extended ^{14}C Data Base and Revised CALIB (version 4.2) ^{14}C Age Calibration Program. *Radiocarbon* 35: 215–30. http://www.depts.washington.edu/qil/calib.

Stuiver, M., P. J. Reimer, E. Bard, J. W. Beck, G. S. Burr, K. A. Hughes, B. Kromer, G. McCormac, J. van der Plicht, and M. Spurk. 1998. INTALC 98 Radiocarbon Age Calibration, 24,000-0 cal BP. *Radiocarbon* 40: 1041–83.

Taylor, R. E. 1987. *Radiocarbon Dating: An Archaeological Perspective*. Orlando, FL: Academic Press.

Thoreau, H. D. 1962. *The Journal of Henry D. Thoreau*. 14 vols. Edited by B. Torrey and F. H. Allen. New York: Dover.

Turcheon, F. H. 1979. *Report on the Archaeological Investigations Conducted on the University of Massachusetts Nantucket Field Station, for the Proposed Field Station Sewage Disposal System*. Report submitted to the Commonwealth of Massachusetts, University of Massachusetts, Boston.

Wagner, G. E. 1987. *The Use of Plants by the Fort Ancient Indians*. PhD dissertation, Washington University, St. Louis.

Williams, S., and V. Talmage. 1977. *Nantucket Elementary School and Teen Center, Phase I and II Report*. Institute for Conservation Archaeology, Harvard University.

Wood, William. 1865[1634]. *New England's Prospect*. Edited by Charles Deane. Boston, MA: The Prince Society.

Wood, William. 1987. Maize Agriculture and the Late Prehistoric: A Characterization of Settlement Location Strategies. In *Emergent Horticultural Economies of the Eastern Woodlands*, ed. W. F. Keegan, 275–94. Occasional Paper No. 7, Center for Archaeological Investigations. Carbondale: Southern Illinois University Press.

10

An Intellectual Biography of Elizabeth Alden Little, 1927–2003

Dena Ferran Dincauze

Childhood to 1970

Dr. Elizabeth Alden Little was drawn into archaeology by a spectrum of lifelong interests that seemed almost to have preselected her, as well as by her formidable research skills. Betty Little's early interests in history, natural science, and outdoor activities expanded throughout her life combined with her formidable research skills to create an outstandingly effective researcher, scholar, and teacher.

Descendants of Mayflower settlers, Betty's family is deeply rooted in New England history, and especially Nantucket whaling. She grew up on Long Island and Nantucket, an alert, intensely curious, and athletic young woman who delighted in horseback riding, skiing, crew racing, and other water sports. Childhood summers passed idyllically at family property on Nantucket. As a Wellesley College student, she taught horseback riding at a French-speaking summer camp.

Her ancestral family includes a notable Nantucket woman, sister of her maternal grandfather, Martha Dunham Summerhayes, whose diary of army life in nineteenth-century Arizona territory, "Vanished Arizona: Recollections of the Army Life of a New England Woman," has been reprinted more than once, most recently by the University of Nebraska Press. The book's introduction by Dan L.Thrapp describes adventurousness similar to Betty's: "She [Martha Summerhayes] received a good education, capped by two years' study abroad." In her book Summerhayes "reveals a saving sense of humor, a compassion and sensitivity to the ordeals of others, a robust earthiness and joy in living" (Thrapp 1979).

At Wellesley College, Betty's intellectual strengths were evident. Her 1948 BA in physics was adorned with honors: she earned the title of Durant Scholar and a Phi Beta Kappa key. Career employment began in 1948 with General Electric in Schenectady, New York, where she contributed to development of phosphor screens for color television (1950–1955); her first publication was coauthored, in typical physics fashion, by her supervisor, Dr. Koller (Koller and Alden 1951). She next enrolled in the Massachusetts Institute of Technology, where she was awarded an ffiM Fellowship, and earned a doctor of philosophy degree in physics (solid state) in 1954, with a minor in mathematics. Her thesis was published with minor reworking as a single-authored paper in *Physical Review* (Little 1955).

Betty married a fellow graduate student, John D. C. Little, in 1953. After many years in Virginia and five years in Cleveland, John rejoined MIT at the Sloan School of Management, ultimately capping his career as institute professor. The Littles settled in Lincoln in 1962, where they raised four children: John, Sarah, Thomas, and Ruel.

As her children required less of her abundant energy, Betty moved her service and research interests into the wider community. In the 1960s (1962–1969), she was active in public service, including volunteering at the Lincoln Public Library, Elementary School, and League of Women Voters. She held offices in the Lincoln Historical Society (1969–1972, vice president; 1983–1996, council member) and began field research on the town's early historic structures. She consulted for the Conservation Commission and the Planning Board, both benefiting greatly from her familiarity with the town's historic landscapes: walls, roads, dams, drainage, and flooded meadows. In preparation for the bicentennial year, she compiled information and explored early house and mill sites in Lincoln, producing with Kerry Glass a prize-winning map of Lincoln buildings and roads in 1775 (Glass and Little 1975). The map is still actively in demand.

Local and State History, 1970–1980

By 1971, Betty was a classroom aide in the Lincoln Public schools, teaching environmental and historical topics involving experimental field projects with children in the fourth and fifth grades. Her success brought wider recognition; in 1973, she was a consultant in history to the public schools of Pennsylvania. That background in teaching and historical research eased her way into Nantucket studies, where she mined the documentary record for evidence of whaleboat technology and then Indian lives. "Live Oak Whaleships" (Little 1971) was her first publication in the kind of social science-historical combination on which she built her later work. "Sachem Nickanoose of Nantucket and the Grass Contest" (Little 1976) began with an incident of folk history and developed into an examination of significant issues in native life and human relationships.

Betty's interests in the human past and the natural world led her to volunteer for a summer excavation of a shell midden on Nantucket. Recognizing that the work standards were haphazard, she sought help from Dr. William A. Ritchie of New York State Museum and from the Massachusetts Archaeological Society. Responses led to her rapid introduction to historical resource conservation. Realizing the advantages of protection of archaeological sites over their inefficient exploitation, she stopped excavating and, as director of research for the Nantucket Historical Association (NHA), she turned her formidable energy and teaching ability toward conservation programs. By 1976 she was a consultant for the Institute for Conservation Archaeology at Harvard, advising productively on a survey and an excavation project at the Nantucket Elementary School. In short order, she revised both the style and substance of archaeological research on Nantucket, to the advantage of both citizens and scholars. In 1978 she was co-coordinator, with Cynthia Young, of a prehistoric site survey of Nantucket County for the Massachusetts Historical Commission and the NHA under a matching grant from the federal Historic Conservation and Recreation Service.

At the NHA, Betty mounted an informative museum exhibit of artifacts displaying changes in styles through time, explaining how the style sequence enabled the chronological ordering of sites. The exhibit attracted artifact collectors on the island and earned their interested cooperation. Soon Betty submitted to the Massachusetts Historical Commission (MHC) an impressive inventory of sites and artifacts on Nantucket, spanning the full range of prehistory in the Northeast. She demonstrated that the island had played an integral role in human activity from shortly after the glacier melted, uninterrupted by its separation from the mainland. In 1978, the grateful MHC bestowed on her its Preservation Award for the first successful survey and catalog of archaeological sites on Nantucket. The report of that work (Little 1979a) initiated the Nantucket Archaeological Studies publication series, the first of what would become fourteen self-published and widely disseminated contributions to scholarship. That same year she initiated her Nantucket Algonquian Studies with a consideration of introduced diseases (Little 1979b) that was enriched by her new acquaintance with the Anthropology Department at the University of Massachusetts Amherst.

Betty's science training prepared her in perseverance toward a goal. She taught herself to read seventeenth-century handwritten historical records, a skill matched by few other researchers. With that tool, she was ready to utilize Indian deeds, wills, and probate records preserved on Nantucket (Little 1980b). By the time such historical research into Indian archives had advanced enough to develop a literature of its own, Betty was an acknowledged member of the research community, and the importance of Nantucket Indians was firmly established. Her roles in the NHA continued well into the 1990s, changing as the NHA itself grew and changed.

Massachusetts History and Archaeology, 1980–1990

A television documentary produced by M. O'Sullivan in 1980, entitled "The Forgotten Tribe," made Betty a television personality. In a letter to a friend, Betty reported: "I was advisor, and contributed talks on wigwams, canoes, inventories, Indian writing, and whaling and sources. As a videocassette, this was presented frequently at Nantucket club meetings and on Channel 3, TV Nantucket. It was also shown at the 1983 semi-annual MAS meeting at Assumption College, Worcester, and at the SAA [Society for American Archaeology] Annual Meeting in Pittsburgh, April 29, 1980." Betty was particularly pleased that the video advocated nondestructive archaeology on Nantucket.

As a scholar, Betty displayed a rare ability to spin gold from straw. Choosing topics widely familiar in local history and folklore, considering regularities as data, she drew new meanings from house ruins, old deeds, artifact scatters, and family legends. She liberally scattered insights for others to gather and develop further. Her natural gifts as a teacher led to numerous presentations to the public and to the conferences and workshops that endeared her to schoolchildren in Lincoln and Nantucket. The dazzling diversity of her research, and its fundamental soundness, resulted in publications that expanded the corpus of New England historical studies and stimulated emulation. Working from home, with imagination and energy her principal tools, she invigorated historical and archaeological studies. The chestnut blight and recovery efforts in Lincoln, Nantucket whaleships and whaling, Indian personalities and oral histories, deeds, houses, territories, diets, and epidemics yielded in turn to her scrutiny (see Little 1979–1994, Nantucket Algonquian Studies).

In the early 1980s, Betty returned to academic study at the University of Massachusetts (UMass) Amherst, taking courses in ethnohistory and regional archaeology, archaeological research methods and site interpretation, geology and paleoenvironments, and medical anthropology, in preparation for a master's degree. To the surprise of her children, she sublet rooms in Amherst to facilitate her study and reduce travel time. At the university she was a valued consultant for UMass students, doing original research in archaeology and ethnohistory and, soon afterward, for people in the larger community of compliance archaeology. She regularly attended local, regional, and national meetings, presenting her own diverse research projects and discussing and inspiring the work of others. In short order, she was an established, respected researcher in several disciplines, with a growing list of publications in both regional and peer-reviewed journals and a graduate degree in anthropology (1985). Instead of a thesis in support of her master's degree, she presented a portfolio of her publications on Indian history, archaeological research, and physical anthropology and isotope studies (see Little's list of publications at the end of this book).

The physicist in her was excited by the potential of radiocarbon studies and isotope analyses of organic materials for a deeper understanding of the human past. Although both topics had proved difficult for many, if not most, student archaeologists, Betty rapidly developed expertise in both. Her work on archaeological radiocarbon had very wide relevance; she demonstrated to archaeologists reluctant to be involved in advanced mathematics that greater precision in dating could be realized only by understanding both the strengths and limitations of the method. She tirelessly showed in publications in the 1980s and 1990s that ages derived by radiometric methods could only be statistical probability statements, but should not be dismissed on those grounds. Her work on the marine radiocarbon reservoir and the importance of that to archaeologists working near shores was original in North America (Little 1993b).

UMass research on burial interpretation inspired her involvement, with Margaret Schoeninger, in the study of dietary isotopes, following an interest evoked before 1983 when the method was innovative. Betty went on to collect samples of Nantucket wild foods to establish chemical signatures essential to the research (Little 1995). Her research and confidence in the field grew, culminating in a publication in *The Journal of Archaeological Sciences*, demonstrating that the converging radiometric signatures of corn and seafood required careful discrimination and showing how that could be done (Little 1997a).

Betty's rapid rise within the Massachusetts archaeological community can be traced to the offices she held: archaeological field director for the Nantucket Historical Association (1976–1977), co-coordinator of a Massachusetts Historical Commission survey grant (1978–1979), Massachusetts Archaeological Society trustee (1979–1984; ex officio 1986–1996), chairman of the Research and Education Committee (1981–1984), and president (1984–1986) and editor of the MAS Bulletin, which she managed for a heroic ten years (1986–1996), encouraging and helping MAS members publish their own research. She was a valued consultant to professional archaeologists doing compliance surveys on the Cape and Islands. Her active involvement in the Massachusetts Archaeological Society for over twenty years significantly enriched the organization, its members in the greater Northeast, and academic archaeology worldwide. Massachusetts Secretary of State Michael J. Connolly presented her with the Massachusetts Historical Commission's 25th Anniversary Preservation Award at the 3rd Annual Massachusetts Preservation Conference in New Bedford, on May 12, 1988.

Publications poured out through the 1980s, in astonishing diversity. Betty's family history in whaling led to research on whaleship construction, a whaling mutiny, pioneering studies of enterprising Indian whalers in southern New England, and a female whaler (Little 1981d, 1987g, 1988d, 1992c, 1994c). Her research convinced her that Native American Nantucketers cooperated reciprocally with Euro-Americans and were not, as many historians held, necessarily exploited. This claim was overlooked, denied, or ignored by historians, to Betty's annoyance. Nor did Betty focus only on glamorous sailing vessels; she tracked down finds of dugout canoes in New England, compiling an inventory that she planned to interpret, noting the wood used, evidence of construction methods, and age of the specimens. A study of inland canoe routes, undertaken for a UMass seminar in Midwestern Cahokia-period trade networks, brought her work to the attention of a wider audience of archaeologists, where its originality evoked both skepticism and awe (Little 1987c).

On Nantucket, it is a small step from ship construction to house construction. Betty demonstrated that Indian houses on the island were built in modular units that are still reflected in more recent vernacular structures in fishing villages on the island. Her study of houses, and earlier the Grass Contest (Nickanoose), led her to issues in Indian land use, and to deeds, land transfers, and house sites remaining in marginal areas on the island. The latter drew her to Abram Quary, whose life she celebrated (Little 1994a), demonstrating the relevance of biography in historical studies.

Betty's notable work in compiling evidence, assuring appropriate care, and recognizing Indian claims to unmarked burials on the island grew out of her native generosity and concern with the comfort and well-being of others. She undertook, on her own initiative, to create a record of burials accidentally exposed by erosion, and in 1985 she became the spokesperson for a burial exposed at Wauwinet. Following the protocols of the then-new Massachusetts law about burial treatment, she collected remains that were otherwise abandoned, reported to the MHC, established contact with John Peters at the Indian Commission, and earned his trust, advocated for burial ground protection, and, in 1986, achieved a resurvey of a historical graveyard that was almost lost to construction.

Betty's generosity and concern for others imbued her editorship of the MAS Bulletin, despite severe trials. She took over the journal in 1987, when publishing was just going electronic. The Bulletin had always been handwork, and Betty had to stand her computer-literate ground against the old guard who wanted things to remain as they had been. She responsibly coached authors to bring the writing and citation standards to levels acceptable to the increasing number of trained researchers who were consulting the Bulletin. She succeeded admirably, with very few wounding encounters on either side, and she brought the Bulletin into the new age over the reluctance of some MAS trustees. At the same time, she was gallantly serving as the replacement for a temporarily absent commissioner on the MHC Review Committee.

International Recognition, 1990–2003

International recognition of Betty's scholarship and contributions bloomed in the years following 1990. She was invited to speak at meetings of both regional and international organizations, was known and consulted by scientists in several disciplines, and accepted numerous responsibilities in organizations devoted to causes she loved. From 1996, she was a research associate of the R. S. Peabody Museum of Archaeology in Andover, an invaluable resource for the museum personnel there. Her research and expertise were widely appreciated; invitations for presentations accumulated (see the list of presentations in the Little Comprehensive List of Works at the end of this book). In 1994, MIT feted the Littles jointly on the fortieth anniversary of the MIT Operations Research Center. In October 1995, Betty was invited to contribute to the 20th Anniversary Whaling History Symposium at the Kendall Whaling Museum in Sharon, where she presented a closely argued case for the contributions of Indian whalers to the development of the industry in Massachusetts ("Behind the Legends: Native American Whaling from Nantucket Island, MA").

As honors accumulated for both John and Elizabeth Little, there were many trips abroad in celebration and recognition of their achievements. Those were typically enjoyable, and sometimes even more; it is hard to place the hot-air balloon tour of French chateaux and vineyards. Betty was alert to opportunities to visit archaeological sites and research locations wherever she went, and she benefited from the visits to pursue her interests. In India, she inquired about local boat-building methods and visited workshops to observe the handcraft. In England, she arranged special access to Stonehenge to observe the sunrise and stirred early from London to go there through the rain.

In 1998, Betty wrote in her Christmas letter about an incident during a trip in France: "At an evening banquet, a contest was run to predict the scores of the opponents at that evening's World Cup game. You had to state whether you were a soccer novice or pro. As an American, I surprised everyone (they laughed) when I said I was a pro. They had never heard of a 'Soccer Mom.' (Three of our children played varsity soccer in college.) Guess what? I won the prediction in the 'professional' category."

Betty's training in physics grounded the research she prized above all else—applications of isotope studies to human diet and archaeological chronology. Manuscripts of presentations at professional meetings, left unpublished, indicate where her research was leading. The complications she handled easily left her colleagues breathless in her wake. A draft in my files, dated September 10, 1996, bears the astounding title "The Effect of Eating Seafood on the Radiocarbon Ages of an Ancient Bostonian, Cape Codder, and Nantucketer from 14c, 13C, and 15N Studies." Another, from 2002, bears an equally daunting draft title "An Hypothesis: That the Increase in Archaeological Visibility (Yield and Preservation) of Maize and Beans in New England after cal. AD 1300 Resulted from Fertilization with Limestone or Shell." These two uncut diamonds bear witness to the way she worked, from insight toward clarity. The work awaits an equally inspired and skilled researcher to achieve the comparisons she was seeking.

Prior to her death, Betty was working eagerly on this study of Indian corn-growing technology, expanding on an insight that growing Indian maize was an advanced technology, requiring specialized knowledge and experience. Particularly, she argued that maize fields tended to be situated on alkaline (low-acid) soils. She worked for months to convince me that the acid-soil values that I knew characterized Northeastern soils were not truly typical of the region. I listened respectfully, knowing as I did that she was usually proven correct, but I was unable to relate her insight to anything I knew about regional soils or bedrock. Recent soils science articles drew my attention to the fact that soils leach rapidly after deforestation and plowing. Present acidity is the result of recent historical processes. The acidity we take for granted today was not characteristic of the Northeast prior to European agricultural practice! The diversity of soils in the Northeast is a product of history, beginning with the glacial dumping of freshly scoured bedrock fragments (which included carbonates), the development of forest litter, flood deposits, and human activities, including shell middens and waste products. Betty's case is strongly supported by new research and deeper insights.

Betty was notable not only for her abilities but especially her generosity. Her own achievements were lightly worn and generously shared. Avocational authors who met her as editor of the Massachusetts Archaeological Society Bulletin, Native Americans in southern New England, students and colleagues in archaeology, internationally respected geophysicists and historians, and other researchers all received her solicitous attention and care. MIT foreign students were regularly guests at the Little home for Thanksgiving celebrations. Betty took singular delight in her family; her children are creative in many disciplines, and her grandchildren charmed everyone as they grew and became interesting persons in their own right.

Betty's numerous and diverse skills allowed her to embody the "two cultures" of scholarship: the literary and historical style of the social sciences and the computational/statistical style of physics. As such, she moved comfortably within and between both styles and published in many kinds of journals. Like bookends, her first and last publications display that diversity and achievement (Little 1951; Little 2002). Her life was a celebration of learning-as-process, not merely as achievement. Even more than a learned woman, she was truly a learning woman, imbued with a joyful curiosity that warmed everyone who met her. Her legacy will inspire others for years to come and will leave us all richer for her expertise and loving care.

Acknowledgments

No appreciation of a person so multifaceted as Betty Little can be produced by any one writer, nor do I think this one approaches completeness. I benefited from information and context provided by John D. C. Little, Tom and Sarah Little, Kerry Glass, and many people who knew Betty at the University of Massachusetts Amherst, and at the Massachusetts Historical Commission.

Works Cited

Little, Elizabeth A. (Note: For all Elizabeth A. Little works cited in this chapter, please see the Publications section in the Comprehensive List of Works at the end of this book.)

Thrapp, D. L. 1979. Introduction. In *Vanished Arizona: Recollections of the Army Life of a New England Woman*, ed. Martha Summerhayes, vii–xxi. Lincoln: University of Nebraska Press.

Afterword

A Presentation at Elizabeth A. Little's Memorial Celebration, September 12, 2003

Ruel Little

Birth Order

Because I am the youngest, I am always the last one. My father informed me a couple of days ago that he didn't want to use birth order for our readings. That is why I am going first.

What I would like to say about my mom is from my perspective as the youngest. I trail my next sibling Tom by three years. So in some ways I had mom to myself for the years before the empty nest.

For much of my life, though, I didn't think of mom as a person. I thought of her as my mom. I expect this phenomenon is probably normal, but in my formative years, while I was learning about myself, I knew little about my mom.

When I was about fifteen, my mom, with newfound time and probably energy, focused on a new career. She went back to school; she turned my bedroom into an office; she began to talk to me about the advantages and disadvantages of radiocarbon dating. (I might add here, she spent much less time talking to me about dating itself.) Yes, this was the mom who got me dressed and fed for school. This was the mom who was the assistant teacher in my fourth and fifth grade classes. She was the one who skied with me, because I wasn't old enough to ski with my siblings.

Now she was going to school part time. On top of that, she took an apartment in Amherst so she could take evening classes or classes on consecutive days. To be honest with you, I didn't even know where Amherst was, and I made no attempt to find out.

I vaguely remember talking to her about the apartment and sleeping nights away from home. She asked me how else she could go to classes with a 2½ hour drive each way. We didn't discuss whether she should go to school or not. Mom knew what she wanted for herself. It wasn't going to be my choice.

Was my mom changing on me? How come she wanted to go to school and not be my mom? She already had her PhD. Was this her way of giving up motherhood to leave the family? Take a U-turn back to who she was before she was my mom? I needed to know mom would be there.

It wasn't that my mom was changing.

It was that I didn't really know my mom.

So I tried to get to know her. Not consciously, but I accepted her new pursuits without making a fuss. She wasn't like other moms I met. But strangely, that surprised me the least. She just became my mom the archeologist.

As time passed, I got married and had a child.

That is when I first realized, as her youngest child, that my experience was destined to be thirty-eight years after her experience. I noted how she was, in many ways, just like I am, or, more correctly, I like her. I began to remember traces of what she taught me about herself as a parent. These traces started showing up like stashes along a trail. Talking to mom directly didn't give too many clues to the mysteries of what she experienced as a parent. Mom didn't give you answers about life in the present. She is a wonderful role model, but she didn't repeat herself.

When my first child was about three years old, mom and I didn't have lots in common, by any means. She was still working hard at her then well-established passion, the passion she created from embers when the kids left home.

What connected me to my mom was a set of pictures of her and my father with their three-year-old son (my brother Jack). At that time my parents only had one child and all the things that come with being a new family.

I saw in the snapshot that her life in the picture was the same as mine. I realized that she had come down this path before me and that she faced the same challenges and rewards that I have. I realized her high school friends were like my high school friends, something I could never understand, because I could never imagine her high school friends in high school. I realized that when she went off exploring the world with her friends, she saw the world not as a mother but as someone who would later use her experiences to tell her children about the world.

When she studied hard in graduate school and got her doctorate, she did it for herself, not so she could be my mom.

She went to work as a physicist on early versions of the color television; she married; she had a family.

I realized looking at that picture that she had a life, and everything that comes with it, a very full life.

I know now looking back that she had the determination to have that full life. She was my mom, but she didn't stop there.

Thinking about that picture of the young woman with a child, I know she is still way ahead of me, but I can see her footsteps in the sand. Her passing has been like a wave washing back into the ocean, pulling sand across my feet. Some of her footprints are harder to make out. Some are very deep. But I see the nature of her path more clearly. And I know I am still following it. And it still isn't really up to me.

A Comprehensive List of the Works of Elizabeth Alden Little

Publications

1951. Electron Penetration and Scattering in Phosphors. *Physical Review* 83(3): 684–85. (Koller, L. R., and E. D. Alden, 1951)

1955. Dynamic Behavior of Domain Walls in Barium Titanate. *Physical Review* 98(4): 978–84.

1971. Live Oak Whaleships. *Historic Nantucket* 19(2): 24–38.

1975. *LINCOLN . . . 1775.* Historical map sponsored by Lincoln Historical Commission, on file at the Lincoln Town Hall, Lincoln, Massachusetts. (Glass, K., and E. A. Little, 1975)

1976. Sachem Nickanoose of Nantucket and the Grass Contest. *Historic Nantucket* 23(4): 14–22; 24(1): 21–30.

1979a. An Inventory of Indian Sites on Nantucket. *Nantucket Archaeological Study No. 1.* Nantucket, MA: Nantucket Historical Association.

1979b. Nantucket Indians Who Died of the Sickness, 1763–1764. *Nantucket Algonquian Study No. 1.* Nantucket, MA: Nantucket Historical Association. (Sussek, M., and E. A. Little, 1979)

1980a. A Brief Historical Sketch of Archaeology on Nantucket. In *Widening Horizons: Studies Presented to Dr. Maurice Robbins*, ed. C. Hoffman, 75–79. Attleboro: Massachusetts Archaeological Society.

1980b. Probate Records of Nantucket Indians. *Nantucket Algonquian Study No. 2.* Nantucket, MA: Nantucket Historical Association.

1980c. Three Kinds of Indian Land Deeds at Nantucket, Massachusetts. *Papers of the Eleventh Algonquian Conference*, ed. W. Cowan, 61–70. Ottawa: Carleton University.

1981a. Essay on Nantucket Timber. *Nantucket Algonquian Study No. 6.* Nantucket, MA: Nantucket Historical Association.

1981b. Historic Indian Houses of Nantucket. *Nantucket Algonquian Study No. 4.* Nantucket, MA: Nantucket Historical Association.

1981c. Index to Mary Starbuck's Account Book with the Indians. *Nantucket Algonquian Study No. 5.* Nantucket, MA: Nantucket Historical Association. (Sussek, M., and E. A. Little, 1981)

1981d. The Indian Contribution to Along-Shore Whaling at Nantucket. *Nantucket Algonquian Study No. 8.* Nantucket, MA: Nantucket Historical Association.

1981e. The Mattequecham Wigwam Murder. *Bulletin of the Massachusetts Archaeological Society* 43(1): 15–23.

1981f. Miscellaneous Papers. *Nantucket Algonquian Study No. 7.* Nantucket, MA: Nantucket Historical Association.

1981g. The Robert Minshall Collection: Nantucket Archaeology. *Historic Nantucket* 28(3): 16–18. (Little, E. A., C. Young, and M. Sussek, 1981)

1981h. The Writings of Nantucket Indians. *Nantucket Algonquian Study No. 3.* Nantucket, MA: Nantucket Historical Association.

1982a. Drift Whales at Nantucket: The Kindness of Moshup. *Man in the Northeast* 23: 17–38. (Little, E. A., and J. C. Andrews, 1982)

1982b. Indian Politics on Nantucket. In *Papers of the Thirteenth Algonquian Conference,* ed. W. Cowan, 285–97. Ottawa: Carleton University.

1983a. *The Algonquian Language of New England: A Vocabulary.* Edited by Jean-Jacques Rivard. Attleboro, MA: Massachusetts Archaeological Society.

1983b. An Archaeologist's Guide to Deed and Literature Research. Edited by Mary K. Johnson. *Bulletin of the Massachusetts Archaeological Society* 44(2): 55–61.

1983c. Initial Predictive Map for Prehistoric Sites on Nantucket. *Nantucket Archaeology Study No. 3.* Nantucket, MA: Archaeology Department, Nantucket Historic Association.

1983d. Locus Q-6, Site M52/65, Quidnet, Nantucket, Massachusetts. *Bulletin of the Massachusetts Archaeological Society* 45(1): 24–41.

1983e. Locus Q-6, Site M52/65, Quidnet, Nantucket, Massachusetts. *Nantucket Archaeological Study No. 2.* Nantucket, MA: Nantucket Historical Association.

1983f. *Nantucket Algonquian Studies* 1–8. Compiled and edited by E. A. Little. Nantucket, MA: Nantucket Historical Association.

1985a. Indian Place Names at Nantucket. In *Papers of the Fifteenth Algonquian Conference,* ed. W. Cowan, 345–62. Ottawa: Carleton University.

1985b. Prehistoric Diet at Nantucket Island, Massachusetts. *Nantucket Archaeological Study No. 6.* Nantucket, MA: Nantucket Historical Association.

1985c (with J. Clinton Andrews). Prehistoric Shellfish Harvesting at Nantucket Island. *Nantucket Archaeological Study No. 5.* Nantucket, MA: Nantucket Historical Association.

1985d. Prehistoric Shellfishing at Nantucket. *Nantucket Archaeological Study No. 4.* Nantucket, MA: Nantucket Historical Association.

1985e. Prevailing Winds and Site Aspects: Testable Hypotheses about the Seasonality of Prehistoric Shell Middens at Nantucket, Massachusetts. *Man in the Northeast* 29: 15–28.

1986a. *Archaeology in Massachusetts, 1980–1985.* Attleboro: Massachusetts Archaeological Society.

1986b. Jethro Coffin in Mendon, Massachusetts, 1708–1726. *Historic Nantucket* 34(2): 20–25. (Little, E. A., and M. Morrison, 1986)
1986c. Observations on Methods of Collection, Use, and Seasonality of Shellfish on the Coasts of Massachusetts. *Bulletin of the Massachusetts Archaeological Society* 47: 46–59.
1986d. Prehistoric Shellfish Harvesting at Nantucket Island. *Bulletin of the Massachusetts Archaeological Society* 47: 18–27. (Little, E. A., and J. C. Andrews, 1986)
1987a. Background Essays for an Archaeological Study of the Jethro Coffin House Lot. *Nantucket Archaeological Study No. 7.* Nantucket, MA: Nantucket Historical Association.
1987b. Bibliography for Historic and Prehistoric Nantucket Indian Studies. *Nantucket Archaeological Study No. 8.* Nantucket, MA: Nantucket Historical Association.
1987c. Inland Waterways in the Northeast. *Mid-Continental Journal of Archaeology* 12: 55–76.
1987d. In Memoriam: Roland W. Robbins. *Bulletin of the Massachusetts Archaeological Society* 48: 59.
1987e. *Nantucket Archaeological Studies* 1–8. Compiled and edited by E. A. Little. Nantucket, MA: Nantucket Historical Association.
1987f. President's Report. *Newsletter of the Massachusetts Archaeological Society* 12(3): 1 and Eastern States Archaeological Bulletin 46: 13–14.
1987g. Whaling off Nova Scotia, Newfoundland, and Greenland in the Early 18th Century by Nantucket Indians. *Nantucket Algonquian Study No. 10.* Nantucket, MA: Nantucket Historical Association.
1988a. History of the Town of Miacomet. *Nantucket Algonquian Study No. 12.* Nantucket, MA: Nantucket Historical Association.
1988b. The Indian Sickness at Nantucket 1763–1764. *Nantucket Algonquian Study No. 11.* Nantucket, MA: Nantucket Historical Association.
1988c. Nantucket: An Archaeological Record from the Far Island. *Bulletin of the Archaeological Society of Connecticut* 51: 47–68. (Pretola, J., and E. A. Little, 1988)
1988d. Nantucket Whaling in the Early Eighteenth Century. In *Papers of the Nineteenth Algonquian Conference*, ed. W. Cowan, 111–31. Ottawa: Carleton University.
1988e. Where Are the Woodland Villages on Cape Cod and the Islands? *Bulletin of the Massachusetts Archaeological Society* 49: 72–82.
1989a. Book Review: Native Writings in Massachusetts. Edited by Ives Goddard and Kathleen Bragdon. Philadelphia, PA: The American Philosophical Society, 1988; *The Nantucket Inquirer and Mirror*, June 29, 1989, 12B.
1989b. Shawkemo Chapter. *Bulletin of the Massachusetts Archaeological Society* 50: 54–55.
1990a. Indian Horse Commons at Nantucket Island, 1660–1760. *Nantucket Algonquian Study No. 9.* Nantucket, MA: Nantucket Historical Association.

1990b. The Indian Sickness at Nantucket 1763-64. In *Papers of the Algonquian Conference*, ed. W. Cowan, 181–96. Ottawa: Carleton University.

1990c. Late Woodland Diet on Nantucket Island: A Study Using Stable Isotope Ratios. *Bulletin of the Massachusetts Archaeological Society* 51(2): 49–60. (Medaglia, C., E. A. Little, and M. J. Schoeninger, 1990)

1990d. Nantucket Test Pit No. 1990-1 at the University of Massachusetts Field Station, Nantucket, Massachusetts. *Nantucket Archaeological Study No. 10.* Nantucket, MA: Nantucket Historical Association.

1991a. From the Sand Eel to the Great Auk: Potential Prehistoric Coastal Diets for Isotope Analysis. *Nantucket Archaeological Study No. 11.* Nantucket, MA: Nantucket Historical Association.

1991b. Late Woodland Nantucket Diet. *Nantucket Archaeological Study No. 9.* Nantucket, MA: Nantucket Historical Association.

1992a. Calibrated Radiocarbon Dates for Paired Marine and Terrestrial Materials from Archaeological Features on Cape Cod and Nantucket Island, Massachusetts. *AMQUA Abstracts*, p. 48. American Quaternary Association 12th Annual Meeting, University of California, Davis.

1992b. Historic and Archaeological Studies of Nantucket's West End. *Nantucket Archaeological Study No. 15.* Nantucket, MA: Nantucket Historical Association.

1992c. Indian Whalemen of Nantucket: The Documentary Evidence. *Nantucket Algonquian Study No. 13.* Nantucket, MA: Nantucket Historical Association.

1992d. Radiocarbon Age Calibration at Archaeological Sites of Nantucket and Other Northeastern Coasts. *Nantucket Archaeological Study No. 12.* Nantucket, MA: Nantucket Historical Association.

1992e. Radiocarbon Ages on Nantucket Island: What Can They Tell Us? *Nantucket Archaeological Study No. 13.* Nantucket, MA: Nantucket Historical Association.

1992f. Whales, Grass and Shellfish: Land Use Issues at Nantucket in the 17th Century. *Nantucket Algonquian Study No. 14.* Nantucket, MA: Nantucket Historical Association.

1993a. From the Sand Eel to the Great Auk: Potential Prehistoric Coastal Diets for Isotope Analysis. Culture and Environment: A Fragile Coexistence. In *Proceedings of the 24th Chacmool Conference of the Archaeological Association of the University of Calgary*, ed. R. W. Jamieson, S. Abonyi, and N. Mirau, 193–201. Alberta: The Archaeological Association of the University of Calgary.

1993b. Radiocarbon Age Calibration at Archaeological Sites of Coastal Massachusetts and Vicinity. *Journal of Archaeological Science* 20: 457–71.

1994a. Abram Quary of Abram's Point, Nantucket Island. *Nantucket Algonquian Study No. 16.* Nantucket, MA: Nantucket Historical Association.

1994b, ed. The Cape Cod-Nantucket-Martha's Vineyard Connection: A Traditional Lineage from Sachems of the Cape and Island. Edited by Russel H. Gardner. *Nantucket Algonquian Study No. 15.* Nantucket, MA: Nantucket Historical Association.

1994c. The Female Sailor on the *CHRISTOPHER MITCHELL:* Fact and Fantasy. *The American Neptune* 54: 252–58.

1994d. Radiocarbon Ages of Different Materials, Maize, Shell, and Charcoal, in One Pit Feature at Myrick's Pond, Brewster MA. *Nantucket Archaeological Study No. 16.* Nantucket, MA: Nantucket Historical Association.

1994e. Radiocarbon Ages of Shell and Charcoal in a Pit Feature at Myrick's Pond, Brewster, MA. *Bulletin of the Massachusetts Archaeological Society* 55: 74–77.

1995. The Late Woodland Diet on Nantucket Island and the Problem of Maize in Coastal New England. *American Antiquity* 60: 351–68. (Little, E. A., and M. J. Schoeninger, 1995)

1996a. Apples and Oranges: Radiocarbon Dates on Shell and Charcoal at Dogan Point. In *Dogan Point: A Shell Matrix Site in the Lower Hudson Valley, Occasional Publications in Northeastern Anthropology #14,* ed. R. W. Moeller, 121–28. Bethlehem, CT: Archaeological Services.

1996b. Daniel Spotso, a Sachem at Nantucket Island, Massachusetts, circa 1691–1741. In *Northeastern Indian Lives, 1632–1816,* ed. R. Grumet, 193–207. Amherst: University of Massachusetts Press.

1996c. NAGPRA Studies, for the Nantucket Historical Association, 1993–1996. *Nantucket Archaeological Study No. 14.* Nantucket, MA: Nantucket Historical Association.

1996d. *Nantucket Archaeological Studies 9–14.* Compiled and edited by E. A. Little. Nantucket, MA: Nantucket Historical Association.

1997a. Analyzing Prehistoric Diets by Linear Programming. *Journal of Archaeological Science* 24: 741–47. (Little, E. A., and J. D. C. Little, 1997)

1997b. Radiocarbon Ages: How to Report. *Bulletin of the Massachusetts Archaeological Society* 58: 64–65.

1999a. Maize Age and Isotopc Values at the Goldkrest Site. In *Corn Cobs and Buttercups: Plant Remains from the Goldkrest Site,* Appendix I, ed. T. B. Largy, L. Lavin, M. E. Mozzi, and K. Furgerson, 81–82; *Current Northeast Paleoethnobotany.* Edited by J. P. Hart. Albany: New York State Museum, Bulletin 494.

1999b. Maize Notes. *Nantucket Archaeological Study No. 17.*

1999c. Radiocarbon Dating of Shell on the Southern Coast of New England. In *The Archaeological Northeast,* ed. M. A. Levine, K. E. Sassaman, and M. S. Nassaney, 201–11. Westport, CT: Bergen and Garvey.

2002. Kautantouwit's Legacy: Calibrated Dates on Prehistoric Maize in New England. *American Antiquity* 67: 109–18.

Research Papers, Presentations, and Interviews

1954. *Dynamic Behavior of Domain Walls in Barium Titanate.* PhD thesis, Massachusetts Institute of Technology, Cambridge.

1970. *Mill History Progress Report. The Newsletter.* Lincoln, MA: Lincoln Historical Society.

1972. *The American Chestnut in Lincoln.* Smith School student paper, directed by Elizabeth A. Little.

1973. *Environmental Studies in Lincoln.* Bound collection of local geographic data, on file at the Lincoln Public Library, Lincoln, Massachusetts.

1976a. *Indians on Nantucket: The History of Our Land.* Nantucket, MA: Daughters of the American Revolution.

1976b. *The Wigwam in Nantucket Indian History.* Nantucket, MA: Nantucket Historical Association, Foulger Museum.

1978a. *Archaeology of the Boat.* Nantucket, MA: Nantucket Historical Association at the University of Massachusetts, Field Station, Nantucket.

1978b. *Exploring 10,000 Years on Nantucket, without Shovels.* Cambridge, MA: Sons and Daughters of Nantucket, Harvard Faculty Club.

1979a. *Digging 10,000 Years on Nantucket, without a Shovel.* Connecticut Archaeological Society Annual Meeting.

1979b. *Historic Values in Lincoln. Undeveloped Land in Lincoln.* Lincoln Planning Board and Conservation Commission, 29–30.

1979e. *Three Kinds of Indian Deeds at Nantucket.* 11th Algonquian Conference, Ottawa, Canada.

1979c. *Local Archaeological Preservation.* Workshop on Historic Preservation for Local Historic Commissions, Massachusetts Historical Commission, Worcester.

1979d. *Nantucket Island Survey.* Massachusetts Archaeological Society Semiannual Meeting, Milton, Massachusetts.

1980a. *The American Chestnut in Lincoln.* Lincoln, MA: Lincoln Historical Society.

1980b. *Drift Whales: The Gift of Moshup.* Annual Meeting of the American Society for Ethnohistory, San Francisco, California.

1980c. *The Forgotten Tribe.* TV documentary, produced by M. O'Sullivan, Nantucket, Massachusetts.

1980d. *Nondestructive Archaeology at Nantucket. An interview with Elizabeth Little.* Nantucket Channel 3 TV, Nantucket, Massachusetts.

1980e. *The Robert Minshall Collection.* Massachusetts Archaeological Society, Cape Cod Chapter, Orleans, Massachusetts.

1980f. *A Study of Probate Inventories for Ten Eighteenth-Century Nantucket Indians: Methodology and Results.* 20th Annual Meeting of the Northeastern Anthropological Association, Amherst, Massachusetts.

1980g. *Workshop on Indian Probate Records.* University of Massachusetts Course Lecture, Suzanne Spencer-Wood, Boston, Massachusetts.

1980h. *Workshop on Inventories as a Source for Archaeology.* Worcester: Massachusetts Archaeological Society, Eckblaw Chapter.

1980i. *Workshop on Probate Records, a Source of Archaeological Data.* Massachusetts Archaeological Society Semiannual meeting, Bridgewater, Massachusetts.

1981a. *Colonial Inventories.* Wednesday Morning Program, Lincoln, Massachusetts, Public Library.

1981b. *Deeds, Wills, and Account Books as Sources for Colonial History.* Quincy, MA: Quincy Historical Society.

1981c. *Indian Politics on Nantucket.* 13th Algonquian Conference, Toronto.

1981d. *Workshops on Nantucket Indians.* Nantucket Elementary School, Grades K–6.

1982a. *Archaeology and the Public: A Symposium.* Panel discussant, Massachusetts Archaeological Society Semiannual Meeting, Salem, Massachusetts.

1982b. *Fossil Coleopteran Assemblages as Indicators of Environmental Change.* Geography 558, R. Bradley. University of Massachusetts Amherst.

1982c. *The Massachusetts Language: Bibliography and Examples of Projects.* Prepared to help schoolteachers initiate projects.

1982d. *Prehistoric and Historic Indian Whaling at Nantucket.* Attleboro: Massachusetts Archaeological Society Annual Meeting.

1982e. *The Taima-Taima Site, Venezuela.* Anthropology 597D, Pre-Clovis Populations, D. F. Dincauze. Amherst: University of Massachusetts.

1983a. *Beetles as Indicators of Environmental Conditions.* Massachusetts Archaeology Society Semiannual Meeting, Assumption College, Worcester, Massachusetts.

1983b. *Historic and Prehistoric Whaling at Nantucket.* The Friday Night Series of the Maria Mitchell Association, Nantucket, Massachusetts.

1983c. *Indian Place Names at Nantucket Island.* 15th Algonquian Conference, Harvard University, Cambridge, Massachusetts.

1983d. *The Preservation of Archaeological Sites at Ram Pasture.* Report submitted to the Nantucket Conservation Foundation, Nantucket, Massachusetts, with Elizabeth Gosnold.

1984a. *A Portfolio of Papers 1976–1984.* Annotated bibliography of published work for MA degree in anthropology, University of Massachusetts Amherst.

1984b. *Shellfish Gathering at Nantucket.* Draft and prospectus for graduate research, University of Massachusetts Amherst.

1985a. *Archaeology in Massachusetts, 1980–1985.* Annual Meeting of the Eastern States Archaeological Federation, Buffalo, New York.

1985b. *Documentary Sources for the Contact Period.* Annual Meeting of the Conference on New England Archaeology, Panel Discussion Group, Sturbridge, Massachusetts.

1985c. *Initial Notes for Comprehensive Planning for Nantucket Archaeology.* Collection of letters, contacts, and ideas.

1985d. *Inland Waterways in the Northeast.* Poster Session, 50th Annual Meeting of the Society for American Archaeology, Denver, Colorado.

1985e. *Jethro Coffin House Lot Archaeology, the Resistivity Study, and the Mendon-Nantucket Connection.* Progress report on Jethro Coffin House research, with slides to the Historic House and Archaeology Committees. Nantucket, MA: Nantucket Historical Association.

1985f. *Nantucket Indians.* Nantucket Historical Association Lecture Series (docents), Nantucket, Massachusetts.

1985g. *Nantucket Indians.* Slide Talk at Our Island Home Open House. Nantucket, Massachusetts.

1985h. *Prehistoric Shellfish Harvesting at Nantucket Island.* 25th Annual Meeting of the Northeastern Anthropological Association, Lake Placid, New York, with J. Clinton Andrews.

1985i. *Scrapbook for an Archaeological Background Study: The Jethro Coffin House Yard.* Nantucket, MA: Nantucket Historical Association.
1986a. *Archaeology in Massachusetts, 1980–1985.* Greenfield: Massachusetts Archaeological Society, Norwottuck Chapter.
1986b. *Archaeology in Massachusetts, 1980–1985.* Lincoln: Lincoln Historical Society Fall Meeting, Lincoln, Massachusetts.
1986c. *Archaeology in Massachusetts, 1980–1985.* Orleans: Massachusetts Archaeological Society, Cape Cod Chapter.
1986d. *Archaeology in Massachusetts, 1980–1985.* Worcester: Massachusetts Archaeological Society, Eckblaw Chapter.
1986e. *Horse Commons at Nantucket Island, 1660–1760.* Annual Meeting of the American Society for Ethnohistory, Charleston, South Carolina.
1986f. *The Mendon-Nantucket Connection: 1708–1737.* Report submitted to the Nantucket Historical Association, Nantucket, Massachusetts, with M. Morrison.
1986g. *Postmolds and Shell Middens at the Quidnet Site, Nantucket.* Massachusetts Archaeological Society Semiannual Meeting, Clark University, Worcester, Massachusetts.
1986h. *The Quidnet Site, Nantucket.* Attleboro: Massachusetts Archaeological Society, Cohannet Chapter.
1986i. *Southeastern Massachusetts Indian Math: Names of Numbers, Counting, and Games.* Nantucket Elementary School 4th Grade Workshop, Nantucket, Massachusetts.
1987a. *Early Canoes and River Routes in the Northeast.* Massachusetts Archaeological Society, W. Elmer Ekblaw Chapter.
1987b. *Nantucket: A Prehistoric Record from the Far Island.* Archaeological Society of Connecticut Annual Meeting, Essex, Connecticut, with John Pretola.
1987c. *Whaling Off Nova Scotia, Newfoundland and Greenland in the Early 18th Century by Nantucket Indians.* 19th Algonquian Conference, Smithsonian Institution, Washington, D.C.
1987d. *Where Are the Woodland Villages? Workshop Panelist, chaired by Peter Thorbahn.* 27th Annual Meeting of the Northeastern Anthropological Association, Amherst, Massachusetts.
1988a. *Current Research on Nantucket Indians.* Coauthor of paper presented by Christian Medaglia at the Maria Mitchell Science Center, Coffin School, Nantucket, Massachusetts.
1988b. *Introduction to Indians at Nantucket.* Nantucket, MA: Nantucket Historical Association (docents).
1988c. *Late Woodland Diet on Nantucket Island (Massachusetts): A Study Using Stable Isotope Ratios.* Coauthor of paper presented by Christian C. Medaglia. 26th Annual Meeting of the Northeastern Anthropological Association, Montreal, Canada.
1988d. *Late Woodland Diet on Nantucket Island: A Study Using Stable Isotope Ratios.* Coauthor of paper presented by Christina Megadalia. 54th Annual Meeting of the Society for American Archaeology, Atlanta, Georgia.

1988e. *Nantucket Canoes, Whaleboats, and Sloops.* Norwell: Massachusetts Archaeological Society, South Shore and North River Chapters, South Shore Natural Science Center.
1988f. *The Nantucket Indian Sickness, 1763–64.* 21st Annual Algonquian Conference, St. John's, Newfoundland.
1988g. *Whales, Whaling, and Rope Making Workshop.* Mohawk High School, 7th grade science classes, Greenfield, Massachusetts.
1989a. Early Historic House Sites at Nantucket and Long Pond and the Madaket Ditch. In *An Intensive Survey of the Madaket Road Bicycle Path, Nantucket, Massachusetts* (ch. 5, 35–43). *PAL Report No. 136*, submitted to Vanasse Hangen Brustlin, Boston, Massachusetts.
1989b. *Historic Indians of the North Shore of Nantucket.* Report submitted to the Nantucket Historic District Commission, Nantucket, Massachusetts.
1989c. *Ruel Lawrence Alden's Family History and Genealogy.* From the files of Harriet Dunham Alden. Lincoln, Massachusetts.
1989d. *The Shack at Miacomet*, vol. 1. Compilation of documents and photographs related to the structure and family that used it.
1990a. *Nantucket Archaeology: Preserving the Heritage of the Past 10,000 Years.* Nantucket, MA: The Maria Mitchell Association.
1990b. *Nantucket Indian Sickness, 1763–64.* The Lincoln Historical Society Winter Meeting, Lincoln, Massachusetts.
1990c. *The Nantucket Indians.* Andover: Massachusetts Archaeological Society, Northeast Chapter.
1990d. *The Nantucket Indians.* Nantucket, MA: The Nantucket Historical Association (new docents).
1991a. *Archaeological Sites of Eskimo and Basque Seamammal Hunting in Newfoundland and Labrador: Precursors of Whaling at Nantucket.* Nantucket, MA: The Nantucket Historical Association.
1991b. *Basques, Eskimos, and Vikings in Canada.* Lincoln, MA: Lincoln Historical Society.
1991c. *Eskimos, Norse, and Basques in Eastern Canada.* Worcester: Massachusetts Archaeological Society, Ekblaw Chapter.
1991d. *From the Sand Eel to the Great Auk: Potential Prehistoric Coastal Diets for Isotope Analysis.* 24th Annual Chacmool Conference, University of Calgary, Alberta.
1991e. *Indian Whalemen of Nantucket: The Documentary Evidence.* The Dublin Conference, Algonkians of New England: Past and Present, Deerfield, Massachusetts.
1991f. *Native American Whaling on the Cape and Islands.* Seminar Series: Whales and Whaling on Cape Cod. Cape Cod Museum of Natural History, Brewster, Massachusetts.
1992a. *Calibrated Radiocarbon Dates for Paired Marine and Terrestrial Materials from Archaeological Features on Cape Cod and Nantucket Island, Massachusetts.* American Quaternary Association Annual Meeting, University of California, Davis.

1992b. *Radiocarbon Ages on Nantucket Island: What Can They Tell Us?* The Natural Science Lecture Series, Maria Mitchell Association, Coffin School, Nantucket, Massachusetts.

1992c. *Update on Nantucket Archaeology.* Massachusetts Archaeology Week, Nantucket Historical Association Whaling Museum, Nantucket, Massachusetts, with Paul C. Morris, Jr.

1992d. *Whales and Grass: Land Use Issues at Nantucket in the 17th Century.* The Peabody Museum Special Exhibit in conjunction with the 500th anniversary of Columbus's discovery of America, "We Claim These Shores: Native Americans and the European Settlement of Massachusetts Bay," and Symposium, "These Quilted Lands," Peabody, Massachusetts.

1993a. *Indian Whale Hunters at Nantucket: The Archaeological and Documentary Evidence.* Paper and rope-making demonstration presented to the Friends of the Robbins Museum, Massachusetts Archaeological Society, Middleboro, Massachusetts.

1993b. *Radiocarbon Age Calibration.* Boston: The Massachusetts Archaeological Society, Boston Chapter.

1994a. *Apples and Oranges: Radiocarbon Dates on Shell and Charcoal at Dogan Point on the Lower Hudson River.* The Conference on the Archaeology of the Hudson Valley, Albany, New York.

1994b. *Looking for Maize on the Coast: Use of Radiocarbon to Estimate Percentages of Marine Foods in Northeastern Woodland Diets.* 93rd Annual Meeting of the American Anthropological Association, Symposium: From Paleoenvironments to Political Complexity: Advances in the Chemical Study and Interpretation of Anthropological Remains, Atlanta, Georgia.

1995a. *Behind the Legends: Native American Whaling from Nantucket Island, MA.* The 20th Anniversary Whaling History Symposium, Kendall Whaling Museum, Sharon, Massachusetts.

1995b. *Coastlines and Interiors: Settlement Patterns on Massachusetts Islands.* 35th Annual Meeting of the Northeastern Anthropological Association, Symposium: Different Kettles of Fish: Approaches to the Study of Human/Marine Interaction, Lake Placid, New York.

1995c. *Nantucket's Native American Whalemen.* The Nantucket Historical Association Symposium: Nantucket and the Native American Legacy of New England, Nantucket, Massachusetts.

1996a. *Changing Cuisines: Prehistoric Coastal Diets of Northeastern North America Explored by Isotopic Measurements of Bone Collagen and Bone Apatite.* Poster Session, International Symposium on Archaeometry, University of Illinois, Urbana, Champaign-Urbana.

1996b. *Marine and Terrestrial Pairs: Radiocarbon Dating in Eastern Massachusetts and Rhode Island.* 36th Annual Meeting of the Northeastern Anthropological Association, Symposium: Cape Cod and the Islands, Plymouth State College, Plymouth, New Hampshire.

1998. *Diet and Reservoir Age: How Seafood Affects the Radiocarbon Ages of Coastal People.* Poster Session, 63rd Annual Meeting of the Society for American Archaeology, Seattle, Washington.

Contributors

J. Clinton Andrews, 1914–1994, combined a lifelong interest in archaeology, Nantucket ecology, and local history with the practical knowledge of the working fisherman. From three generations of detailed observation, he drew on a vast body of local knowledge that he frequently made available to researchers and students at the University of Massachusetts Nantucket Field Station where he worked. Among other projects, he collaborated on grey seal, land mammal, seabird, and archaeological research. He published *An Annotated List of the Salt Water Fishes of Nantucket* (1973), *Fishing around Nantucket* (which he also illustrated) (1990, both published by the Maria Mitchell Association, Nantucket), and several articles for *National Fisherman* magazine.

Dr. Marshall Joseph Becker has studied the Native peoples of the Delaware River and Delaware Bay regions for more than forty years. He was trained at the University of Pennsylvania in all four fields of anthropology and now applies multiple anthropological approaches to gather information about the Lenape ("Delaware Indians") and their neighbors. Becker has published nearly 200 articles on the Lenape and other Native Americans in scholarly as well as popular journals. He also has published a number of book chapters and monographs on the peoples of the lowland Maya region. His studies of skeletal populations from archaeological sites in Italy, the Czech Republic, and elsewhere in the European Union have appeared in dozens of articles. Becker's research has been supported by grants from the National Science Foundation, the National Endowment for the Humanities, the American Philosophical Society, the National Geographic Society, and the Social Science Research Council.

Shirley Blancke is associate curator of Archaeology and Native American Studies at the Concord Museum, Concord, Massachusetts. Specializing in local archaeology, she is a longtime member of the Massachusetts

Archaeological Society and served as the Massachusetts Archaeological Society Bulletin editor from 1997 to 2003. Originally from Britain, she received an MA in archaeology and anthropology from Cambridge University and a PhD from Boston University. She created some of the exhibits for the Hall of Man in Africa at the American Museum of Natural History in New York.

Dr. Kathleen J. Bragdon is a professor in the Department of Anthropology at the College of William and Mary. Her research focuses on the ethnohistory and sociolinguistic history of Native southern New England. Bragdon has published several books on New England Native language and culture. Her latest, *Native People of Southern New England 1650–1775* (2009), represents her recent focus on "ethnohistorical linguistics." Bragdon has received the Erminie Wheeler Voegelin Best Book Prize from the American Society for Ethnohistory and (with Ives Goddard) the Kenneth Hale Prize from the Linguistic Society of America.

Elizabeth S. Chilton is an associate professor, the department chair of anthropology, and the director of the Center for Heritage and Society at the University of Massachusetts (UMass) Amherst. Her research, publications, and teaching focus on the archaeology of New England, Native history, maize horticulture, social complexity, cultural resource management, and the analysis of material culture. She is the director of the UMass Amherst Field School in Archaeology, and she has directed or codirected eleven such field scho ols at UMass and Harvard University over the past twenty years. She received her MA in 1991 and her PhD in 1996, both from the Department of Anthropology at UMass Amherst. She was an assistant and then an associate professor of anthropology at Harvard University from 1996 to 2001, and she has been on the University of Massachusetts Amherst faculty since 2001.

Dena Ferran Dincauze is a Massachusetts native whose nascent interest in American archaeology was supported by members of the Massachusetts Archaeological Society (MAS)—Benjamin Smith, Alfred Mansfield, and Eugene Winter. She met Betty Little at an MAS meeting, and the two were colleagues and friends almost immediately. Dincauze received her BA at Barnard College, New York City, where the encouragement of Nathalie and Richard Woodbury launched her career. Graduate study at Cambridge University in England and at Harvard completed her career training; early fieldwork in South Dakota, England, and southern New England helped her decipher the riddle of soils. Dincauze was active in the Society for American Archaeology and editor of *American Antiquity*. She represented MAS on the Massachusetts Historical Commission.

Tonya Baroody Largy is an archaeological consultant specializing in the analyses of both plant and animal remains from archaeological sites and also is on the staff of the Zooarchaeology Laboratory of the Peabody Museum, Harvard University. She received her BA from the University of Massachusetts, Boston, and her MA from the University of Massachusetts Amherst. She has been active in Massachusetts archaeology since the late 1970s. She has conducted excavations in the Sudbury/Assabet/Concord River basin and has participated in excavations sponsored by the National Park Service and several Cultural Resource Management firms in the broader Northeast and as far away as Harappa, Pakistan. She is past president of the Massachusetts Archaeological Society.

Ruel Little is the youngest son of John and Elizabeth Little. He received a BA in physics from Johns Hopkins University and an MS in mechanical engineering from the Massachusetts Institute of Technology. However, his real educational opportunities were lifted from the woods of Lincoln and the shores of Nantucket, where he followed a less formal syllabus. His knowledge of anthropology and archaeology is exclusively learned from field trips to little-known destinations in both places. He is proud of this heritage of curiosity, learning, and poking his nose into unnoticed places. Little is currently the vice president of Technology at GreenRay, a start-up developing a labor-saving solar module.

Mitchell T. Mulholland is a research professor in the Department of Anthropology at the University of Massachusetts Amherst. His research interests are the archaeology of New England, especially Native American occupation, seventeenth-century Euro-American settlement, pollen and archaeology, and public archaeology. He received a BA in anthropology from Connecticut College in New London and an MA and a PhD in anthropology from the University of Massachusetts Amherst. He presently serves as director of UMass Archaeological Services, a cultural resource management organization, and he has more than thirty years of experience in his field.

Mary Lynne Rainey worked in the field of cultural resource management from 1979 through 2006 in the mid-Atlantic and New England regions. She holds an MA in anthropology from the University of Connecticut and is a registered professional archaeologist. As an employee of the firm PAL from 1988 to 2005, she directed over twenty Nantucket projects in the areas of Siasconset, Sesachacha Pond, Pocomo, Polpis, Plainfield, Nobadeer, Madequecham, and Miacomet valleys, the Creeks region, downtown, and in the Eel Point neighborhood. She has been a guest speaker at the Nantucket Historical Association, the Nantucket

New School, the Nantucket Elementary School, and the University of Massachusetts Field School. Currently she is an independent research consultant.

Duncan Ritchie received his BA from Franklin Pierce College and his MA from Brown University. He is a senior archaeologist at PAL in Pawtucket, Rhode Island. He has over thirty years of experience in cultural resource management, which has included many archaeological investigations of both the precontact Native American and historic period Euro-American sites on Nantucket. His primary research interests are the New England Precontact period and historical archaeology, ethnohistory, and lithic material sourcing using petrography and trace element analysis.

Index